VICTOR TRUMPER AND THE
1902 AUSTRALIANS

Victor Trumper and the 1902 Australians

LIONEL H. BROWN

Secker & Warburg
London

First published in England 1981 by
Martin Secker & Warburg Limited
54 Poland Street, London W1V 3DF

Foreword copyright © David Frith 1981
Text copyright © Lionel H. Brown 1981

British Library Cataloguing in Publication Data
Brown, Lionel H.
Victor Trumper and the 1902 Australians.
1. Trumper, Victor
2. Cricket – England – History
I. Title
796.35'865'0924   GV915.T74

ISBN 0-436-07107-X

Printed in Great Britain by
Redwood Burn Limited, Trowbridge & Esher

Contents

List of Illustrations		vi
Foreword by David Frith		vii
Preface and Acknowledgements		ix
Introduction		xi
A Note on Statistics		xv
Chapter 1	The Arrival of the Cornstalks	1
Chapter 2	"Got a frost-bite in your tail, Kangaroo?"	12
Chapter 3	"And it's even cold for May, Kangaroo?"	26
Chapter 4	Birmingham – The First Test	38
Chapter 5	Holocaust at Headingley	52
Chapter 6	Rain at Lord's – The Second Test	67
Chapter 7	By all the "flaming" gods of June	72
Chapter 8	Smokestack Sheffield – The Third Test	84
Chapter 9	The Midland Tour	95
Chapter 10	Somerset, Surrey and Rain	108
Chapter 11	Victor Victorious – The Fourth Test	116
Chapter 12	"To play the divil wid the bowlin'"	134
Chapter 13	Jessop's Match – The Fifth Test	146
Chapter 14	Darling's Darlings – Five Wins in a Row	163
Chapter 15	Festival Cricket	176
Chapter 16	The Tour in Retrospect	187
Appendix	Statistics of the Tour	195
Bibliography		199
Index		201

List of Illustrations

Between pages 80 and 81

The Eleventh Australian Touring Team
The England Eleven at Birmingham
Victor Trumper
J. Darling
C. Hill
R. A. Duff
M. A. Noble
H. Trumble
W. W. Armstrong

Between pages 112 and 113

S. E. Gregory
A. J. Y. Hopkins
J. J. Kelly
A. C. MacLaren
F. S. Jackson
G. L. Jessop
J. T. Tyldesley
L. C. Braund
G. H. Hirst
W. Rhodes
Trumper cutting at Lockwood
The end of the Oval Test

Foreword
by David Frith

It becomes increasingly difficult, as years pass, to get emotional about cricketers. They are just men in flannels, often smaller in character as well as stature when acquainted close-up. It is our fault for setting them up as gods in the first place.

This might explain how it is easier to revere a cricketer from a past age, one who can never now let himself down. Even then there are stories handed down or even newly cast which can tarnish the image.

One whose reputation survives all tests is Victor Trumper, "modest as a daisy". The worst part of him was his name. He seems to have been too good to be true. Such men have walked the earth, and – so I am told – still do. But they rarely play Test cricket.

So strong was the Trumper legend, passionately upheld by old men in Sydney when I was a boy, that I ventured out to Waverley Cemetery and found his final resting place. It is pleasantly sited, high above the pure blue Pacific as it touches the coast above Coogee Bay. Later I visited Crown Street School and tried in vain to find the initials the boy Trumper was said to have scored into his desk-top.

A few years on, I changed clubs, joining Paddington for no better reason than that I wanted to play at Trumper Park. There, in the tumbledown wooden pavilion, hung the most famous photo in cricket: Trumper thrillingly leaping out to straight-drive. Small wonder that a dreaming fielder was sometimes caught unawares as he fixed on illusions of the smiling, pigeon-toed, silken-skinned, local-born batting genius who enchanted the down-to-earth "Paddo" crowds half-a-century ago – when he was not representing Australia over the hill at the Sydney Cricket Ground, or further afield.

Victor Trumper died unfairly young, yet the grief surrounding his death in 1915 was not responsible for enhancing the story, as so often happens in cult matters. His charming, shy, generous personality and his magical powers as batsman had, years earlier, ensured a kind of immortality.

I have never heard a tale to his discredit – except that he made occasional mistakes at the crease and in business: both forgivable. For his virtuosity as batsman he will always be one of my two "all-time" batsmen to face two "all-time" bowlers if I should have to be seated before a cricket contest for eternity. I want to savour his audacity, his inventiveness, his fencer's wristwork. I want to see command with a smile and without arrogance, batsmanship of a peerless order displayed in the purest spirit and with a suppleness which is generally held to be the exclusive speciality of non-Caucasians.

Lionel Brown has done the right thing, I believe, in concentrating on Victor Trumper's 1902 *tour de force*. Reading of those extraordinary Test matches and the easy-going crowd-pleasers who played in them will assuredly cause many to curse yet again that television recordings came so late. But the torch of youthful gladness is bound to re-ignite in all our hearts in celebration of the magnificence of Trumper, Guy Eden's "saucy darlin' ".

To curl up with this account of the 1902 tour is to be whisked back down the tunnel of time to a sometimes showery, often sunlit, and utterly memorable cricket season, and to taste the performance of a cricketer of classic beauty.

Preface and Acknowledgements

The detailed research for this book has taken comparatively little time, though in the broader sense it dates back to the early nineteen-thirties of a grandfather's lively memory of the tour in question and the giants of the "Golden Age". Later, much fact and substance was garnered by "the luck of the toss" during the war years when I found myself with the free run of a library of cricket literature previously undreamed-of. From then on the study of cricket history became as important as playing the game itself. Once decided upon and the formalities of research undertaken, the act of writing became a pleasure as I attempted to relive the events of that rainwashed but glorious summer of so long ago.

First, I wish to thank the following publishers for kindly giving their permission to quote from various works: Associated Book Publishers Ltd for *Life Worth Living*, C. B. Fry (Eyre & Spottiswoode Ltd), *The Complete Cricketer*, A. E. Knight (Methuen & Co. Ltd), and *Cricket and Cricketers*, Col. Philip Trevor (Chapman & Hall Ltd); the Hutchinson Group Ltd for *Cricket in Firelight*, Richard Binns (Selwyn & Blount), *Who's Won the Toss?*, E. H. D. Sewell (Stanley Paul), and *Sydney Barnes – Master Bowler*, L. Duckworth (Hutchinson); Mills & Boon Ltd for *Twenty-Fours Years of Cricket*, A. A. Lilley; *Country Life* for *Cricket*, edited by H. Hutchinson; Cassell Ltd for *The Game's the Thing*, M. A. Noble; Anthony Sheil Associates Ltd for *A Cricketer's Log*, G. L. Jessop (Hodder & Stoughton Ltd); London Magazine Editions Ltd for *The Croucher* and *Maurice Tate*, both by Gerald Brodribb; William Collins Ltd for *Autobiography*, Neville Cardus; George Weidenfeld & Nicholson Ltd for *Rothmans Jubilee History of Cricket*, John Arlott (Arthur Barker Ltd); Epworth Press for *Hirst and Rhodes*, A. A. Thomson; and Macmillan Ltd for *Great Batsmen – Their Methods at a Glance*, G. W. Beldam and C. B. Fry. Also, a debt of gratitude is due to all the authors whose works were found invaluable in research and appear listed in the Bibliography.

ix

This book would be much the poorer without the poems and verses, which I hope might enliven any dullness, and I thank warmly the Editor of the *Evening News* for permission to quote "Does your circulation fail, Kangaroo?" by Samuel J. Looker, which first appeared in that newspaper.

As some of the verses used first appeared in long defunct periodicals I have been unable to trace copyright, and I therefore crave indulgence for any infringement from persons concerned.

I wish to record my heartfelt thanks to my Publishers and their most willing staff, and it is a great pleasure for me to acknowledge the real enthusiasm and assistance of their Managing Editor, Bill Neill-Hall. Whilst last, but not least, my grateful thanks are due to my niece, Mrs Glynis Barritt, for undertaking the task of typing the manuscript, and to my wife for her invaluable help, encouragement and for living with "The 1902 Australians" for so long.

Lionel H. Brown
Woodford Green
Essex
1981

Introduction

There is a certain fascination about the cricket season of the year
1902. Once more England was being visited by an Australian touring
team – the eleventh; an outstanding one under the captaincy of
Joseph Darling. English cricket had never been stronger, with an
embarrassing wealth of talent available, both amateur and professional. The game itself was played with a pace, keenness and
enthusiasm that can only be guessed at today.

It was a very cold, wet summer, and, in spite of the strange
conditions under which the Tourists had to play most of their
matches, the ill health and misfortune which for a time dogged
them, they produced, day after day, bright, attractive and attacking
cricket. Far from using the county matches as practice for the
sterner and more important Tests, they played them with zest as
games to be won; and only when too much time had been lost
through the vagaries of the elements, did a result terminate in a
draw. Admirably captained by Joe Darling, they soon settled down
into a splendid team where every player had his rightful place and
knew what was expected of him.

Their visit had been anticipated with considerable interest; of the
batsmen, Darling himself, Clem Hill, Syd Gregory, Monty Noble,
and, most of all, the brilliant Victor Trumper were names for the
home cricketing public to conjure with. All had visited "the mother
country" before and their past achievements were very much alive
in the memory. Reg Duff, Warwick Armstrong and Albert Hopkins
came for the first time with reputations to live up to. Besides Noble,
the bowling department had the fiery Ernie Jones, the "Jonah"
who had once bowled a ball through W. G. Grace's beard, and
Hughie Trumble, the tallest Australian cricketer and deadliest
bowler in the side. Medium-paced Bill Howell, tireless, economical
and steady as ever, was with them once more. Their exploits
on previous tours were only too well known and remembered.

xi

Of left-armed Jack Saunders much was expected from his recent performances in the Antipodes. Two wicketkeepers completed the party: the well liked and heavily moustachioed Jim Kelly had been here before, and the lesser moustachioed Hanson Carter had not. The indefatigable, experienced and much travelled Major Benjamin Wardill managed, arranged and advised the team. In this good work he was assisted unofficially by a former Australian player, who had come over here on holiday for the cricket, Dr Rowley Pope, a medical practitioner of considerable charm, of whom it was often said that he materially helped with the social polish that was not always found to be necessary back home in the new Commonwealth. His medical advice and knowledge, too, were to prove invaluable.

Of the English counties they were about to visit, Yorkshire were pre-eminent, and were to be winners of the county championship for the third year running. They were an immensely strong team of all round talents, mainly professional. Nottinghamshire, Lancashire, Sussex, Surrey and Kent, too, could regularly put powerful sides in the field. Practically every county club retained the services of at least one fast bowler and some boasted two, and there was a wealth of bowling talent of every variety of that time available.

The "Golden Age" was approaching its midway point, and was probably at its zenith in terms of the great players of the era, nearly all being at the high-water-mark of their powers. The number of them to choose from was both embarrassing and bewildering for any would-be selector. MacLaren, Tyldesley, Garnett, Hallows, Sharp and Barnes, together with Jackson, Taylor, Denton, Brown, Hirst, Rhodes, Haigh and Hunter, meant that the two "roses" counties alone could have fielded almost a side and half of inter-national standard. From Notts, there were the three Gunns, William, George and John, with A. O. Jones, Iremonger, Wass and Hallam, and from Derbyshire, Lawton, Ashcroft, Storer and Bestwick were all in their prime. Warwickshire could boast Lilley, W. G. Quaife, Kinneir, Field, Hargreave and Santall, and Worcestershire the Foster brothers (H. K. and R. E.), Bowley and Arnold, while Leicestershire retained Knight, Wood, J. H. King and R. T. Crawford. From the south-western shires, there were Jessop, Townsend and Board of Gloucestershire, and Lionel Palairet, Braund, Robson and Cranfield from Somerset. Hampshire could contribute Llewellyn, Major Poore and A. J. L. Hill, and Sussex Ranji and Fry, Vine, A. E. Relf and Killick. Kent could boast Mason, Burnup, Sam Day, Dillon, Blythe, Bradley and Huish. Of the London based clubs, Surrey possessed Abel and Hayward, Dowson, Lockwood, Richardson and another Crawford, V. F. S., while Middlesex claimed Warner, Wells, G. Beldam, the Douglases, Bosanquet and Trott (if allowed). Finally, from Essex, there were Fane, Perrin, McGahey, Mead and "Sailor" Young. A roll-call of honour; talents to conjure with indeed!

The Test rubber of 1902, gradually building up to the exciting climaxes of the last two games, remains a fascinating enigma of what might have been. The weather robbed England of certain victory at Edgbaston, and selection muddles an undoubted win at Old Trafford. The host country could well have won the series regardless of what might have happened at Lord's without rain. But, putting all speculation aside, the concluded Test matches in themselves remain as three of the most satisfying games ever played in England, with thrills and suspense continually vying with each other, high drama, the ebb and flow of fortune, and superb skill in every facet for players, spectators and future historians of cricket.

Throughout the season of 1902, whether from the Tourists' point of view or from that of the cricketing public at large, one phenomenon emerges above all – Victor Trumper. This most polished and beautiful batsman scored 2,570 runs, including eleven innings over 100, in a very wet season. He made them, moreover, in the most handsome fashion, by brilliant hitting and attacking batsmanship at the rate of over 60 runs an hour on all kinds and conditions of pitches against every type of bowling. Never playing himself in, he went down the pitch and drove, cut or pulled the bowlers off their length from the first ball he received. Nothing quite like it in so elegant a manner had the cricketing crowds seen before, not even from Ranji and Jessop! And such a modest and unassuming young man – they took him to their hearts.

Looking back upon these exploits from some seventy-nine years on, we can, of course, see it all in a perspective that was denied to the onlookers of 1902. We at least know what came afterwards in subsequent seasons. Within but twelve years what remained of the Golden Age was gone forever and a more utilitarian cricket became the order of a post-war world. With but an occasional flash of brilliance from an ageless Hobbs or Woolley, a Bradman, a Tate or a Hammond on form, the rest was honest workaday toil by comparison. But cricket's later history does not concern us here; it is still the year 1902. Three days are considered sufficient for a Test match, runs are expected to be scored at the rate of well over 300 a day, wickets are still uncovered, a hit over the ring is only four (a sixer has to be hit out of the ground), bowlers are expected to get the batsmen out and batsmen to score runs – at a lively rate and in a striking fashion.

Perhaps we may now attempt to look back into the past and see how they did those stirring deeds during that glorious rain-soaked summer with the encouragement, and no little assistance, from the 1902 Australians and Victor Trumper.

A Note on Statistics

The bulk of the statistical material in this book has been drawn from the 1903 edition of *Wisden* and *Cricket: A Weekly Record*. However, given the methods employed at the time, the scorecards in the above show but the barest details. Items such as the fall of wickets, altered batting orders in the second innings and indications of captains and wicketkeepers were not usually recorded. Therefore, it is with particular pleasure that I would like to thank the following County representatives and others for researching the original scorebooks to provide this information and the correction of some longstanding errors: P. Wynne-Thomas (Nottinghamshire); V. Gray (Essex); E. E. Snow (Leicestershire); J. Pratt (Oxford University); J. Lister (Yorkshire); R. Warburton (Lancashire); A. J. Pocock (Cambridge University); F. G. Peach (Derbyshire); A. C. Smith (Warwickshire); H. A. Osborne (Sussex); A. K. James (Hampshire); B. E. Simmonds (Kent).

Sadly, the records are incomplete as, through the passage of time or the ravages of war, some scorebooks have been lost or destroyed. But I would like nevertheless to offer my appreciation to all who replied to my request.

Regarding the Tests, I am indebted to *The Wisden Book of Test Cricket*, edited by Bill Frindall, for rectifying some mistakes contained elsewhere.

CHAPTER 1
The Arrival of the Cornstalks

As the S S *Omrah* docked at Tilbury on a wintry April day in King
Edward VII's Coronation year, the eleventh Australian touring
team under Joseph Darling prepared to disembark together with
the returning England side of Archie MacLaren, which they had
decisively beaten four games to one in the season that had just
closed in the new Commonwealth.

During the voyage both teams had been on the friendliest of
terms, perhaps not so surprising when one realises that these young
men had been playing cricket together and associating with each
other closely for the previous few months. Nevertheless, although
the returning Englishmen were relaxing after a hard tour, the
"Cornstalks" were taking very seriously their endeavours to keep
fit in their determination to beat the full strength of the mother
country on her home grounds.

The English cricketing public had not taken the four-to-one
defeat of MacLaren's team too seriously. Australia was a long way
off and that tour, a private venture of MacLaren's, was far from
being representative of our real strength; and, after all, fortune
had not favoured the team in the way of luck. But the previous
Australian side to visit us three years before in 1899 under the very
same Joseph Darling had undoubtedly fairly beaten the flower of
English cricket by handsomely winning the only completed match
of the rubber. There was no question but that the Australians had,
at least for the time being, proved themselves the stronger at our
national game; they had impressed us enormously. However,
everyone felt that now, in the year of grace 1902, was our real
chance to show our colonial cousins from the new Commonwealth
what the might of England would do to them on the cricket field.
There is no doubt that this Test rubber was keenly awaited, not
only by the cricketing public in both countries, but by the ordinary
man in the street, who normally took a cursory interest in the game

1

through his daily newspaper. For the popularity of cricket at first-class level had never before been higher in England and Australia.

It was not entirely certain that, owing to business commitments, Joe Darling would be able to make the trip, for he had recently moved from South Australia to take up sheep farming in Tasmania. Presumably, in his absence, the captaincy would have fallen on the broad shoulders of Hugh Trumble, who had led Australia in the last two Tests and had previously visited England on four occasions. The composition of the side was far from easy for the Australian State selectors to choose because not all the finally selected players picked themselves automatically, so to speak, and on form the N S W batsman L. O. S. Poidevin could have been chosen, as might his fellow-State fast bowler Alex Kermode. Likewise, A. McBeth of N S W was a possible contender for a time, but his bowling had fallen away towards the end of the 1901–2 season. The Victorians C. E. McLeod and Frank Laver, both all rounders who had visited England in 1899, were possibles, as were their batsmen colleagues Peter McAllister and H. Stuckey. It appears to have been but a last minute decision to include the fast bowler Ernest Jones, now past his peak but still formidable on his day, as Kermode had not lived up to his early promise and there was no one else under consideration. Many in Australia thought the side was not as strong as it might have been, but Joe Darling was completely confident in his players and they, for their part, were fully confident in themselves and, above all, their astute captain.

The fourteen young men who disembarked from the *Omrah* constituting the official eleventh Australian Touring Team were as follows:

Joseph Darling, captain (South Australia)
Hugh Trumble (Victoria)
Sydney E. Gregory (N S W)
Montague Alfred Noble (N S W)
Clement Hill (South Australia)
Ernest Jones (South Australia)
James J. Kelly (N S W)
Victor Thomas Trumper (N S W)
Albert J. Hopkins (N S W)
Reginald A. Duff (N S W)
John V. Saunders (Victoria)
Warwick W. Armstrong (Victoria)
William P. Howell (N S W)
Hanson Carter (N S W)

Major Benjamin J. Wardill, the Secretary of the Melbourne Club, accompanied the team as manager.

The tour had been arranged by the old established Melbourne Cricket Club in conjunction with the trustees of the Sydney Cricket

Ground, who previously had been responsible for inviting Stoddart's 1894 and 1897 sides and MacLaren's recent venture to Australia, as well as promoting the Australian tours to England. The State selectors, Darling, Trumble and Gregory, after having chosen their side, according to time-honoured custom called the selected players together to appoint their own manager, captain and vice-captain. In addition to this, an executive committee of three players was agreed upon which acted jointly with the manager to make all decisions affecting the party on tour.

They chose as their shrewd and most astute captain Joe Darling, a dominant personality with his own opinions and a rugged hard-hitting left-hand batsman who gloried in powerful drives. Equable in temperament, with inexhaustible patience and rock-like defence, he was a most difficult batsman to dislodge and could alternate his game between violent attack to hit his side out of trouble and stern defence. His heavily moustached, shortish thick-set figure and deep blue eyes exuded an air of quiet confidence to his team as he walked out to bat with the rolling gait of a countryman. Already he had scored three centuries in the 1897–98 series against England with an aggregate of 537 runs, and his tally in Test matches so far was 1,293. On the 1899 tour in all matches, he had scored a record for Australia of 1,941 runs at an average of 41.29. He controlled his team with a stern yet benign authority and was the possessor of a quiet, dry sense of humour which always put the young player at his ease. The members of the team thought highly of him as a captain and a man, for he would scorn to do an underhand action and could not be imposed upon. He fielded well and observantly from the slips or mid-on. *Wisden* had honoured him as one of the cricketers of the year for 1900.

A towering figure of a man who looked down from the bowling crease at the batsman, Hugh Trumble used his great height and long arm to full advantage when bowling his slow to medium off-spinners with superb control, flight and subtle variations in pace and direction. On English pitches he had proved on previous tours how devastating he could be even when the pitch did not help him. He was the prop man of the bowling and had already taken 91 English wickets in Test matches including a remarkable performance of 12 wickets for 89 runs in the Third Test at The Oval in 1896, on which tour as a whole he secured 148 wickets at an average of 15.81. Then, on the following visit in 1899, he was top of the bowling again with 142 for 18.43. A great slip, but a versatile field anywhere, he was the possessor of the next largest pair of hands to Albert Trott's in contemporary cricket, which were as safe as they were capacious. He was a capable batsman of perhaps somewhat limited method, a dogged defender who could hold up one end, or at times score runs freely. He was useful as an opener, middle order or

3

a number nine in this formidable batting array, and had a reputation as a practical joker both on and off the field. Trumble was very much the thinking bowler, ever ready to search out the opposing batsman's weaknesses or favourite strokes, which he tempted. Along with Jim Kelly he was the oldest member of the side, both being born within two days of each other in May 1867. An elder brother of his had toured England in 1886.

Lack of inches in little Syd Gregory was made up for by the sparkle with which he did everything. He sparkled in the field at cover point or extra cover, where he had few equals and no superiors. Like Jessop he could field deeper than most covers and run in to save the single, stoop and return the ball underarm in one movement equally well with either hand. With his superb long throw he could field anywhere; if he had never scored a run in a Test match, he would have been chosen for his fielding alone. But Syd Gregory was a dazzling batsman as well (he preferred to bat number five) who could always be relied upon to score runs in handsome fashion, and as a cutter he was unsurpassed. If anybody wanted to illustrate all the classic strokes of the art of batsmanship, here was the man to use as a model. He first came to England at the age of twenty in 1890 and had played in every Test match (except two in Australia in 1891–2) since; no team would have been considered complete without him. Already he had scored three hundreds in Test matches, the highest being 201 at Sydney in 1894 during the First Test, and altogether had tallied some 1,365 runs against England. This dapper, compact little man with his habitual waxed moustache and bright, cheery countenance was nearly thirty-two and was always ready with a fund of humorous stories and anecdotes to keep any party lively and amused. A sparkling little man indeed.

The Cornstalks took their cricket very seriously, but none more seriously and earnestly than variously known Monty or Alf Noble, who sometimes was referred to by his colleagues as "Mary Ann", as misleading a sobriquet as would be possible to find for this individual. He had the hallmark of the studious cricketer who thought the game out in detail at all its levels. Noble was one of the great all-rounders in the side, who, when he wished, could be a delightfully free-scoring batsman all round the wicket for his Paddington Club in Sydney, but who often, because of the dictates of the game and the good of his side, had to curb his powers to a stern and patient defence. A fine on-side player with a selection of leg deflecting scoring shots when defending and a neat cutter, he was at all times the man for a crisis in an important match, but his rock-like defence could be a trifle monotonous for the spectator. The easy run up to the wickets belied a fine, medium pace off-spin bowler with a curious flight and pronounced break-back. He had been developing a surprising out swerve (from leg to off) to the occasional ball which

4

batsmen found very disconcerting and gave him many wickets. He varied his pace from almost fast to about slow-medium with artful concealment; his well disguised slower ball would sometimes drop or "duck" – a technique he had apparently developed from studying baseball pitching.

On his only previous visit to the mother country three years before, "Monty" soon found English pitches suited his style of bowling, taking in all 82 for an average of 22.90. Playing against England for the first time in 1897–98 he had already scored 611 runs at the highest level and captured 64 wickets. More recently against MacLaren's side on the tour just completed, Monty Noble had secured a record of 32 wickets in the Test match series for an average of 19.00 runs apiece, including a splendid 7 for 17 in the first Melbourne Test. A great fielder, as one would expect, he would field anywhere with distinction but preferred to be at old fashioned point – the point of the bat. Standing six feet tall with the body of an athlete, his handsome clean-shaven features under the wavy hair did not belie the studious thinker within. For all that, he possessed a disarming smile, a dry sense of humour and a fine baritone voice. One day he would make Australia an outstanding captain.

Clem Hill, probably the finest left-hand batsman in the game, could be best described as a pugnacious hitter. With a slightly crouching stance at the crease, he scored by late and square cutting or by off driving through the covers, a powerful bat with a complete set of strokes all round the wicket who delighted in batting just for its own sake and not just to score runs alone. He was very fleet of foot for a rather thick-set and solid young man, having the grace of a dancer as he chassied down the pitch sliding his left foot behind the right to attack a slow bowler. But amongst his armoury were the forcing strokes to the on side, and fast bowlers he drove with the power of a cannon shot through the leg-side field. His defence was his attack, and rarely could the poor trundler keep him quiet let alone dislodge his bails. A superb field anywhere but, owing to an extremely safe pair of hands and superlative throwing, he would naturally be used in the country. Just to witness Clem and Victor Trumper throwing the cricket ball to each other from one side of the playing arena to the other after the fall of a wicket was added value indeed for the spectator. It may not be recalled by many but, at the outset of his career, he also kept wicket.

First playing for Australia against England in 1896, when he came as the youngster of the side, he appeared, apart from ill health depriving him of two games, with distinction in every Test match since. Clem always liked to bat at number three and had scored 1,304 runs at an average of 44.97 already against England, including scores of 96, 188, 135, 99, 98 and 97. The highest personal total he had achieved was during an inter-State game – 365 not out against

5

New South Wales. A forthright character, but one of the friendliest of cricketers, he had a long solemn face, merry eyes and a busy, alert mind. Humorously known as "Kruger", owing to a supposed resemblance to the Boer worthy, he was a first-rate sportsman – win or lose.

Australia had always produced bowlers who did well in England. To be a good bowler on the often iron hard pitches of Australia and get wickets, you had to resort to techniques of which not all English bowlers were capable. Subtle variations of pace and flight – as important as just spinning the ball – and extreme pace, provided it could be kept up for lengthy periods, were yardsticks for success. From the earlier colonial days of Spofforth and Boyle, Garrett and Palmer, Turner and Ferris, and then briefly Sammy Woods to George Giffen, the Trott brothers and Hugh Trumble, we see a line of bowlers who had confused and confounded the English batsmen whenever they met in combat. In 1896 the body of English cricket was rather sorely bruised and battered by the terrific pace of one Ernest Jones of Adelaide (some say Broken Hill), one-time stevedore, miner and dust-cart driver. "Jonah", on his first outing of that tour at Sheffield Park against Lord Sheffield's XI, ousted the cream of home cricket, virtually an England Test side – W. G. Grace, F. S. Jackson, Ranjitsinhji, C. B. Fry, Shrewsbury, William Gunn and Davidson – for 84 runs. This was the celebrated occasion when he bowled the ball that bounded through the Champion's beard and soared over the wicket-keeper, standing far back, for four byes. W. G.'s annoyance had exploded – "What's this? What's this?" After Harry Trott had said, "Steady, Jonah," the fast bowler made his classic and oft quoted apology, "Sorry, Doc, she slipped!" He could and often did short pitch the ball to make it rear head high so you had to hook him, run out and cut him – or duck! A tall, burly, heavily built man, bushily moustached, with enormously powerful forearms and shoulders, he proceeded to demoralise 121 batsmen on that tour. In 1899 he shortened his run up to the wicket, but his pace remained as fast as ever. On the hard pitches of that season, he proceeded to take 135 wickets with sheer pace. England's batsmen compared him to Charles Kortright at his fastest; even faster than Tom Richardson at his peak, they thought. Although now a little older, he was thirty-three, on hard pitches his powers were undiminished. As a batsman, Jones could chance his arm for a lofted four or just as easily be bowled, but as a fielder he had no peer for such a heavily built man and was magnificent at mid-off.

To successfully follow J. McCarthy Blackham and "Affie" Jarvis as stumper to an official Australian Test side was no mean feat on the part of James Kelly. Carefully modelling his style of keeping on Blackham's methods, Kelly was a safe but never showy performer, who never appealed unless he was pretty certain. It was probably due to his neat unobtrusive work that when he occasionally rose to make either a remarkable catch or superb stumping, it was then realised how much his safe keeping was taken for granted. A capable batsman with many attractive strokes and an extremely confident watcher of the ball, as one might expect of a wicketkeeper, he was considered good enough to open for his own Sydney Club, Paddington, and sometimes even for New South Wales. An admirable knock of 103 during his last visit here was still remembered. Thirty-four dismissals stood to his credit already in the eighteen representative matches in which he had officiated. His humorous countenance was half hidden by an enormous walrus moustache from which he periodically extracted his briar pipe to make some amusing comment on or about the game. A popular and lovable character, he delighted in the nickname of "Mother" for obvious reasons.

There are but few batsmen to have graced the game of cricket who dazzled the eye and entranced the beholder as could Victor Trumper. Probably one can think only of Ranji and Jessop, and in their quite differing ways both had much in common with him. He was the classic batsman extraordinary, and was to lift the art of batsmanship to a plane as yet undreamed of. Being so complete a master of his craft with such superlatively quick reaction and eye, he could determine on a stroke yet change his mind and play another dazzling, stylish scoring shot which still seemed perfection. He had at least three different strokes for each ball and many more entirely his own which he was constantly improvising. As C. B. Fry was to later say of him, "He has no style, and yet he is all style . . . His whole bent is aggressiveness towards the bowling, and he plays a defensive stroke only as a very last resort. Yet such is his command of his strokes, that even when he is scoring his fastest he gives an impression of perfect safety."* Victor could walk out to bat and, regardless of the good bowling, make lovely strokes from the first ball he received. As likely as not, that first ball would be over the ropes for four runs, for unlike most other batsmen he never played himself in. No combination of pitches and bowlers seemed difficult to him; he made batting appear the easiest thing in the world. If one observed him from behind the bowler's arm or his own wicket, one could appreciate the apparent risks he took in cutting or pulling good length balls pitched right up on his middle stump. He was a perfect timer of the ball, and many of his strokes were made on wrist work alone. Oft were the occasions when he would dance down the pitch or jump out to make a half volley or full toss out of what might have been a fatal leg- or off-break.

It is not surprising, then, that Victor Trumper scored his runs at a

*G. W. Beldam and C. B. Fry, *Great Batsmen–Their Methods at a Glance*, Macmillan, 1905, p. 97.

much faster rate than most batsmen, Australian or English. Of that, our home cricketers and sporting public were only too well aware, for hadn't they seen him three years previously score a magnificent 135 not out when Australia won at Lord's? Hadn't they also watched him reduce the Sussex bowlers to impotence while scoring 300 not out at Brighton? With the help of another 104 against Gloucester, he scored 1,556 runs during that tour and had only been a last-minute inclusion in the side, mainly at the insistence of Monty Noble, who had known him since his school days and watched over him with growing wonder. Victor first shone into full prominence in the season of 1897–8 when he joined the Sydney First Grade Club, Paddington. In just eight innings, 1,021 runs flowed from his bat with three not outs and an average of 204.20. Six of those innings were centuries; his highest score was 191 not out and his lowest being run out for 82! Selected for New South Wales, he made 292 not out against Tasmania, 208 against Queensland, then 253 against New Zealand and 230 against Victoria. Small wonder he was expected to be one of the prime run-getters in the Cornstalks' touring side. This lithe, good-looking young man, now twenty-four years old, just played cricket for the pleasure it gave him. Modest almost to the point of shyness, kind hearted and generous in thought as well as in deed, he had a chivalry on and off the field which was remarked upon by all who knew him. His fielding was moulded on the same lines as his batting; he could field anywhere, but with his magnificent long throw, safe hands and brilliant returns he was usually in the outfield, especially at long off or third man. Victor was also a very good change bowler; with a clinking pace on the fast side of medium, he commanded both a very fast ball and a slower one, all with the same action. The cricketers of England were to see quite a lot of this charming young man in the months to come.

A newcomer to England was Albert Hopkins, who had already appeared in two Test matches for Australia in the recently closed tour of MacLaren's and for his first appearance contributed a valuable 43 after the early batting had failed. A very attractive bat with all the classic strokes, but a partiality to the hook shot which sometimes got him out, he played in a lively polished fashion and certainly, like Trumper, took risks. He was nearly twenty-six, still improving, and it was thought that he would do well on the softer English pitches where he could be used as an opener or to stiffen the middle-order batting. Additionally, it was thought he would give variety to the bowling; although he bowled break-backs at a medium pace he cut the ball with a hand action rather than the use of finger spin. Typically of this fine team of athletes, he was an excellent outfield and could be used in any position whether on the off side or in the leg trap to Armstrong's bowling. Hopkins, of medium height and clean shaven, probably owed much for his inclusion in this side to his innings of 117 for N S W in their home State engagement with Victoria.

Brown as a berry was Reggie Duff, and described by C. B. Fry as having "a face like a good looking brown trout"*, this handsome young twenty-three-year-old batsman came for the first time to England, but with the wrong label. He had been described in the English cricket press as a stonewaller with very stubborn back play, which was really little less than libellous of Reg Duff's superb batting technique and bustling for runs. He was one of the new players to emerge during the recent MacLaren tour, appearing in four of the Tests with considerable distinction, as he had scored 104 in his first Test match. Thus, he fully vindicated the selectors' choice, in the face of considerable criticism, in materially helping Australia to victory and shaping as a batsman of the first class. In all, he scored 311 runs in eight innings, and in the last match had been promoted to open with Victor Trumper. He was a lovely timer of the ball; thus, when he played a lofted drive on either side of the wicket, he hit the good length ball not at its pitch but on the rise. This kind of stroke was rather uncommon; it called for a good eye. He possessed all the class batsman's strokes and was willing to use them, including a lovely slicing sort of cut from which he often scored, and a slashing pull shot off the rising ball. Nevertheless, when conditions required it he had an excellent defence; but he was always looking for runs. A short, sturdy, smiling young man sporting a fashionable military moustache, he was a marvellous mid-off, rivalling Ernie Jones for that position, but could field anywhere with customary Antipodean ability. At a pinch, too, Duff could be brought on to bowl his slow off-breaks or take over the stumper's gloves. A most useful fellow for the Tourists to have on their strength.

Jack Saunders, too, had just come into prominence in the newly closed season. This tall, dark, wavy-haired young man, with his upturned military moustache, was an unusual product to appear in Australia – a slow-medium left-hand bowler. He had been increasingly successful in Victorian cricket, but it was because of his fine performance of 11 for 130 against N S W that he was chosen for the Fourth Test at Sydney, where he took 9 for 162. It was considered that he would be ideal to send to England where pitches were thought to be eminently suited to him, for he had proved to be a fine wet-pitch bowler on which he could make the ball turn abruptly from the leg. Bowling often from around the wicket with a high action, he cleverly "yorked" batsmen and would produce the occasional faster one that went straight through. It was thought, too, that Englishmen would find it difficult to score off him on the leg side. G. L. Jessop questioned his action, and he was not alone in considering Saunders' flicky wrist on delivery to be illegal. Little

*C. B. Fry, *Life Worth Living*, Eyre & Spottiswoode, p. 241.

need be said of Jack Saunders' ability with the bat; he was a typical
tail-ender, but could fill any position in the field with complete
confidence.

There was something rather saturnine about the look of Warwick
Armstrong. He was tall and, at the age of twenty-two, athletic. He
has been described as rather a "rum cove", and his cricket could
be as dour and determined as he appeared. A trifle ungainly at the
crease, nevertheless a long reach enabled him to smother the
good length ball, and he was an awkward customer to bowl to when
set. Often defensive by method, and in this he was very sound,
Armstrong could be relied upon to hold up one end so would be
a useful individual to send in at a crisis. There were occasions,
however, when the mood took him when he hit out with powerfully
timed drives and forced the fielders to spread out around the
boundary. Already enjoying his third season in the first-class game,
he was chosen to represent Australia in the Second Test against
MacLaren's touring side, in large measure due to an impressive
innings of 137 for Victoria at Melbourne against New South Wales.
How he justified the selectors' faith was borne out with a score of 45
not out on his first appearance during the Second Test, then with 55
at a critical stage when the early batting slumped in the Fourth
Test. Notably, Armstrong was not out four times in seven innings.
He subsequently broke his collar-bone and, although it had healed,
was still suffering from soreness at the commencement of his first
visit to England. As a bowler, in 1902 he was still considered as
of the change variety to be useful for resting the main bowlers
in county matches. His leg-breaks, or, more precisely, leg-rollers,
could be sent down with a persistently nagging accuracy and length,
and would keep the runs down. He might, of course, prove more
suitable on the softer English pitches, as had already been proved
when the pitch helped him at home, where the ball really could
"break" using his leg spin. If the pitch was unhelpful, at least
bowling on the leg stump with such accuracy could force batsmen
into rash strokes. Then there was always the occasional ball that
Warwick overspun with the same apparent action, a straight break
which came straight through and made pace off the pitch. Less
mobile in the field than some, the tall Victorian was a safe slip and
sure close field.

No newcomer to the mother country, burly bee-farmer Bill
Howell had done exceedingly well on the Cornstalks' last tour in
1899, taking 117 wickets. But he had first made his mark against
English batsmen when, for New South Wales against Stoddart's
side in 1894–5, he surprised them by taking 5 for 44 on an unhelpful
Sydney pitch. MacLaren described it as a very fine performance,
and was even more impressed by him during the Australian season
of 1897–8, when Howell did most of the damage (4 for 70) on an

excellent pitch in the first innings of the Adelaide Test, bowling much better even than his figures showed. He was a right-arm medium-pace bowler with considerable powers of finger spin, having a rotary wrist action which part twisted and part cut the ball on leaving the hand. The effect of this, even on perfect pitches, was a smart break-back from the off. His pace tended to be on the fast side of medium, and, on Howell's first appearance on the 1899 tour, he so foxed the Surrey batsmen at The Oval that he took all 10 wickets for only 28 runs in the first innings, and 5 for 29 in the second. So far he had taken 20 wickets since 1897–8 in Test matches. Genial, thirty-two-year-old Bill Howell was probably a better left-hand bat than most people imagined, and going in generally between eight and eleven for N S W during the season just over, he scored successively 44, 18 not out and 27, then 67 in inter-colonial State matches. Against MacLaren's touring side he hit 34 and 27 for his State, and had scores as high as 35 and 31 not out in the Tests. Always a trier, in the Antipodes he was known as "Billy the Plugger"; ever active and loose-limbed, he fielded well anywhere.

The final member the Cornstalks included in their touring team was, of course, the deputy wicketkeeper. Choice unhesitatingly devolved on twenty-four-year-old Yorkshire-born, but Australian-brought-up, Hanson Carter. This young man was, surprisingly, an undertaker by profession. As well as being an expert wicketkeeper, he was developing as a capable batsman with all the strokes, a fine fielder anywhere, and could also bowl if required. Unfortunately for him, he was often kept out of the N S W side by Jim Kelly and only had the occasional chance to show his abilities when that worthy was absent through Test match duty. Carter had officiated behind the sticks for the N S W team while MacLaren's side totted up 769 runs. Possibly, his fine keeping in this match earned him the reserve place for the tour. It had already been noted how well he took the ball on the leg side, and he was thought of as a shrewd tactician of the game. We now know, of course, that "Sammy" Carter had to wait for a long time after 1902 before finally taking over the gloves from James J. Kelly, which he was to do eventually with such distinction.

These, then, were the young men who immediately became the focus of public attention, honorary "amateurs" for the cricket season, swelling the volume of colonials in England for the forthcoming Coronation, but here for a sterner purpose than the rest. Their prime objective was the retention of the legendary Ashes, but they also intended to play attractive cricket and win, if possible, every match in which they were engaged.

11

CHAPTER 2

"Got a frost-bite in your tail, Kangaroo?"

The weather at the end of April and the beginning of the "merry" month of May was, even for England, dreadful. As the Australians attempted their initial practice at Lord's, they had to put up with wintry showers of sleet and hail. The temperature was little above thirty-two degrees and, when it did rise, it changed to rain. Spring was bitterly cold. That it must have been a miserable introduction to the Old Country for these young men from the new Commonwealth, one need not question, for they had just arrived from the heat of an Australian summer and were quite unprepared for such bitter and intense cold. From the superb period photographs taken of them on the practice ground at Lord's, they all appear attired in long-sleeved sweaters posing in batting array on an obviously saturated and well cut-up pitch. The latter was due to a lacrosse match having been played by the Canadian lacrosse champions just previously, which had been attended by the King.

Owing to the extreme climatic conditions the Cornstalks were able to obtain little satisfactory practice, but at least they had the opportunity to pose for the photographs taken by George Beldam, and Foster and Hawkins, both of Brighton. Their first casualty occurred when Trumble slipped on the wet turf and, as it turned out, badly dislocated one of the fingers of his bowling hand. This was most unfortunate, for Trumble was to be out of action until early in June; thus the Tourists were deprived of one of their main bowlers before the first match had even been played, and their opening fixture was to be against a powerful London County side, got together by Dr W. G. Grace himself.

On former Australian tours up to 1896, "The Champion" had always led a very strong side against the Tourists at Sheffield Park in Sussex under the patronage of Lord Sheffield as the curtain-raiser to the tour. His Lordship, however, was abroad and Sheffield Park had been leased to visiting notabilities for the forthcoming

Coronation. Therefore, Crystal Palace was to be the venue of the first game, as in 1899, and the services of a fine array of talent for London County had been engaged for the occasion. Fry and Jessop were included among the regulars of this period consisting of C. J. B. Wood, G. Beldam, Len Braund, Billy Murdoch, Jack Board, Joe Vine, W. Smith and C. B. Llewellyn, as well as W. G. himself. London County had already played their first three fixtures: two against Surrey, both of which they had won, and a drawn match with Warwickshire very much in London County's favour. Charles Fry, by the way, some nine days earlier had taken part here at Crystal Palace in the replay of the F A Cup Final. He was a fine amateur footballer and played regularly for Southampton and the Corinthians. (The "Saints" lost 2–1 to Sheffield United in very windy conditions.)

Incessant rain on the Sunday and still more on the morning of 5 May delayed the start until 3 o'clock in the afternoon. Darling left out the injured Trumble, Ernie Jones – because the wet wicket would not suit him – and reserve wicketkeeper Carter. The visitors won the toss, and Duff, Hill and Noble were soon back in the pavilion – three wickets being down for but 33 runs. A far from auspicious start. Duff had gone for eight and Hill was bowled first ball, both by Hampshire's young South African all-rounder Charles Llewellyn, whose vicious left-handed away-spinners gave most of the Australian batsmen considerable trouble. But as soon as Darling joined Syd Gregory, they attempted to hit out against the offending Llewellyn in an excellent stand before the left-hander struck again when the score was 80. Trumper started well but was unfortunately run out for nine, the only other resistance being given by Armstrong, and so the Tourists were all out for a mere 117 runs. W. G. had taken two wickets, but the main damage had been done by Llewellyn on a pitch which gave him a deal of help. There was another brief interruption for rain when London County took possession and the Champion played on to Noble in the first over. Fry at the other end, however, batted with care, though George Beldam was soon sent back having been leg before to Noble. Thus, at close of play London County were 34 for two.

On the Tuesday "Cis" Wood, who normally took some shifting and never chanced a run in his life, was soon removed by Kelly. Braund, however, played up well from the commencement, but London County were very soon in further trouble when Fry was bowled by Noble, and four wickets were down for 52 runs. Now joined by Jessop they set about the bowling, batting in such a dashing fashion as to add 93 runs in only forty minutes. They were particularly hard on Monty Noble, who was "knocked about as if he had been a club bowler"; in one over alone Braund hit him for four fours. Unfortunately, Gilbert Jessop ended his fine display going

13

down the wicket missing Saunders and being stumped. Braund continued his masterly innings in spite of stoppages for bad light and rain. Murdoch, Smith and Llewellyn added but little to the score and Braund was on 72 when he was joined by Vine. Going on to score the first century against the Tourists, he was last man out, caught and bowled by Noble for 104 runs, which he had scored in just under 150 minutes.

London County's score of 235 left the Australians 118 runs in arrears, and they immediately lost three wickets on the still wet pitch, but their ability to fight an uphill task was shown when Victor Trumper joined his captain. A glimpse of batting delights to come was seen when together they added 85 in three-quarters of an hour; sixty-four of them came from Trumper, who was finally stumped dancing down the wicket to one of Braund's leg-breaks. He had hit all round the wicket brilliantly. After having been the more passive partner, Darling, now with Armstrong's assistance, drove fiercely whenever he was able. He was most unlucky to be caught by Joe Vine off the "Old Man's" bowling when eight runs short of the coveted century in the evening's gloom. Warwick Armstrong lasted little longer than his captain and, at close of play, the Australians were but 85 runs on with three wickets in hand. The last day was as wet and cold as ever and the few spectators who turned up witnessed little cricket, for only a quarter of an hour's play was possible before the match had to be abandoned.

The wretched weather had doubtless saved the Cornstalks from defeat on their first appearance, for had London County been able to bat again they would have most likely knocked off the deficit. There is no doubt many critics scoffed and said that this was not a very strong Australian side, scarcely allowing for the Tourists having had little pre-match practice and being thoroughly unhappy with the elements. Their bowling had not impressed and their batting, with the exception of Darling and Trumper, had often been quite at sea, but their fielding, in spite of the dreadful conditions, was keen, alert and up to the best Australian traditions. It had been an opening gambit and as yet the Tourists needed match practice, but they had shown in the second innings their ability to hit themselves out of trouble in conditions quite foreign to them. So to the discerning eye it was obvious that they would soon strike form and that they were going to be a side well worth watching.

AUSTRALIANS *v* LONDON COUNTY

At Crystal Palace, 5, 6, 7 May.

Match drawn.

AUSTRALIANS

M. A. Noble c Jessop b Braund	10	lbw, b Llewellyn	4
R. A. Duff b Llewellyn	8	b Llewellyn	1
C. Hill b Llewellyn	0	b Llewellyn	7
S. E. Gregory c Braund b Llewellyn	34	b Vine	2
*J. Darling c Fry b Llewellyn	26	c Vine b Grace	92
V. T. Trumper run out	9	st Board b Braund	64
W. W. Armstrong run out	13	c Wood b Vine	29
A. J. Hopkins b Grace	3	not out	7
†J. J. Kelly not out	5	not out	3
W. P. Howell c Grace b Llewellyn	4		
J. V. Saunders c Beldam b Grace	0		
Extras (B 3, LB 2)	5	(B 3, LB 1)	4
	117	(7 wkts)	**213**

LONDON COUNTY

*Dr W. G. Grace b Noble	1	Mr W. Smith c Darling b Howell	1
Mr C. B. Fry b Noble	31	C. B. Llewellyn b Howell	5
Mr G. W. Beldam lbw, b Noble	8	J. Vine c Darling b Hopkins	18
Mr C. J. B. Wood st Kelly b Howell	4	†J. H. Board not out	4
L. C. Braund c and b Noble	104	Extras (B 3, NB 2)	5
Mr G. L. Jessop st Kelly b Saunders	47		
Mr W. L. Murdoch b Saunders	7		**235**

LONDON COUNTY	O.	M.	R.	W.	O.	M.	R.	W.
Llewellyn	18	3	52	5	17	2	80	3
Braund	3	1	8	1	13	1	61	1
Vine	6	1	27	0	13	2	40	2
Grace	8.5	1	25	2	9	1	28	1
AUSTRALIANS								
Noble	23.1	2	90	4				
Saunders	10	0	43	2				
Howell	26	4	75	3				
Hopkins	3	0	22	1				

Umpires: G. Porter and G. Bean

It was after this match that the *Evening News* printed an amusing poem by Samuel J. Looker, dedicated to the Australians' plight during the London County game and the wintry conditions they had so far suffered since they arrived:

> "Does your circulation fail, Kangaroo?
> Got a frost-bite in your tail, Kangaroo?
> Do you find it hard to play
> When it's hailing half the day,
> And it's even cold for May, Kangaroo?

"Are your Noble, Duff and Hill, Kangaroo?
And poor Trumper feeling ill, Kangaroo?
Has the voyage made them stale,
Since Llewellyn did not fail
When he started 'finding bail', Kangaroo?

" 'Tis no doubt a sudden change, Kangaroo?
But you'd sooner find your range, Kangaroo?
If in coming o'er the seas,
In the chambers where they freeze,
You were hardened by degrees, Kangaroo?"*

The same evening the frozen "Kangaroos" travelled by train from St Pancras station to Nottingham where the following day, 8 May, they were due to meet the strength of Nottinghamshire on the fine Trent Bridge ground. So commenced one of the best games that the Tourists played in during a season of many thrilling matches. Ernest Jones was included in the attack and Saunders rested. When the Notts skipper, Arthur Jones, won the toss and elected to bat, the elements were described as being more suitable for football than cricket. Notts were without one of the three Gunns – George – but otherwise a full strength side turned out, including those veteran run-getters Arthur Shrewsbury, William Gunn and Mr J. A. Dixon, their former captain of the Victorian age.

Noble struck immediately. Jim Iremonger, the young opener – who also played soccer for Notts County – and William Gunn were both bowled. Two valuable wickets for the Visitors, but Arthur Shrewsbury now joined his captain and they commenced to pull the game round, at first slowly, then with increasing vigour. The pitch was too wet for Ernie Jones to demoralise them, but Howell was more successful. He finally broke the stand when A. O. Jones was caught for 45. Manfully, Bill Howell toiled on with Noble at the other end, only to suffer at the hands of John Gunn (80), who meanwhile had joined Shrewsbury. In two hours they added 139 runs to the score, playing the attack with ease, and in Shrewsbury's case, the pads as well. The watching public now saw Trumper in a new role – as a bowler. He sent down twenty-one overs, more in this innings than he had on the whole of the 1899 tour, with his fast medium deliveries. Trumper had a knack of spotting a batsman's weakness very quickly. He soon found the veteran Arthur's, who padded up too late and in the wrong place for Victor's quicker one. Out for 73, the small figure slowly walked to the pavilion, bowled by a young man who had been only a few months old at the time that he, Arthur Shrewsbury, had played in the first match against the

*P. C. Standing, *Cricket of Today and Yesterday*, T. C. & E. C. Jack, Vol. 2, p. 112.

16

first Australian touring team of David Gregory's in 1878, some twenty-four years before.

Notts, having stayed at the wicket for the whole of the first day's play, were finally all out for 287. Howell with 4 for 74 had borne the brunt of the attack, but Trumper in his new "English" role as a trundler had taken 3 valuable wickets for 59 runs.

Now the Tourists had not been entirely certain as to their opening pair; they had tried many permutations, but Darling decided to send Reg Duff in first with Trumper as they had done previously in Australia, and they came off. Runs came immediately; T. Wass and G. Anthony, who opened the Notts' attack, were soon changed to John Gunn and A. Hallam, but the flow was not abated. Trumper hit beautifully clean and hard, putting the bowlers on the defensive, scoring at twice the rate of his partner, but they were both seen to fine advantage. No matter how Jones changed his field, they found gaps. This was entertaining cricket enough to keep the spectators warm on a cold day. With the scoreboard displaying 75 runs for no wicket and looking "as safe as houses", Trumper went down the pitch to Hallam and was bowled for 47. Clem Hill came in to assist the confident Duff, who was timing the ball beautifully and often hitting it on the rise. The run-rate had slowed after the opening partnership, and Hill, followed quickly by Syd Gregory, were both beautifully caught by Goodacre off John Gunn whilst looking for runs. Soon after Darling got off the mark, Reg Duff was dismissed by Hallam, caught Wass, for a valuable 49, and the fortunes were swinging back to Notts' favour, more especially so when Noble over-cautiously popped up one of John Gunn's deliveries to point, where Shrewsbury pouched it and Australia were 5 down for 137. Darling, ever watchful, phlegmatic even, waited patiently for the right ball and hit with great power. Meanwhile, he had been joined by Armstrong, and 38 runs were added before Armstrong was deceived by Hallam's pace. 175 for 6 and Notts were back in the game.

The Australians were now in trouble. Albert Hopkins made an unsteady start, he was out of touch, as was Darling himself, being twice nearly caught, missed each time by Tom Wass at mid-on. Never let Darling off once, let alone twice, it will be expensive. They settled down and hit carefully and with power. No matter how A. O. Jones rang the bowling changes, Gunn, Hallam, Wass, Anthony, even Dixon, the scoreboard clicked steadily. Hopkins now batted delightfully, producing beautifully timed strokes all round the wicket, cutting square and late with many runs coming from a long pull over square leg; to the spectators, he looked like another Trumper. Together they added another 131 runs, of which Bert Hopkins' contribution was 80 before John Gunn bowled him. 306 for 7 looked far more healthy when Jim Kelly came out to join

17

his captain, and they hit the tired bowling to reach 353 at the drawing of stumps.

The following morning, Saturday, the Australians needed quick runs to have any chance of winning – they were only 66 runs on; so Darling and Kelly chanced their arms and added a quick 72 before John Gunn struck again, Darling having made 128 runs in nearly five hours. 425 for 8 and the burly "Jonah", with considerable luck, giving the "long handle", drove Gunn and Anthony, relishing his fortune until he mistimed the latter for a caught and bowled. The Cornstalks had reached 474, thanks to Darling's two let-offs; a healthy total.

Obviously, Nottinghamshire could only play for a draw and it seemed most likely, the pitch still playing well was in their favour, that they must bat out time. A. O. Jones and Iremonger started carefully enough, Howell and Noble having no great success with the ball. Jones, however, was caught for 19 and William Gunn played watchfully in his stead. Just after half past three with the score at 80 for 1, Darling decided to try Armstrong instead of Noble. Twenty minutes passed, twelve runs were added, then Armstrong had Gunn LBW and, a couple of balls later, he induced Shrewsbury to touch one to Noble at short square leg. Iremonger, who had played so steadily for 46 runs, now gave a return catch to Warwick and four wickets were down, three of them mesmerised by the Armstrong leg-break. They still had a chance to draw if only the remaining batsmen did nothing rash; after all, the pitch was still good and Armstrong was only rolling them, no *savage* break to contend with. But the Notts batsmen must have been "mesmerised" by the frowning countenance that rolled those leg-spinners down with such precision. Apart from John Gunn, who, for a time, tried to play him before he pitched to the tune of 30 good runs, the remainder played recklessly against him. Three of Armstrong's remaining victims were clean bowled. Now the end came inevitably, and Notts went down to defeat by an innings and four runs with three-quarters of an hour playing time left. Warwick Armstrong had bowled with remarkable success to take 8 second innings wickets for 47 runs in 17 overs and 5 balls, so giving the Australians their first win of the tour in only their second match. They were knitting together well as a side; the spectators were delighted with Darling's darlings.

From Nottingham, the Australian players returned to their London hotel to rest for the weekend; they were due to meet Surrey at Kennington Oval on the Monday. It was still bitterly cold and still it rained! It felt more like February than 12 May when Darling's men arrived at The Oval in their horse-brake, wrapped in heavy sweaters. The few spectators that were in evidence, heavily clad in overcoats and mackintoshes, shivered as they sat or paced

AUSTRALIANS
v
NOTTINGHAMSHIRE

At Trent Bridge, Nottingham, 8, 9, 10 May.

Australians won by an innings and 4 runs.

NOTTINGHAMSHIRE

*Mr A. O. Jones c Hill b Howell	45	c Duff b Howell	19
J. Iremonger b Noble	4	c and b Armstrong	46
W. Gunn lbw, b Noble	0	lbw, b Armstrong	23
A. Shrewsbury b Trumper	73	c Noble b Armstrong	2
Mr W. B. Goodacre b Trumper	20	c Howell b Armstrong	16
J. R. Gunn c and b Howell	80	c Darling b Armstrong	30
Mr J. A. Dixon c Kelly b Howell	3	b Armstrong	17
G. Anthony b Jones	30	b Armstrong	1
†T. W. Oates c Kelly b Trumper	11	b Noble	0
A. W. Hallam b Howell	4	not out	8
T. G. Wass not out	8	b Armstrong	4
Extras (B 7, LB 2)	9	(B 9, LB 8)	17
	287		**183**

AUSTRALIANS

V. T. Trumper b Hallam	47	A. J. Hopkins b J. Gunn	80
R. A. Duff c Wass b Hallam	49	†J. J. Kelly c Jones b J. Gunn	66
C. Hill c Goodacre b J. Gunn	14	E. Jones c and b Anthony	38
S. E. Gregory c Goodacre b J. Gunn	6	W. P. Howell not out	4
*J. Darling c Hallam b J. Gunn	128	Extras (B 5, LB 3, NB 3)	11
M. A. Noble c Shrewsbury b J. Gunn	10		
W. Armstrong b Hallam	21		**474**

AUSTRALIANS	O.	M.	R.	W.	O.	M.	R.	W.
Jones	17	5	33	1				
Noble	16	7	46	2	... 14	5	32	1
Howell	35.3	14	74	4	... 22	7	66	1
Armstrong	21	4	59	0	... 17.5	6	47	8
Hopkins	2	0	7	0				
Trumper	21	6	59	3	... 8	1	21	0
NOTTS.								
Wass	21	0	79	0				
Anthony	11	2	53	1				
J. Gunn	63	15	174	6				
Hallam	45	12	126	3				
Dixon	12	3	31	0				

FALL OF WICKETS			
	Notts.	Aus.	Notts.
Wkt.	1st	1st	2nd
1st	27	75	56
2nd	27	104	92
3rd	51	116	97
4th	200	125	104
5th	214	137	145
6th	223	175	154
7th	249	306	156
8th	270	425	171
9th	279	468	179
10th	287	474	183

Umpires: V. A. Titchmarsh and T. Mycroft

up and down hopefully waiting for the rain to cease. There was no need to worry about picking a favourite viewpoint for the far famed "Surrey Crowd" was conspicuous by its absence, in spite of the auspiciousness of the occasion, so poor Craig, "the Surrey poet", and the match card sellers were having a thin time.

Digby Jephson and Darling tossed hopefully; Darling won. In view of the conditions, he left out Jones, bringing Saunders back; Hugh Trumble was still unfit, and Kelly had unfortunately damaged a finger at Trent Bridge so Hanson Carter came into the team for the first time. Whilst the Surrey side was a good one, it was not their strongest available by any means – no Holland, Captain Bush or "Shrimp" Leveson Gower, no "Razor" Smith – and the pitch obviously would not suit Lockwood and Richardson, who were playing. Nevertheless, a team including Bobby Abel ("The Guv'nor"), Tom Hayward, Bill Brockwell, E. G. Hayes, E. M. Dowson, and V. F. S. Crawford would give a good account of themselves; that is, provided it stopped raining. Play was finally possible at tea time; Trumper and Duff came quickly down the pavilion steps, Richardson and Dowson opened the bowling. Trumper danced out on the heavy waterlogged pitch and drove them. Duff was soon bowled for eight rather uncomfortable runs, but Victor seemed in his element. Now with Clem Hill they were making up for lost time under glowering skies; in sixteen minutes these two elegant batsmen plundered 37 runs. After little more than an hour, the scoreboard read 87 for 1 wicket – and then down came the rain again.

On Tuesday, rain delayed the resumption, and it was still frightfully cold and gloomy. Eventually, Trumper and Hill carried on where they had left off; Lockwood was tried in an attempt to stem the flow, but he could not get a foothold. Unfortunately, Clem Hill ran himself out, though Trumper batted stylishly onward. He was hard on the bowlers, driving, cutting and pulling in fearless fashion even balls pitched on the middle stump. Gregory played faultlessly, but was second fiddle to the glorious, strokemaking Trumper, who soon reached his century. Those who witnessed it realised it was inevitable, for he played with such an easy style and grace, and his perfection of technique ensured he was safeness itself in attack. His previous two innings had shown that, in spite of the chances he took, he would soon reach the coveted hundred. Now, as soon as he had done so, he played a bad ball from Hayward into the hands of Hayes, one that normally he would have hit into the crowd: there seemed little chance of a result, there was plenty of batting to come and his team-mates badly needed batting experience on wet pitches; he had had his! The still sparse crowd applauded the lithe figure of Trumper as he walked towards the pavilion. It was a pity that their Royal Highnesses the Prince of Wales and Prince Charles of Denmark had not arrived at the ground before lunch instead of afterwards; they missed seeing Victor Trumper in action. After another interruption for rain of about an hour, umpires Jim Phillips, himself an Australian, and the redoubtable Alfred Shaw came out again and play continued. Now the royal party saw the brilliant partnership of Noble and Armstrong, who put their bats to almost everything. Richardson toiled manfully, getting little real pace out of the heavy turf, and Digby Jephson even put himself on.

Probably, Armstrong was surprised to see an underhand lob bowler in action. After little more than three hours at the wicket, the Tourists having added some 209 runs, Darling called his players in. At 296 for 5 with small prospect of a result, he might as well let Surrey bat. They were 18 for 0 at the close.

Little Bobby Abel, "The Guv'nor" to "The Surrey Crowd", was, at the age of forty-four, still one of the finest professional batsmen of the day. He had opened the Surrey innings, and continued on the morrow on what could only be described as a treacherous sticky wicket. The previous evening's rain, a dry night and early morning sun had fortuitously given the Australians an unexpected advantage. Saunders and Howell bowled Surrey out for 96 runs, but Bobby Abel scored 34 of these and he kept up his wicket carefully on the difficult pitch whilst his comrades were in dire distress. Carter did very well behind the stumps, standing close up and being quick, neat and effective, catching two and conceding only three byes and two leg-byes.

Surrey were invited to follow on and, although the pitch was still difficult, the most likely result seemed to be a draw. This time Bill Howell, a fine bowler on any pitch, keeping up a good pace and accurate length and sometimes bringing the ball back awkwardly, caused suicidal tendencies among most of the Surrey side. But "The Guv'nor" knew instinctively which balls to hit and which to leave alone. He played many fine innings during this season for much higher scores, but few were more skilful in application. As each other wicket fell for a small score, Stedman and Dowson hit out in sheer desperation towards the end, thus enabling the home side to reach three figures, which at one time seemed unlikely. Four hours on this day had sufficed for Surrey to lose 20 wickets for a total of 200 runs, thereby leaving the Australians the victors by an innings and 78 runs. It was a fine win, which, at the beginning of the day's play, had seemed most improbable. Noble and Saunders had contributed liberally, but the architect of the victory was William Howell, who had taken 11 wickets for a mere 56 runs. It was a popular and well-earned win.

By hansom-cab in small parties, Darling's young men were taken to theatres and music halls during their sojourn in the metropolis. This had always proved a popular diversion with touring sides after a hard day in the cricket field. They visited the Apollo Theatre to see and hear the delightful Miss Edna May in the musical play *Three Little Maids*, which had just opened.

And so to Leyton, just beyond the River Lea in metropolitan Essex, on Thursday 15 May to meet the county that had beaten them in 1899 in a surprise victory. Essex had already taken part in two waterlogged fixtures, versus Surrey at The Oval and as hosts to Yorkshire at Leyton, where the home side had been dismissed by

AUSTRALIANS *v* SURREY

At Kennington Oval, 12, 13, 14 May.

Australians won by an innings and 78 runs.

AUSTRALIANS

V. T. Trumper c Hayes b Hayward ...	101
R. A. Duff b Richardson	8
C. Hill run out	33
S. E. Gregory c Abel b Hayward	38
*J. Darling c Brockwell b Hayward	19
M. A. Noble not out	44
W. W. Armstrong not out	41

A. Hopkins
†H. Carter
W. Howell   } did not bat
J. V. Saunders

Extras (B 9, W 2, NB 1) 12

(5 wkts dec.) 296

SURREY

R. Abel b Howell	34	c and b Howell	36
A. Baker c Carter b Noble	3	b Noble	3
E. G. Hayes b Howell	17	c Armstrong b Howell	4
W. H. Lockwood b Howell	20	c Trumper b Saunders	12
T. Hayward c Carter b Saunders	0	b Howell	2
W. Brockwell c Noble b Saunders	13	b Howell	3
Mr E. M. Dowson c Howell b Saunders	0	not out	20
Mr V. F. S. Crawford c Armstrong b Howell	0	b Howell	12
*Mr D. L. A. Jephson c Darling b Saunders	3	b Howell	0
†A. Stedman b Howell	0	b Noble	23
T. Richardson not out	0	b Noble	0
Extras (B 3, LB 2, NB 1)	6	(B 7)	7
	96		122

SURREY	O.	M.	R.	W.	O.	M.	R.	W.
Richardson	34	10	89	1				
Dowson	14	2	49	0				
Hayward	27	2	94	3				
Lockwood	1	0	3	0				
Brockwell	9	0	37	0				
Jephson	3	0	12	0				
AUSTRALIANS								
Armstrong	19	12	20	0				
Saunders	12.3	6	26	4	13	1	39	1
Noble	14	4	21	1	10	2	43	3
Howell	8	1	23	5	22	7	33	6

Umpires: A. Shaw and J. Phillips

Haigh and Rhodes for 89. With one completed innings in each of two matches, the Essex batsmen had had little opportunity to achieve anything of note. Perrin had made 42 not out and McGahey 48 not out. Fane and newcomer Sewell had as yet done nothing, whilst the bowling had already been walloped by Bobby Abel and F. S. Jackson for a 101 apiece.

Welcomed by inveterate pipe-smoker Harry Owen (it was, needless to say, still raining), the Tourists found that the side opposing them, although strong in batting, were not quite up to the standard of the 1899 combination with the ball. Although Charles Kortright, "Sailor" Young and Walter Mead were playing, they all had passed their prime, and young Claude Buckenham had not been chosen, the pitch and the weather hardly suiting him. Many of Darling's men remembered "Sailor" Young, the fast medium left-arm bowler who had proved almost unplayable in the 1899 match with 11 wickets for 74 runs. He bowled round the wicket and the ball came with his arm, and it sometimes pitched on the blind spot outside the off stump. He had twice got Trumper out in the 1899 Tests. "Korty's" legendary speed was not legendary to them, either, having faced him in 1899. He might well be faster than "Jonah" – many English players thought him the fastest ever – and he bowled a capital yorker. Walter Mead would be well known to Gregory and Trumble for his right-hand medium slows that he held in both hands until the last moment, and disguised to be either a rolled leg-break or a finger-spun off-break. In 1893, here at Leyton, he had demoralised them to the tune of 17 wickets for 205 runs. The Cornstalks had good reason to remember these Essex bowlers.

Kelly came back into the side and Ernie Jones returned in place of Saunders, although the wicket would have been more suitable for the latter. Trumble's hand had not yet recovered. There was no possibility of play until after 3 p.m., and the pitch was soft and difficult. Mr F. L. Fane and "Bob" Carpenter were quickly removed (2 for 25). But once the Essex "twins" Peter Perrin (known as Percy) and Charlie McGahey came together, they made light of a bad wicket and added 83 excellent runs until Trumper had "Charlie Mac" caught: 108 for 3. Now Victor Trumper had a fine spell of bowling, quickly sending back Owen and Sewell, both bowled, the latter from a crashing yorker, and Kortright caught off a hefty smack by Hopkins in the outfield, whilst Armstrong finally disposed of Perrin for 63. So, as umpire West called time, the home side had tumbled to 157 for eight.

After a late start on Friday, Essex were finally removed for 178. When bowling wicketkeeper Tom Russell, Trumper thus raised his tally to 5 wickets for 33 runs including 4 maidens in 13 overs; it was as surprising to Victor himself as it must have been to his colleagues and foes alike. A splendid piece of bowling. But Noble had also bowled well in taking 3 for 42. Immediately the Australians took possession, Victor, in tackling a ball from "Sailor" Young, pulled it on to his wicket for 9, so Clem Hill assisted Duff to raise the score quickly to 59 at lunch. The heavy skies could contain themselves no longer and only seventy minutes play had been possible.

Although the last day came with a bright, dry start on a still damp pitch, the Essex bowlers initially had no success. It should have suited both Mead and Young! It was Charlie McGahey who kidded Reg Duff into thinking he was bowling leg-breaks to enable Russell to stump him for 47. He had scored well and quickly, but it was Clement Hill playing a driving game who really impressed on this bad pitch. Although he was missed once, he made no other mistake

23

and he was particularly severe on Mead and Young. Syd Gregory, who had started to play well in support, was unlucky to be caught behind. Joe Darling attempted to force the pace without success, and the Australians were 4 down for 200 runs with Hill having reached his century, a most impressive display, amid much acclaim. Given instructions to hit out, Hopkins and Jones were sent in and fell to the wiles of Mead, while McGahey at this point took three splendid catches in succession. First it was Hill for 104 (209 for 6), then Jones, followed by Howell to be 210 for 8. Armstrong and Noble steadied the side until Darling closed the innings at 249 without further loss as the skies turned nasty again. Fane and Carpenter immediately fell to Monty Noble (13–2) before scudding rain forced the players to seek the welcome shelter of the pavilion once more. The match was later abandoned, unfortunately for the Australians, for it was unlikely that Essex would have lasted very long on that pitch.

With the tour but two weeks old and considering the terrible weather conditions, without a precedent in the history of the game, Darling, Trumper, and now Hill had each reached the century mark, whilst Hopkins and Duff had also shown good form. In spite of Hugh Trumble being *hors de combat* and the wickets unsuitable to Jones, Howell had bowled marvellously, and Saunders, Noble and Armstrong had had their moments of success. Thus, it was beginning to be realised that the English critics had underestimated them, and this eleventh touring team might prove to be the strongest and most dangerous side to visit us from the Commonwealth.

The magazine *World* included a rather humorous poem referring to the bleak wintry conditions in which cricketers were endeavouring to play our summer game:

"The bowlers bowled amid the snow,
And blue was every finger-tip,
And all the batsmen looked as though
King Frost firm held them in his grip.

"The Umpire knit his thoughtful brow,
And sighed as off he tried to slink,
'The only kind of cricket now
Is cricket on the hearth, I think.' "*

*P. C. Standing, *Cricket of Today and Yesterday*, T. C. & E. C. Jack, Vol. 2, p. 119.

AUSTRALIANS *v* ESSEX

At Leyton, 15, 16, 17 May.

Match drawn.

ESSEX

Mr F. L. Fane b Jones	9	c Howell b Noble	6
H. Carpenter b Noble	9	b Howell	1
Mr P. Perrin b Armstrong	63	not out	1
Mr C. McGahey c Howell b Trumper	36	not out	0
*Mr H. G. Owen b Trumper	6		
E. H. D. Sewell b Trumper	12		
Mr C. J. Kortright c Hopkins b Trumper	9		
H. Young b Noble	0		
†T. M. Russell b Trumper	4		
W. Reeves not out	15		
W. Mead c Hill b Noble	6		
Extras (B 8, NB 1)	9	(B 5)	5
	178	**(2 wkts)**	**13**

AUSTRALIANS

R. A. Duff st Russell b McGahey	47	W. P. Howell c McGahey b Young	0
V. T. Trumper b Young	9	W. Armstrong not out	12
C. Hill c McGahey b Young	104	M. A. Noble not out	25
S. E. Gregory c Russell b Mead	23	Extras (B 6, LB 4, NB 5)	15
*J. Darling c Russell b Mead	7		
A. J. Hopkins c Reeves b Mead	7	**(8 wkts dec.)**	**249**
E. Jones c McGahey b Mead	0	†J. J. Kelly did not bat.	

AUSTRALIANS	O.	M.	R.	W.	O.	M.	R.	W.
Jones	10	2	33	1				
Noble	18.1	7	42	3	3	2	1	1
Howell	8	1	25	0	4	2	7	1
Armstrong	12	4	36	1				
Trumper	13	4	33	5				
ESSEX								
Mead	30	3	105	4				
Young	31	6	75	3				
McGahey	6	0	22	1				
Reeves	6	0	32	0				

FALL OF WICKETS

Wkt.	Ess. 1st	Aus. 1st	Ess. 2nd
1st	17	24	10
2nd	25	107	12
3rd	108	176	—
4th	122	190	—
5th	143	200	—
6th	150	209	—
7th	153	209	—
8th	157	210	—
9th	157	—	—
10th	178	—	—

Umpires: W. A. J. West and J. Carlin

CHAPTER 3

"And it's even cold for May, Kangaroo?"

It was the Whitsun weekend, and whilst in far away South Africa the Boer leaders were arriving in Pretoria preparing to sue for peace with Lord Kitchener and Lord Milner, the Australian touring team entrained for Leicester, their next encounter being with the shire of that name at Aylestone Road, due to commence on Whit Monday, 19 May. In the last few days Leicester had had by far the worst of a drawn game with Yorkshire at Huddersfield, and in the previous encounter, their first match of the season, the Midland county had narrowly escaped defeat at the hands of Lancashire, Archie MacLaren showing fine form with 112, being saved only by the weather.

Leicester were not one of the stronger county sides, but they did have some very competent batting in C. J. B. Wood, R. T. Crawford, J. H. King, A. E. Knight and H. Whitehead. They were less strong in bowling, however. They no longer had Pougher and Parnham, but Woodcock and King were the mainstays of the attack ably supported by two twenty-year-old amateurs: Reggie Crawford, Parson Crawford's second son and the younger brother of V. F. S., and W. W. Odell, a promising new slow bowler. Arthur Woodcock at thirty-six, "Timber" to his friends, took a long run up and still sent them down very fast indeed from his powerful frame. Surrey-born, he had spent some time in America as coach to Haverford College, Philadelphia. For a time during the 1890s he was thought to be almost as fast as Kortright. He still kept himself very fit, but, like many pace men in their later years, was prone to knee trouble. J. H. King was a reliable left-handed all-rounder, yet to reach his maturity. In Albert Knight they possessed a classic batsman of rather unusual capabilities. Four years later, he was to write a quite remarkable book on the game, *The Complete Cricketer*, full of shrewd observations showing the deep thinker and scholar within him. He was also a deeply religious man. Opening batsman "Cis" Wood had met the Tourists before in their first match at Crystal Palace. He was usually partnered by Whitehead, and they were as reliable an opening pair as any county could wish for.

No doubt the Australians remembered the last time they visited Leicester in 1899, having dismissed the Midlanders for only 20 runs off the bat, Monty Noble (7 for 15) and Ernie Jones (3 for 5) having caused the rout, thus winning by 248 runs. That they might try to emulate their former success may well have been in Darling's mind, for he decided to retain Jones and replace Bill Howell with Jack Saunders. Carter was brought in again behind the stumps, for Kelly's hand was still troublesome.

Under a pale and watery sun after overnight rain, C. E. de Trafford won a toss that he would perhaps have preferred to lose. Joe Darling, with the success of three summers ago in his mind, handed the ball to Jones and Noble in turn. They bowled unchanged and, for thirty-five overs and one ball between them, attempted a repeat performance. They knocked out the Leicester side before lunch for 51 runs. Only Wood reached double figures on that cold and miserable morning, and three of his colleagues collected ducks. "Jonah's" success in taking 6 wickets for 26 runs must have been satisfying to him, for it was already being suggested by commentators on the game that he was no longer the great performer of previous tours. This, of course, was patently unfair, for until now he had not been able to operate on a pitch that remotely suited him. Noble, backing him up admirably with 4 for 21, also had every reason to be pleased with himself.

The afternoon provided further shocks, this time for the Australians, for the pitch also suited "Timber" Woodcock and King, and for a time it seemed they might emulate Jones and Noble. Arthur Woodcock, bowling with all the pace he could command, nearly brought off a hat-trick: he had Duff, Hill and Gregory in four balls. It was only when Darling joined Trumper that they managed to contain the bowling for a time. Victor played with all his ease and grace, quite untroubled, and Joe got his runs grimly; then King, with his medium slow left-handers, drew Trumper forward and deceived him. The pitch was quite difficult and the visitors were soon 9 down for only 77 runs. It was at this point that Ernie Jones started to hit while Saunders kept his end up. Missed twice before reaching 11, "Jonah" came to the rescue vigorously, giving King and Woodcock the long handle to reach 40 runs in twenty minutes before being well caught by Odell off the bowling of King. Thanks to this last wicket stand the Tourists had managed 126 – far more than at one time had seemed likely. All credit, though, is due to the fine penetrative bowling of Woodcock and King, operating unchanged for 5 wickets apiece against this formidable batting array.

27

On Leicester's resumption at the wicket, after more rain, Wood and Whitehead were not parted until they had cleared 54 of the outstanding 75 in little longer than half an hour. The county side had started in fine fettle, but could not maintain the headway in the face of a persistent attack on the stumps by Noble and Jones, for by the time the arrears were cleared three wickets had fallen. Knight and Reggie Crawford tried their best to stay; the latter was bowled in attempting to collar Noble, as was Knight soon afterwards.

Came the final morning: although Saunders and Trumper bowled a few overs, the tail was swept up by Monty Noble assisted by Jones. The last four wickets were worth 26 runs to the County, thus leaving the Tourists to obtain a mere 69 with most of the day ahead of them. As in the first innings, it was Noble and Jones who shared the plunder. Noble's figures were splendid, 12 wickets for 69 runs, and "Jonah's" all-round effort of 40 runs from the bat and 8 wickets for 55 was heart-warming for the Australians. So, under heavy skies, they went out to knock off the deficit. Neither Duff, caught by Wood off Odell, nor Hopkins, leg-before to Woodcock, could stay with Trumper, but then Syd Gregory joined him; they both hit hard until Victor mistimed Odell. It took the captain himself, hard driving and completely overhauling Gregory, to make the seven-wicket win in just one hour. The Australians could afford to be very pleased with themselves – everybody in the side had now done something of note.

And so to Oxford, the city of dreaming spires, did our Antipodean friends repair to meet the Dark Blues on the famous Christ Church Ground. The Oxonians, apart from the experience of the usual University trial matches, had only enjoyed two games, both twelve-a-side events. They had played against a strong team raised by H. D. G. Leveson Gower, in which they went down with all colours flying and great credit to themselves, followed immediately by a drawn fixture with Somerset, during which much time was lost through the inevitable elements. The Dark Blues' captain, C. H. B. Marsham, was in good form with the bat, but so was his fellow-Kent amateur, the left-handed E. W. Dillon, who had played a fine knock of 114 against Somerset. The young freshman W. H. B. Evans from Malvern had covered himself with glory, too, for his brilliant hitting in the same match. In W. Findlay, they had a class wicketkeeper, but their bowling was not a strong feature. G. W. F. Kelly and A. C. von Ernsthausen were fast, "Bertie" Evans and R. A. Williams were both of medium pace, and Dillon could trundle some fair leg-breaks.

Darling intended to field the same side that was victorious at Leicester, but in view of the dreadful weather on the first day, 22 May, not a single ball was able to be sent down; thus the Varsity men were able to entertain the famous Australians in their pavilion.

AUSTRALIANS *v* LEICESTERSHIRE

At Leicester, 19, 20, 21 May.
Australians won by 7 wickets.

LEICESTERSHIRE

Mr C. J. B. Wood b Jones	13	b Jones		33
H. Whitehead b Noble	2	lbw, b Noble		24
J. H. King b Jones	8	c Saunders b Noble		12
A. E. Knight c Noble b Jones	6	b Noble		24
Mr R. T. Crawford c and b Jones	8	b Noble		17
*Mr C. E. de Trafford c Saunders b Jones	6	c and b Jones		1
S. Coe b Noble	0	c Gregory b Noble		11
F. Geeson b Jones	0	lbw, b Noble		1
Mr W. W. Odell c Carter b Noble	0	b Noble		6
A. Woodcock c Armstrong b Noble	4	c and b Noble		5
†J. P. Whiteside not out	0	not out		0
Extras (B 2, NB 1, LB 1)	4	(B 3, LB 5, W 1)		9
	51			**143**

AUSTRALIANS

V. T. Trumper b King	20	b Odell		14
R. A. Duff c Whiteside b Woodcock	0	c Wood b Odell		3
C. Hill b Woodcock	0			
S. E. Gregory b Woodcock	2	not out		18
*J. Darling c Whitehead b King	25	not out		22
M. A. Noble c Crawford b Woodcock	13			
W. W. Armstrong c Odell b King	7			
A. J. Hopkins b King	9	lbw, b Woodcock		1
†H. Carter c Coe b Woodcock	1			
E. Jones c Odell b King	40			
J. V. Saunders not out	9	Extras (B 11)		11
	126	(3 wkts)		**69**

AUSTRALIANS	O.	M.	R.	W.		O.	M.	R.	W.
Jones	18	9	26	6	...	17	8	29	2
Noble	17.1	7	21	4	...	20.1	6	48	8
Saunders					...	3	0	24	0
Trumper					...	6	0	33	0
LEICESTERSHIRE									
Woodcock	19	5	54	5	...	6	1	16	1
King	19	0	72	5					
Odell					...	10	2	23	2
Geeson					...	3	0	12	0
Crawford					...	1	0	7	0

FALL OF WICKETS

	Leics.	Aus.	Leics.	Aus.
Wkt.	1st	1st	2nd	2nd
1st	6	1	54	3
2nd	23	1	64	14
3rd	26	7	74	40
4th	37	35	94	—
5th	37	54	99	—
6th	39	63	112	—
7th	39	75	126	—
8th	39	76	136	—
9th	49	77	142	—
10th	51	126	143	—

Umpires: W. A. J. West and V. A. Titchmarsh

Once play began on the second day, Dillon and Marsham hoisted 40 runs for the first wicket, but from the moment Jones and Noble removed them for 21 apiece, the remainder of the Varsity collapsed to the swerve of Monty Noble and the leg-spin wiles of Warwick Armstrong for the addition of a paltry 35, the latter mopping up 4 wickets for 9 runs in only 6 overs.

Right from the start Trumper, aided and abetted by Reg Duff, went for the runs and the Oxford bowling, which they treated with total disrespect. When Duff was well caught behind by Findlay for 41 off the fast bowling of von Ernsthausen, Clem Hill continued the grand work of supporting Victor in the run feast. Trumper's first 50 had come in 40 minutes hitting in beautiful style, placing the ball through the field at will. Continuing in this happy vein, playing many strokes improvised at the merest whim, for the sheer joy of it almost, he raced to his century. His stylish and magnificent strokeplay delighted both spectators and opponents alike, and although he gave chances at 86 and 117, these were but small blemishes on a marvellous display of the art of batsmanship; until finally he offered up a catch to Mr Wyld at cover point for 121. The scoreboard read 2 wickets for 213. After adding another 13 pugnacious runs, Clem Hill was most cleverly stumped by Findlay for a well-hit 64.

On the Saturday the spectators witnessed a bright 39 from the attractive bat of Albert Hopkins when, after seven Oxonians had taken a turn with the leather, Darling decided to declare the innings closed whilst he was in possession himself. The Cornstalks came in at 6 for 314 runs.

Oxford were now struggling again, overwhelmed by bowling and fielding of a class so much above them. Voss, however, managed much better than his fellows, and the 28 runs to his credit were attractively made against this superb bowling. Darling had decided to bring on Saunders when the score was 53 for 3 – he immediately bowled "Bertie" Evans. During this innings Carter, behind the stumps, was hit in the eye by the ball after it had hit the bails. His right eye was so badly cut that he had to be treated by Dr Pope, and although he returned to the field he was to be out of action for some time. The Dark Blues were trying hopefully to play out time, Darling may have left his declaration a little too late, but Jack Saunders, bowling an immaculate length and coming quickly off the pitch, had the Varsity men in trouble for they found his break so difficult to gauge. Although Kelly and Findlay held up the proceedings for an unconscionable time – they almost saved the game – Saunders had them both in the end with ten minutes to spare. He would not be denied; seven wickets for 67 runs had won the match, and just in time!

Back to the metropolis for a day's respite, the Australians need-ing warmth and rest before turning out to play the M C C on their first public appearance at Lord's. This fixture would provide them with far sterner opposition than they had encountered of late. The first Test match was only five days distant and the side they were due to meet on the morrow was composed almost entirely of Test players, past, present, and potential. The weather had

AUSTRALIANS
v
OXFORD UNIVERSITY

At Oxford, 22, 23, 24 May.

Australians won by an innings and 54 runs.

OXFORD UNIVERSITY

Mr E. W. Dillon c Darling b Jones	21	c Duff b Jones	3
*Mr C. H. B. Marsham c Hopkins b Noble	21	b Noble	5
Mr H. J. Wyld c Saunders b Noble	1	b Jones	19
Mr W. H. B. Evans c Trumper b Noble	7	b Saunders	13
Mr R. Z. H. Voss b Armstrong	10	b Saunders	28
Mr M. Bonham-Carter c Jones b Noble	7	(7) lbw, b Saunders	9
Mr R. A. Williams c Trumper b Armstrong	0	(8) c Noble b Saunders	26
Mr E. G. Whately b Armstrong	0	(9) c Jones b Saunders	8
Mr G. W. F. Kelly b Armstrong	0	(10) lbw, b Saunders	31
†Mr W. Findlay not out	5	(6) b Saunders	21
Mr A. C. von Ernsthausen b Noble	4	not out	3
Extras (NB 1)	1	(B 11, LB 6)	17
	77		183

AUSTRALIANS

V. T. Trumper c Wyld b Evans	121	M. A. Noble not out	4
R. A. Duff c Findlay b Ernsthausen	41	*J. Darling not out	5
C. Hill st Findlay b Whately	64	Extras (B 10, LB 2, W 3, NB 2)	17
S. E. Gregory b Whately	6		
A. J. Hopkins c Bonham-Carter		(6 wkts dec.)	314
b Ernsthausen	39	E. Jones	
W. Armstrong c Bonham-Carter b Kelly	17	†H. Carter } did not bat	
		J. V. Saunders	

AUSTRALIANS	O.	M.	R.	W.	O.	M.	R.	W.
Noble	20.3	7	38	5	18	9	25	1
Jones	14	5	29	1	16	5	38	2
Armstrong	6	1	9	4	15	6	19	0
Saunders					26.5	3	67	7
Trumper					3	0	17	0

OXFORD	O.	M.	R.	W.
Ernsthausen	19	4	80	2
Whately	20	2	76	2
Dillon	4	0	17	0
Williams	15	2	63	0
Bonham-Carter	4	0	18	0
Kelly	8	0	21	1
Evans	3	0	22	1

FALL OF WICKETS

Wkt.	Oxon. 1st	Aus. 1st	Oxon. 2nd
1st	42	108	14
2nd	43	213	28
3rd	43	228	33
4th	60	263	73
5th	61	300	74
6th	64	360	94
7th	64	—	138
8th	68	—	141
9th	68	—	180
10th	77	—	183

Umpires: A. Pike and Shaw

shown little sign of abatement; it continued to be so cold and wet for late May that some witty enthusiast had penned the following notice:

"In order to meet the wishes of our customers, we have decided to offer the following useful outfit at inclusive prices to cricketers:

One tarpaulin hat made in the style of the Panama.
One winter overcoat covering the knees.
One pair waterproof boots.
One suit thick winter tweeds.
Two sweaters extra thick, one a size larger than the other.
One ounce best cough lozenges.
One best novel to read in the pavilion while waiting.
One bat.†
One pair pads.†
One pair gloves.†

† These are, of course, not generally necessary for a cricketer this year, but we advise them to be included in case of accidents."*

It may occasion a matter of surprise that the Tourists' programme was arranged in such a manner, having so heavy an encounter before the First Test, but it must be remembered that although the Test rubber was the prime object of the visit, it had not as yet so completely overshadowed the importance of the other matches on a tour. We may be sure that Darling's team took them all in the same spirit – each a match to be won.

On perusal of the Sunday newspapers, they became acquainted with the strength of their antagonists chosen to sport the M C C colours under the command of "The Champion" himself. In addition to Dr W. G. Grace, there were C. B. Fry and K. S. Ranjitsinhji from Sussex, Lionel Palairet and Leonard Braund from Somerset, Pelham Warner, J. T. Hearne and fellow-countryman Albert Trott of Middlesex, Frank Mitchell of Yorkshire, wicket-keeper William Storer of Derbyshire and, finally, B. Cranfield, the Somerset slow left-hander. Originally, Llewellyn, the Hampshire left-arm spinner, who had such a successful bowl against the Cornstalks in their first match (against London County), was invited to turn out but, alas, was indisposed. Cranfield was the last-minute replacement.

The "Old Man" brought memories to this match – he had been in the M C C side in 1878 when Spofforth and the Australians over-whelmed them for 33 and 19 and beat them by 9 wickets, all in one day. This was the feat which caused English cricket to begin to take these Australians seriously.

Fry and Braund (both Test players) they had already met this season at Crystal Palace, Prince Ranjitsinhji – the "Wizard of the Orient" – was an old adversary, having already displayed, at their expense, his magic in England and Australia – 62 and 154 not out in his first Test encounter with them six years ago, with many subsequent innings of artistry since. Lionel Palairet, considered by

*P. C. Standing, *Cricket of Today*, T. C. & E. C. Jack, Vol. 2, p. 120.

many the classic batsman *par excellence*, had been in sparkling form the previous summer; nearly 2,000 runs and five hundreds in 34 innings would have made him a certainty for Test status had there been any touring side that year. Warner, too, another fine batsman in the best public school tradition and the Middlesex captain's apprentice, they had met before in 1899.

Jack Hearne was a bowler of world class, and had given successive Australian sides problems to deal with for the past six years; he had taken 257 wickets for 14.28 runs six years ago; Ranji thought his action perfect, he could vary his pace ever so subtly at will. He possessed a marvellous off-breaker of perfect length, a faster ball that went with his arm, and the ability to spin with either fingers or wrist as conditions required; he could also break to leg.

A bowler of infinite resource was genial, giant–like Albert Trott, and, as a fellow-Australian, they knew him well. "Alberto", as he was known fondly by Lord's devotees, was a character. Younger brother of Harry Trott, and one of the successes of the 1894–5 Australian season, he came to join Middlesex in 1896 after not being chosen for the touring party. Probably one of the finest all-round cricketers of the day, he had in both 1899 and 1900 performed the unusual feat of taking 200 wickets and scoring over 1,000 runs. He was a very powerful hitter – Monty Noble would recall ruefully that in this very fixture three years before Trott hit him harder and harder. Then came one stupendous drive which put the ball into the top balcony of the Lord's pavilion; a few balls later came the historic hit for which Trott will always be remembered. From a half volley of Noble's, "Alberto" made a huge drive which sent the ball ballooning over the top of the pavilion, bouncing off a small roof at the back into a garden below. As a bowler he would be likely to send you down anything: every degree of pace, any amount of off-break, a slow leg-break, a full pitch to your blockhole, or one which hung back; untiringly he would bowl these all day. He was also a superb fielder, especially to his own bowling.

As a wicketkeeper, Bill Storer had been vying with Dick Lilley for possession of the England gloves for years; there was little to choose between them, either behind the wicket or wielding the willow. He had performed remarkably well on MacLaren's 1897–8 tour of Australia, assisting in twelve dismissals in the six Tests he had already played in.

The Cambridge captain of 1896, Frank Mitchell, had really come to the fore in the previous season of 1901, when for Yorkshire he had scored seven separate hundreds in a total of 1,807 runs. A keen batsman of orthodox style and Yorkshire grit, the Australians had played against him on both previous tours.

Surprised by the appearance of a fine morning, and in front of some 12,000 eager spectators, W. G. won the toss. Again the luck of

33

the coin was of little advantage, for the pitch was not at all helpful to the side electing to bat, nor bad enough to send in one's opponents. Nevertheless, Fry and Palairet opened for M C C with care. The attack was accurate and persistent without being penetrating. Runs came slowly but steadily, Darling manipulating his bowling assets with some frequency, and 79 had been notched up before the first wicket fell. Ernie Jones struck immediately afterwards – Braund was bowled before he could settle, "Coo" Palairet went for a purposeful 39, and "Jonah" shattered Warner's stumps. A change in fortunes. Ranji at the other end, plainly not his usual self, survived two chances off Jones whilst in his teens: the first fielding lapses of the tour!

Perhaps concentration had been affected by a curious incident which occurred whilst Jones was bowling. A sparrow near the pitch had been struck and knocked over by the ball. "Jonah" was about to resume bowling when there were cries from some of the spectators of, "Kill it! Kill it!", one of whom dashed onto the outfield presumably to carry out the deed. He was accompanied by shouts of approval from a section of the crowd; this, of course, held up play. As he neared the stricken sparrow it recovered and, to the surprise of all, flew off, much to the amusement of spectators and players alike, and a few minutes elapsed before play could be resumed. Ranji settled down and batted with all his old brilliance. He showed that he had lost none of the skill that the onlookers expected from him; his 67 runs were the high-water mark of the M C C innings.

Meanwhile, Albert Trott had come in to the pleasure of the Lord's crowd, who were hoping to see him repeat his great hit of three years before. Alas for them, Duff finely caught him in the out-field trying to drive Noble. "The Champion" and Mitchell stayed for a time, each scored 29, until both were removed by the steadiness and accuracy of Bill Howell, Gregory catching Grace at cover point. They were finally all out for 240. The Australians had about an hour's batting, being 74 for the loss of Duff (16) at the close. Trumper carried on just where he had left off at Oxford.

Before another large crowd on Tuesday, Trumper collared the bowling unmercifully from the first ball of the day. To quote Percy Cross Standing, who witnessed the match, "He gave an exhibition at once masterly and elegant," and, "He proved himself possessed of a greater variety of strokes than any player of the day."[*] As W. G. rang his bowling changes, Victor played them all with ease and alacrity. It did not take him long to reach his third century of the tour; his 105 runs were brilliantly made and he gave no sign of a chance before he was bowled by Hearne. Neither Hopkins nor Hill had lasted long; Clem had been seeing the ball well until he got

[*] P. C. Standing, *Cricket of Today*, T. C. & E. C. Jack, Vol. 2, p. 123.

34

himself awkwardly over a nasty one from Hearne to be caught and bowled for 24. Now Gregory and Darling were well set, and it looked as if a long score might be distinctly possible, until Trott came back and yorked Syd Gregory for 30. Regardless of the Australian captain's rough treatment of him, "Alberto", amid cheers, soon disposed of Darling (bowled), and then Monty Noble (caught and bowled). Armstrong played like a barn door, but "The Champion" put himself on again and quickly wound up the tail, taking the last three wickets. The Australians were only 31 ahead, and W. G. had taken 5 for 29 with his round-arm deliveries.

With the pitch somewhat improved, Charles Fry and Lionel Palairet again got off the mark for what looked like another promising start. But the perspiring and persistent Howell soon had Fry caught by Armstrong for 21. Then the guile of Armstrong's leg-spin immediately tricked Len Braund into falling leg before. Ranji started quickly enough with all his magic until Trumper induced him to offer the ball to Syd Gregory at cover for 26. Then "Jonah" bowled Palairet, the sheet-anchor, who had made a graceful 44, and Trott tried to loft Hopkins out of the ground and was bowled. Five M C C wickets had now fallen; it was up to Warner, in his Harlequin cap, to stop the rot. He steadied the side with a well-knit and circumspect innings; W. G. stayed with him for a time and had reached 23 carefully before Trumper was through his defence with a faster one. Thus, Frank Mitchell, full of Yorkshire pluck, came out to join "Plum" Warner. Gamely, Warner battled on until he reached his well-earned 50, then, going forward to Noble, he was snapped up behind by Kelly.

Rain, which had been conspicuously absent on the previous two days, now contrived to delay the start on the third day. Storer's tenure at the crease was brief, so Jack Hearne, who could bat better than his present position of number ten indicated, joined Mitchell. Together they punished the attack which the previous day had their colleagues in such trouble. By determination, they added 73 runs in 80 minutes without being parted. It was at this juncture that Dr Grace, wrestling with his calculations, decided that the remaining three hours of play would prove too difficult a task for his enemy to obtain the outstanding 250 runs, so he waved in the not out pair.

It had been agreed previously that stumps would be drawn early to enable the Australians to catch their train from Euston to arrive in Birmingham at a reasonable hour, in view of the first Test match starting the very next day.

That the gentlemen from "down under" viewed Dr Grace's declaration as a challenge became quite obvious in the way that Victor Trumper and Reggie Duff started their second innings. Victor commenced scoring at an even faster rate and hitting harder than in his first venture. He badly mauled Albert Trott, one hit being a memorable "smash" into the delighted crowd. Looking set for his second century of the match in well under even time, he danced down the pitch again to Trott and was bowled for 86. The spectators rose again to him. Just previously, Duff had been caught by Trott's outsized hands off left-hander Cranfield for a well-made 37 to the delighted shout of, "Well cot! Well cot!" from W. G.

AUSTRALIANS *v* MCC

At Lord's, 26, 27, 28 May.

Match drawn.

MCC AND GROUND

Mr C. B. Fry lbw, b Howell	36	c Armstrong b Howell	21
Mr L. C. H. Palairet b Trumper	39	b Jones	44
L. C. Braund b Jones	2	lbw, b Armstrong	4
K. S. Ranjitsinhji b Armstrong	67	c Gregory b Trumper	26
Mr P. F. Warner b Jones	2	c Kelly b Noble	50
A. E. Trott c Duff b Noble	8	b Hopkins	4
*Dr W. G. Grace c Gregory b Howell	29	b Trumper	23
Mr F. Mitchell b Howell	29	not out	55
†W. Storer lbw, b Howell	0	c Howell b Noble	4
J. T. Hearne b Noble	11	not out	35
B. Cranfield not out	4		
Extras (B 6, LB 6, W 1)	13	(B 8, LB 3, W 1, NB 2)	14
	240	(8 wkts dec.)	**280**

AUSTRALIANS

V. T. Trumper b Hearne	105	b Trott	86
R. Duff lbw, b Grace	16	c Trott b Cranfield	37
A. J. Hopkins lbw, b Grace	7		
C. Hill c and b Hearne	24	b Hearne	22
S. E. Gregory b Trott	30	not out	24
*J. Darling b Trott	28	not out	42
M. A. Noble c and b Trott	21		
W. Armstrong not out	12		
†J. J. Kelly b Grace	3		
E. Jones b Grace	0		
W. P. Howell c Palairet b Grace	3		
Extras (B 17, LB 5)	22	(B 4, LB 2)	6
	271	(3 wkts)	**217**

AUSTRALIANS	O.	M.	R.	W.	O.	M.	R.	W.
Jones	22	6	62	2	15	4	44	1
Noble	33	13	96	2	19	7	44	2
Howell	25.3	7	54	4	30	11	62	1
Trumper	5	3	7	1	14	4	23	2
Armstrong	11	6	8	1	19	7	52	1
Hopkins					17	5	41	1
MCC								
Cranfield	9	0	45	0	5	0	26	1
Trott	24	1	96	3	19	0	102	1
Braund	8	2	29	0				
Hearne	14	5	50	2	14	2	53	1
Grace	19.5	5	29	5	10	4	12	0
Ranjitsinhji					2	0	18	0

Umpires: W. A. J. West and J. Carlin

himself. Clem Hill forced the pace when Trumper left, only to fall to Hearne for 22. "The Champion" put himself on to try to slow the run-rate, so he must have felt terribly relieved when they had to come in because of rain. This cost thirty minutes playing time. Joe Darling still thought of winning, so, together with Gregory, they forced the pace by hitting at everything. Darling hammered the M C C bowlers unmercifully in making 42 in the twenty minutes left. Together they had added 56 runs in that time, more than enough to worry W. G. that he had declared too soon. They were only 33 runs short of the target and had seven wickets in hand. If it had not been for the half-hour delay for rain, let alone an early finish, they must have won comfortably. Certainly, it was a moral victory for the Cornstalks, and one which enabled them to travel to Birmingham with the highest expectations of their coming encounter with the might of England.

CHAPTER 4

Birmingham – The First Test

Thursday 29 May dawned fair. Whilst the Australians were attempting to relax and soothe any pre-match nerves preparatory to travelling in their horse-brake to the Edgbaston ground, many distinguished visitors from abroad were arriving in England for the forthcoming Coronation of H M King Edward VII (due to take place in one month's time on 26 June). Good news was also coming in by telegraph from South Africa concerning the Boer leaders, who had now decided amongst themselves the manner in which they intended to sue for peace. Among the multitude of cricket followers who were entering the ground the atmosphere was one of light-hearted enjoyment, both at the turn of national events and the prospect of a magnificent entertainment from the teams about to represent their respective countries. The weather seemed to have taken a turn for the better, so they anticipated an absorbing day's cricket. The Australians had impressed the public enormously with the fine cricket they had so far displayed, and the pleasantness and affability of the team to those lucky enough to have met them personally. All contributed to the high regard for them and the intense interest with which they were followed.

Joe Darling's selection problems were far easier than England's; the team was already decided for him. Most unfortunately, in addition to Hugh Trumble's damaged bowling hand, Jack Saunders had, during the previous day, felt the symptoms of tonsilitis coming upon him – he had already been suffering with inflammation of the eyes, for which Dr Pope had treated him. He, perforce, had to be placed in medical care and left in London. Fortunately, Jim Kelly's hand had quite recovered (Carter was out of action from his badly cut eye), so Australia would not have to call on Reg Duff to keep wicket. A fine team, but they would be without the services of two of their best bowlers.

The selectors were Lord Hawke of Yorkshire (the Chairman),

Mr Gregor MacGregor, the Middlesex captain, and Mr H. W. Bainbridge, the captain of Warwickshire. They in their turn decided to co-opt their elected captain Archie MacLaren, whom they had selected to lead in all five Tests, Mr A. G. Steel, the former Lancastrian Test all-rounder who had just been elected President of the M C C, and Mr Charles Fry. Now in their deliberations, during which Lord Hawke would produce from his pockets innumerable newspaper clippings, the selection body decided to choose a team for all conditions and circumstances and, in so doing, they did not let themselves be guided entirely by current form but more on the known abilities of the cricketers concerned. Thus, fourteen players were invited to attend the Edgbaston ground and hold themselves in readiness to play if called upon to do so. They were as follows:

Mr Archie MacLaren, captain (Lancashire)
The Hon. Francis S. Jackson (Yorkshire)
Kumar Shri Ranjitsinhji (Sussex)
Mr Charles B. Fry (Sussex)
Mr Gilbert L. Jessop (Gloucestershire)
Mr John R. Mason (Kent)
Augustus A. Lilley, wicketkeeper (Warwickshire)
John T. Tyldesley (Lancashire)
Thomas Hayward (Surrey)
Leonard C. Braund (Somerset)
George H. Hirst (Yorkshire)
Wilfred Rhodes (Yorkshire)
William H. Lockwood (Surrey)
Charles B. Llewellyn (Hampshire)

After deliberations as to the state of the ground (Bates, the Warwickshire groundsman, had produced a beautiful pitch), and the weather, it was decided to leave out Jack Mason, Tom Hayward and Charles Llewellyn. Now the England team that went into the field, in the opinions of many critics then and subsequently, was probably the strongest side that ever represented the Mother country. Every member of the team was a first-rate bat, six could be considered genuine all-rounders in every sense of the term, and the bowling had quality and every variety: Rhodes was the best slow left-hand bowler of the day, Hirst a fast medium left-hander now approaching his peak, who swerved the ball into the bat, Jackson a good military medium right-hand of considerable guile, Bill Lockwood a genuine right-hand fast bowler of tremendous pace and skill, and Len Braund the most skilful right-arm leg-break bowler of the day. Additionally, if required, Jessop could still bowl very fast for a few overs, or medium-paced cutters as necessary.

Another reason was that here was a fielding side for once every bit as good as the Australians (many thought better) which would certainly save many runs even if through ill chance they were unable to score them.

MacLaren said during a Selection Committee meeting (for the later 1909 series), "I want Jessopus for every Test, as he'll run Trumper out for me at least once."* That this was his attitude in 1902 is undoubted, for he always thought highly of Jessop as a smasher of opponents' bowling and a fielder extraordinary, particularly in his favourite positions of extra cover or cover point. Most batsmen were afraid to run if the ball went anywhere near Jessop, and this applied to the Cornstalks as well, with the possible exception of Trumper, Hill and Gregory. As first slip MacLaren himself had no equal, excepting perhaps Ranji and Len Braund, who together formed an outstanding combination of slip fielders, the best that England probably ever had. They were backed up in the deep at third man by the remarkable Tyldesley in his specialist position. F. S. Jackson would be at cover point with, for Lockwood's pace bowling, Rhodes at deep point, Jessop at extra cover and George Hirst at mid-off to complete the off-side field. With Lilley standing fairly well back and Fry at a roving mid-on position looking after the leg side, we have an outstanding combination with every member of the team fielding where he would normally for his own county. In addition, every man in this side, except Lockwood, could field anywhere else, thus being quite capable of filling other positions when slow, left-hand or medium-paced bowlers were operating.

As to the batting, every man was capable of making a century, even numbers ten and eleven – Lockwood and Rhodes. Furthermore, all the other nine were just as capable on a turning pitch as on a plumb one, MacLaren, Ranji and Johnny Tyldesley being outstanding in this respect. In Jessop they had the fastest scorer in the game, christened by the sporting press as "Croucher" from his unorthodox stance, and also known as the "Human Catapult" for his prodigious hitting; he was likely to turn the result of a match in half an hour of spectacular batting. Nobody knew quite how to set a field to him when he got going.

MacLaren, the Lancashire captain, was an outstanding performer with the bat, who had made his mark whilst still at Harrow School. He played his cricket as captain, batsman or fielder in the grand manner. Extraordinarily perceptive as a tactician, popular and trusted by his players, and a born leader, he was nevertheless a realist in his approach to captaincy. He rarely underestimated the opposition, and it may be for this reason that he has sometimes been criticised for being a pessimist. This was rather unfair. The Australians had the highest regard for him as a captain, and as a

*E. H. D. Sewell, *Who's Won the Toss?*, Stanley Paul, p. 82.

sportsman *par excellence*, while as a batsman they thought him the finest Englishman to have visited the Antipodes. Monty Noble in his book *The Game's the Thing* pays high tribute to all these attributes in the man, speaks of him in glowing terms and learned much from him of the art of captaincy. With his unique upright stance at the wicket, the bat lifted high behind his head, and an imperious look, he swept his bat beautifully downwards for each stroke, following it through in an arc and rising high above the head again. A dominant, attacking player, there were no half measures about Archie; even when forced into a defensive shot, the stroke was made deliberately in the grand manner.

To accompany his captain to the wicket, Charles Fry was in many ways a contrast and a complement. He, too, developed early as a games player at Repton, but his batting in the early days, although of marked ability, was somewhat stiff and unyielding. However, with his analytical eye and mind, by watching the great batsmen of the day, and by constant practice, he altered his style until he became a polished and fluent performer. Much of this was due, of course, to his association with Ranjitsinhji, whom he greatly admired. Fry, by this time, had become the acknowledged expert on the art and science of batsmanship: he thought about it, wrote about it, and practised it. It was only by applying himself with such thoroughness that he had also developed an upright stance from which he could play any particular stroke at will, although the Australians always felt he had a penchant for the strokes on the leg side. His drive, according to A. E. Knight, who studied him well, "is a clean and honest lift straight from the shoulders".* He hooked fiercely and played what can only be called a long-leg hit to the slightly wide ball short of a length, to which he would step across the wicket, sweep right round, and hit as it rose past the body with his bat parallel to the pitch. His remarkable powers as a "wielder of willow" can be observed from his scoring capacities of recent years. In 1898 he scored 1,788 runs at 54.18 average, in 1899 it was 2,366 at 43.81, in 1900 he made nine centuries in collecting 2,325 runs at an average of 61.18, and in 1901 he was top of averages scoring as many as thirteen centuries in a total of 3,147 runs at 78.67.

Ranjitsinhji, the remarkable cricketer from India, a close personal friend of Fry's, was a natural genius at the game. Even so, at Cambridge he did not gain his Blue until his fourth year. He had learned his early cricket in India, but, by dint of assiduous practice at Cambridge under the best professional tutelage of Richardson, Lockwood and Hayward, he blossomed into the magical player of late-Victorian and early-Edwardian memory, when he became as great a drawer of the crowds as had W. G. Grace. The cricket-going public were fascinated by this slender and athletic noble Rajput

*A. E. Knight, *The Complete Cricketer*, Methuen, p. 268.

41

who played such marvellously electrifying cricket. Fry commented, "He had no technical faults whatever; the substratum of his play was absolutely sound," and "It is characteristic of all great batsmen that they play their strokes at the last instant; but I have never seen a batsman able to reserve his stroke so late as Ranji nor apply his bat to the ball with such electric quickness."* It was also Charles Fry's opinion that he had three strokes for every ball, and that some of them were entirely his own; for example, his famous leg glance, which was achieved by perfect timing and wrist-work. Another close friend of Ranji's, E. H. D. Sewell, who played for Essex, says, "During the first half of his career he made the majority of his runs by wonderful cutting and leg-side wrist-strokes and by off-drives all along the turf," and "During the second half of his cricket life he was really a hitter, and going in for driving, some of it high."† Ranji had been captain of Sussex for the past two seasons; he was a fine leader and the cares of the Sussex throne had little effect upon his scoring. In 1899, when he shared the captaincy with "Billy" Murdoch, he amassed 3,159 runs for an average of 63.18, the following season the score was 3,065 at a then unbelievable 87.57, whilst in the season that had just passed his aggregate was 2,468 at an average of 70.51. In these three seasons he had scored twenty-seven centuries. No wonder he was thought of as an Oriental wizard with "blue flames shimmering round his bat"!

Another product of Harrow cricket who rose to the highest echelon of the game was the Hon. Francis S. Jackson, known colloquially to the sporting public and fellow-amateurs alike as "Jacker". His fine physique, easy affability and general military bearing had quite a hold on the cricketing crowd, and he was idolised in Yorkshire. Immaculately clad, he always looked good on the cricket field no matter what he was doing at the time, a sound forcing bat with all the strokes who always seemed to be at his best when things were going against his side. He had already played many fine innings for England against the friendly enemy from "down under". His début in a Test match, whilst still at Cambridge, was signalled by an innings of 91 when helping Arthur Shrewsbury to add 137 runs in 105 minutes to recover a bad start at Lord's in 1893. In the next game at The Oval he scored 103. In 1896 he suffered a cracked rib when facing "Jonah" at Sheffield Park. Nevertheless, in the two matches England won he helped materially with knocks of 44 and 45. In 1899 his best efforts were 73, 44 and 118. His 118 in the Fifth Test that year came from an opening partnership of 185 in 170 minutes with Hayward, before he finally fell to the South Australian express. Many pursuits had combined to keep him away from the cricket field, his father's business interests and service as a Guards

*C. B. Fry, *Life Worth Living*, Eyre & Spottiswoode, p. 222.
†E. H. D. Sewell, *Who's Won the Toss?*, Stanley Paul, p. 64.

Officer among them, so that he rarely had the opportunity to play regular county cricket. Nonetheless, Yorkshire always played him if he was available and he was practically an automatic choice for England.

The only professional in this team chosen for his batting alone, and with the ability to stand alongside the great amateurs of the period on an equal footing, was Johnny Tyldesley. Far removed in style, manner and approach to his art from the average professional batsman was gentleman John Thomas; he looked every inch the amateur in his brilliance. He was the most beautiful cutter in the game, his late cuts were breathlessly late, crisp and sure, but his driving particularly impressed, as when he turned a delivery into a perfect length by hitting the ball on the rise. Many strokes he played like a ballet-dancer on the tips of his toes, but it was as a bad-pitch player that he rose to the heights; when others were in constant trouble Tyldesley danced like a cat as he played back in as graceful a manner as the artist in him. Perhaps another reason that the selectors chose him was for his marked partiality to the Edgbaston ground; his scoring here had been as prolific as on his own rain-soaked Old Trafford. In the previous season he had amassed 3,041 runs, which included nine separate hundreds for an average of 55.29. Knowing Tyldesley as he did, MacLaren thought him indispensable.

These, then, were the main batsmen in whom the selectors pinned their faith, but it must be remembered that Dick Lilley was a very capable bat, and George Hirst had already achieved the double three times. In each of his last two seasons of solid, reliable batting, Hirst scored nearly 2,000 runs. Leonard Braund had already proved his excellent skill with the bat on the recent tour of Australia and in the opening London County match (it must be remembered that he, too, had done the double in the previous season), and although Lockwood had missed this feat in the past year, he had been successful with the double in 1899 and 1900. In Yorkshire it was already known how well Wilfred Rhodes could score runs when the dictates of the game demanded, but what was remarkable about young Wilfred's abilities was the number of wickets he had taken with slow left-armed away-spinners since commencing first-class cricket. In his first season, 1898, his bag was 154 at 14.60, in 1899 he tallied 179 slightly more expensive wickets at 17.10, followed by an outstanding performance of 261 at 13.80 in the batsmen's summer of 1900. This superb effort was repeated in yet another batsmen's season of 1901 to the tune of 251 wickets at 15.12 runs per dismissal. On paper, the team that Lord Hawke and Company had chosen was invincible.

It was a certainty that whoever won the toss would elect to bat, and, when MacLaren did so, it was expected that England would

43

make a long score on such a beautiful pitch. MacLaren and Fry opened the innings, and the imperious Archie took one run off Jones, who was bowling flat out for his first over. He made four off Monty Noble; this left Fry to face Jones again. Now came Australia's initial breakthrough. "Jonah's" great pace forced Fry to play off the edge of the bat and Jim Kelly, standing well back, took the ball cleanly. A confident appeal from the Cornstalks, and Fry's "favourite" umpire, Jim Phillips, lifted his finger; 5 for 1. Ranji came in to bat to a tumultuous ovation; it may have unsettled him for, anxious to get off the mark, he nearly ran himself out from the first ball he received. Another seven runs were added when MacLaren, appearing quite at ease looking for runs, having made nine of the thirteen on the board, played a stroke in the direction of Hill. He started out of his crease, saw Hill closing on the ball, stopped and shouted, "Get back," to Ranji, whom he thought had backed up too far. Now Ranji, who probably had a better view of the ball, in his turn shouted to his captain to get back himself. MacLaren must have momentarily misunderstood the Prince's warning, for he hesitated as Ranji was still several yards out of his own ground and facing his direction. It was while this comedy of errors was being enacted that Hill smartly returned the ball to the striker's end, and both batsmen, stranded in mid pitch, saw with horror Kelly breaking the wicket. A terrible misunderstanding, and the England captain was out: 13 for 2. The Australians were jubilant, they fielded on the tips of their toes. Jackson attempted to stop the rot; poor Ranji, however, had been terribly upset over the run out and appeared quite ill at ease, and some of his runs were a trifle streaky. They added twenty-two, thirteen coming from Jackson's careful bat. Meanwhile, Darling had brought on Trumper to bowl in place of Jones, followed by Armstrong; then a simple straight ball from the latter clean bowled the uneasy Prince.

Three down for 35 runs! No wonder the Australians felt the cricketing gods were on their side. They came in closer ready for yet another wicket. But they had not bargained for the pride of Old Trafford, John Tyldesley, determined to turn the tide as he took centre at 12.35 p.m. Taking his time, waiting for the right ball to punish, Tyldesley helped "Jacker" to face the crisis. Darling changed his bowlers every few overs, but, playing with careful judgement and self restraint, the Lancashire and Yorkshire pair scored runs. Tyldesley's timing was superb, off driving through the field, cutting with great power and perfect in defence, while the Hon. F. S. played many powerful strokes off the back foot or dropped his bat half cock to smother the good one. In fifty-five minutes the partnership had added 64 runs, and when luncheon was taken at 1.30 p.m. they had raised England's total to a more respectable 99 for 3. Of these runs Jackson had made 34 and

Tyldesley 29, and they had shown up weaknesses in Australia's attack.

Thirteen runs after the interval "Jacker" chopped one of Jones' expresses onto his wicket: his stroke was a fraction too late. This very valuable contribution to England's cause could be measured in terms other than his 53 runs, but even so the scoreboard read only 112 for 4. Tyldesley was on 36 when Dick Lilley joined him, and he immediately added another seven runs to raise his score to 43. It was at this point that he gave a certain chance to Noble's bowling when he was missed low down by "Jonah", of all people, at mid-off. After a leg bye, however, the burly South Australian made no mistake when Lilley skied up an easy catch from another of Noble's swerving deliveries. 121 for 5 and things looked black for England – half the side were back in the pavilion. His concentration most likely unsettled, Tyldesley now had an alarming over from Warwick Armstrong, whose leg-breaks he normally played with consummate ease. Missed by Joe Darling at mid-on and from the very next ball nearly caught and bowled by the tall Victorian, he almost caused heart failure among the spectators – three bad errors in Tyldesley's fine batting display and three lapses in Australia's fielding which, until then, had been immaculate. This had been their great chance to break through once and for all, but Tyldesley was the wrong player to let off the hook three times.

Partnered now by solid and reliable George Hirst, he proceeded to put the Cornstalks at a discount and together they slowly pulled the innings round. His hitting, particularly through the off side field, was superb. He often used his famous half-drive, half-cut stroke, and in 80 minutes they added a further 94 runs. He reached his 50 in an hour and three-quarters and when tea was taken out to the players (as was the practice) at 4.30 p.m. he had made 85. This was the turning-point of England's innings. Immediately after the resumption the hard-hitting George Hirst was taken in the slips by Armstrong off Trumper – 212 for 6. Jessop came in, had little of the bowling, scored six, then hitting wildly at Trumper, holed out to Hopkins at deep cover point – 230 for 7. Braund was a more steady partner and, immediately after his arrival, John T. Tyldesley scored the single to give him his century. It had taken almost three and a half hours, and it was now 5 p.m. Together they added 34 more runs (20 to Tyldesley) before Jones bowled Braund for 14. At 264 for 8 Lockwood joined him. Tyldesley cut and drove his way onwards, no matter how Darling rang his bowling changes, until a few minutes before six o'clock when Howell induced the Lancashire stalwart to get his leg in front to a straight one. So at 295 for 9 wickets, having scored 138 runs, Tyldesley came in to a deafening ovation. His innings had included 20 fours and a five – all run – and had lasted in all 4 hours and 22 minutes. The time he had taken was less important

45

than the valuable runs; he had been the sheet-anchor of the side and his batting display had been brilliant.

With the bowling now quite wearied, Lockwood and Rhodes scored easily: during the remaining thirty-six minutes before close of play they added another 56 runs, remaining undefeated to the end. Throughout the innings Joe Darling had shown considerable skill in handling his bowling forces and displayed dogged courage in time of stress, and the Australian fielding had always been keen and full of anticipation, apart from the three lapses. So the homegoing crowd had had their money's worth of excitement at seeing England forge their way from a disastrous start to the fairly healthy position of 351 for 9 wickets.

During the night it rained long and heavily, and still on Friday morning it drizzled. The re-start was therefore delayed until nearly three o'clock in the afternoon, the outfield, of course, being extremely wet. The clouds were heavy and the light was far from good. It was expected that MacLaren would declare the England innings closed, but to most of the crowd's surprise the Australians came out to take the field followed by Lockwood and Rhodes. It would appear that MacLaren, after a careful inspection of the pitch and acting on Dick Lilley's advice (it was, of course, the latter's home ground), decided to bat on to allow the turf more time to dry for England's bowlers to get a better foothold and not have a slippery ball to handle. So for half an hour the last pair quite comfortably added another 25 runs to bring their stand up to 81 before the England skipper decided to declare at 376 for 9. Time was becoming precious and the sky threatened more rain.

The pitch was rolled out, and Trumper and Duff walked out in poor light to a drying pitch. Now, opinions have differed as to the conditions of the pitch and of the players engaged. Lilley, who knew the square intimately, thought it was scarcely affected and felt the Australians were under the impression that the pitch was helping the bowlers more than it was. Fry said it was unpleasant but not too terrible, yet Jessop, on the other hand, regarded it as genuinely "sticky". Writing shortly afterwards, MacLaren's view was, "The wicket was quite on the wet side, and by no means unplayable."[*] He also says that "the ball was not turning to any great extent".

In view of the débâcle which followed, and for which neither spectators nor players on either side could possibly have been prepared, the state of the pitch is probably of some considerable importance. By taking the secondary evidence of the umpires, Jim Phillips and W. Hearn, that the pitch was by no means so difficult, and Percy Cross Standing in *Cricket of Today*, who concurs, it would seem, then, that MacLaren's recollections shortly afterwards were probably correct.

[*]A. C. MacLaren, in *Cricket*, Ed. H. G. Hutchinson, Country Life, p. 293.

In less than ninety minutes the whole of this fine Australian side was disposed of, indeed vanquished, for just 36 runs. Admittedly the light was poor, but England did not employ anyone faster than Hirst, and the Tourists did not complain of bad light. The pitch, we must assume, was "by no means unplayable", and the ball was not turning very much. How did it happen?

Hirst opened the bowling to Victor Trumper, who opened his account and then faced the next over from Rhodes, scoring again. Hirst bowled a maiden to an uneasy Duff, but Trumper scored two more off Rhodes with easy confidence. It was at this point, presumably, that Rhodes, after consulting with his Yorkshire colleague, asked his captain about the possibility of changing ends. Therefore, Braund was brought on for a solitary over to enable them to do so. It resulted in a single from Reg Duff, who now had to face Hirst from the other end. He was in difficulties and tried to drive himself out of trouble. The fielding was tight. With Australia seven runs up, Duff played at Hirst and snicked one through the slips; Braund at first slip got a hand to it but could not hold it. Hirst, losing control of his swerve, bowled a wide to Trumper. Now Rhodes operated from his desired end and immediately had Duff in two minds; a shorter one next had Reggie Duff put one straight into Jessop's hands at extra cover. One wicket for nine runs, first blood to Rhodes and England. Clement Hill of the flashing blade came in as the usual number three and stole an eager single off Rhodes. Now, facing Hirst, he attempted a leg glide to a ball which got up rather awkwardly and steered it to fine leg; with no one there it should have been four all the way. He had reckoned without the superlative anticipation of Len Braund. Braund, sore about missing Duff, felt that he owed George Hirst a catch; he saw Hill shaping to make the stroke and noticed Dick Lilley moving across to the leg side, so from his place at first slip he ran behind the wicketkeeper and took a miraculous right-handed running catch, inches from the ground, at fine leg! Jessop thought it the finest close to the wicket catch he had ever seen. Hill, disbelieving that such a safe stroke should be his downfall, returned to the pavilion rather dejectedly; 10 for 2. If Victor Trumper was dismayed at the quick exits of two of his comrades, he did not show it. He took four more runs off Rhodes' next over to bring his score up to 9, then Syd Gregory, without troubling the scorers, put his leg in front to Hirst. Three down for fourteen!

Darling managed a single from the last ball of Hirst's over and so faced Rhodes, who was spinning the ball with great skill and varying his length almost imperceptibly. Darling drove for two runs then, drawn forward, he hit hard into the covers. "Jessopus" took it cleanly and poor Darling found himself walking back, duped by Rhodes. Seventeen for four! Having attempted a run the batsmen had crossed; Victor always backed up well. So tall, erect and broad

47

of bat, Alf Noble came to the wicket to face a new over from George Hirst. Surely he could hold up one end while Trumper obtained the runs. But no. He quickly got off the mark with a two followed by a single, and Victor took yet another to face the wily Rhodes once more. The over was a duel between a bowler and a batsman each at the peak of their skill, neither giving any quarter, but Trumper scored a single. Hirst to Trumper again; another wide when George momentarily lost control of his swerve once more; the next delivery and, quick as lightning, Victor jumped down the pitch, pulling him to the leg side for two runs. If the outfield had not been so wet it would easily have reached the boundary; Trumper made it look so simple. Up until now Hirst had seemed the more difficult proposition; less runs had come from him than from his Yorkshire colleague.

Came now the decisive over as Rhodes came in with his graceful run up to the wicket and easy-motioned delivery. Noble played back with great care, waiting for the ball to turn; Rhodes in again and this time a dead-bat stroke. Now a slightly shorter one, Noble forward; it beat the bat and Lilley smartly had the ball in his hands and the bails were off with Monty Noble's back foot just out of the crease. Five down for twenty-five. The very next ball had Armstrong caught at the wicket by a jubilant Lilley. Twenty-five for six, and even Rhodes permitted himself a smile. Each bowler managed another maiden; they were bowling tight and the fielders crept in. Trumper pulled Hirst again, when he dropped short, for two more on the empty leg side; then an off drive along the turf which Jessop somehow managed to keep down to a single. Hirst to Hopkins, who covered up at the last second, then a stylish stroke to get him off the mark. Another maiden from Rhodes to Hopkins, who must have felt pleased when it was over.

The Yorkshire pair had now bowled nine overs each; they were a perfect foil for each other. Hirst had taken two wickets and Rhodes had beguiled four Australians with his remarkable left-armed spin. George Hirst hitched up his trousers for another bowl at Trumper, who came out to meet him with a devastating pull worth four runs that dazzled the spectators, but the wet turf kept it down to two. Now Hirst obtained what he had been striving for – the master's wicket – he bowled him! Victor Trumper, the mainstay of the Australian side, who had made batting look easy when his colleagues at the other end were in the direst distress, had fallen at last, and the light of the Southern Cross had all but gone out. Seven wickets for 31 runs; even the formerly cheering spectators were awestruck. As he came off the field he gained tremendous applause, for 18 of those 31 runs had come in sublime fashion from his bat alone, but it had taken seventy minutes.

The end was obviously now in sight; Jim Kelly was missed in the heat of the moment by Jackson at cover when he fumbled the ball, Hopkins managed to score four more runs, and Rhodes started his eleventh over. Off the third ball, with the score at 35, Hopkins, who was beginning to come good, was caught behind by Lilley. From the fourth ball Ernie Jones holed out to Jackson at cover. The batsmen had crossed and Kelly touched Rhodes' next ball through the slips. Ranji was unsighted and they ran a single. Howell now faced the last ball of the over, which he lofted high into the waiting hands of Fry at long-on; Australia were all out for an unbelievable 36 runs. Wilfred Rhodes had seven wickets to his credit for only seventeen runs and his compatriot George Hirst had taken the remaining three for fifteen.

It had been a sensational collapse, but it was due entirely to the Yorkshire pair of bowlers backed up by superlative fielding. Lilley had been brilliantly anticipative behind the stumps. Fry thought that Hirst had been the most troublesome to the Australians, "their batsmen hurried to the other end and tried to hit Rhodes, without success".* MacLaren's opinion was that "Rhodes did what he liked with his opponents, although the ball was not turning to any great extent."† Be that as it may, our Yorkshire pair both bowled magnificently; they were to be heroes again before the 1902 Test rubber had ended.

Jessop felt there was an excuse for Australia's showing; they had played the previous match at Lord's which, although wet, was still appreciably faster than the slow pitch at Edgbaston on which they now found themselves; and the way in which Rhodes and Hirst performed, it would have been a great achievement for them to have scored a hundred runs.

Darling was invited to follow on; an hour's play still remained, but the light was now so bad that after three overs, during which Trumper and Duff scored eight runs, they successfully appealed and the players came in. With no improvement in the light conditions, stumps were finally drawn at six o'clock and, as the crowds of spectators were leaving the ground, it started to rain once more.

It fell in torrents that night for twelve hours, but by late morning on Saturday the sun was out and thousands of would-be spectators were hopeful of some cricket, although the playing area was saturated. By afternoon the crowd had increased but the umpires on inspecting the pitch declared it unfit for play. At four o'clock the gates were opened, and as the crowd surged in many people were trodden underfoot, so keen were they to see England win; it was a miracle that nobody was killed. As they waited patiently, the two captains consulted and advised the umpires to allow play to continue. As Lilley opines, "This was purely out of kindly consideration

*C. B. Fry, *Life Worth Living*, Eyre & Spottiswoode, p. 231.
†A. C. MacLaren in *Cricket*, Ed. H. G. Hutchinson, Country Life, p. 293.

49

for the huge waiting crowd, who thus had the satisfaction of seeing an hour's play at the close of the afternoon."*

Thus seventy-five minutes playing time was all that remained. Trumper left first at 16 having made 15 of them. Then, with the additional loss of Duff (14) when the score was 41, the Australians played quietly until the close. So in this unsatisfactory way the First Test ended tamely in a draw. If the overnight rain had not been so devastating to the pitch, it is certain that England would have won comfortably, for even allowing for the remarkable tenacity of the

*A. A. Lilley, *Twenty-Four Years of Cricket*, Mills & Boon, p. 120.

ENGLAND *v* AUSTRALIA
(1st TEST)
At Birmingham, 29, 30, 31 May.
Match drawn.

ENGLAND

*Mr A. C. MacLaren run out	9	Mr G. L. Jessop c Hopkins b Trumper		6
Mr C. B. Fry c Kelly b Jones	0	L. C. Braund b Jones		14
K. S. Ranjitsinhji b Armstrong	13	W. H. Lockwood not out		52
Hon. F. S. Jackson b Jones	53	W. Rhodes not out		38
J. T. Tyldesley lbw, b Howell	138	Extras (LB 3)		3
†A. A. Lilley c Jones b Noble	2			
G. H. Hirst c Armstrong b Trumper	48		(9 wkts dec.)	376

AUSTRALIA

V. T. Trumper b Hirst	18	c Braund b Rhodes	15
R. A. Duff c Jessop b Rhodes	2	c Fry b Braund	14
C. Hill c Braund b Hirst	1	not out	10
S. E. Gregory lbw, b Hirst	0	not out	1
*J. Darling c Jessop b Rhodes	3		
M. A. Noble st Lilley b Rhodes	3		
W. W. Armstrong c Lilley b Rhodes	0		
A. J. Hopkins c Lilley b Rhodes	5		
†J. J. Kelly not out	1		
E. Jones c Jackson b Rhodes	0		
W. P. Howell c Fry b Rhodes	0		
Extras (B 3)	3	(LB 4, W 1, NB 1)	6
	36	(2 wkts)	46

AUSTRALIA	O.	M.	R.	W.	O.	M.	R.	W.		FALL OF WICKETS		
										Eng.	Aus.	Aus.
Jones	28	9	76	3					Wkt.	1st	1st	2nd
Noble	44	15	112	1					1st	5	9	16
Trumper	13	5	35	2					2nd	13	10	41
Armstrong	25	6	64	1					3rd	35	14	—
Howell	26	8	58	1					4th	112	17	—
Hopkins	6	2	28	0					5th	121	25	—
ENGLAND									6th	212	25	—
Hirst	11	4	15	3	9	6	10	0	7th	230	31	—
Rhodes	11	3	17	7	10	5	9	1	8th	264	35	—
Braund	1	0	1	0	5	0	14	1	9th	295	35	—
Jackson					4	2	7	0	10th	—	36	—

Umpires: J. Phillips and W. Hearn

Tourists and their recuperative powers from seemingly hopeless positions, it is extremely doubtful whether they could have managed to save themselves. In the event it was a moral victory for England, and the Australians' morale was somewhat shaken.

A punning cricket poet wrote the following lines in epitaph for the Edgbaston Test match:

"Our Cornstalk cousins like us well,
Our country, our abodes,
And yet the truth they fain must tell –
They cannot face our *Rhodes*."*

*P. C. Standing, *Cricket of Today*, T. C. & E. C. Jack, Vol. 2, p. 128.

CHAPTER 5

Holocaust at Headingley

On Sunday 1 June the Australians travelled to Leeds to meet the champion county of the last two seasons. Of all the counties Yorkshire were the toughest proposition, for unlike most others they did not rely for their greatest strength on the availability of amateurs; they had a predominantly professional side of first-class ability. The amateur contingent ready to wear the White Rose cap was formidable enough but, with the exception of F. S. Jackson and T. L. Taylor, could not always gain a place in the eleven. This particular meeting had excited the public imagination; the more so in view of the nearness to defeat that the Cornstalks had been brought in the Edgbaston Test and that their arch slayers had been Hirst and Rhodes.

It was on this very day that the good news spread across the land of the final surrender of the Boers in Pretoria. With the war at last over and church bells ringing throughout the countryside, the populace was in a holiday mood; little work was to be done for days. What better way to celebrate for the good folk of Yorkshire – and their Lancastrian neighbours – than to make their way to Headingley cricket ground.

Lord Hawke, in a letter to Percy Cross Standing, mentions "33,705 people on the ground today [1st day] and they fairly took everything, wickets and stands by storm".* It was a record attendance at a cricket match in England. Mounted police were needed to control the vast assemblage inside Headingley and the many thousands more who were unfortunate enough not to gain admittance. There had been overnight rain and the pitch was too soft to start on time.

The Australians were relying on the same side as had appeared at Birmingham; they had little choice. Martin Hawke selected his usual triumphant "Tykes"; he could do little else. He knew his men

*P. C. Standing, *Cricket of Today*, T. C. & E. C. Jack, Vol. 2, p. 128.

thoroughly, and no matter what may be said of his Lordship as a captain and a cricketer, he was a fine judge of character and an even finer one of cricketing ability. Moreover, he took a great personal interest in his professionals and did much for their welfare.

Brown and Tunnicliffe to open! As a pair of professional opening batsmen, and on their day prolific run-getters, they could compare with the Surrey stalwarts Abel and Hayward, or perhaps in years gone by with Shrewsbury and William Gunn; there were no others. As unalike his partner as possible, short, moustachioed John Thomas Brown could bat like quicksilver and score at a handsome rate with pugnacious strokes all round the wicket. But it was his very late cuts for which he had the highest repute, and his far-famed short-armed hook strokes; he was good enough to have been chosen eight times for England. Brown was responsible for an excellent match-winning hundred (140) at Melbourne in 1895, and he had already made two scores over 300. He fielded nowadays close to the wicket as cleverly as he had done in the outfield in earlier times. John Tunnicliffe, "Long John O'Pudsey" they called him, for he was six feet two inches tall, was the more sedate member of the pair, his long reach enabling him to smother anything, but he could open his shoulders if required and drive with great force. His slip fielding was so remarkable, even for Yorkshire, it is still spoken of. As senior "pro" he was Lord Hawke's aide, and was much respected by all. This pair had many long opening partnerships to their credit, the most notable being 378 against Sussex in 1897 and a staggering, for those days, 554 off Derbyshire in William Sugg's benefit match at Chesterfield in 1898.

Next in the batting order came David Denton, known as "Lucky" Denton – for at times he was a chancy starter – who was just flowering into the mature, stylish batsman of the years to come. He was considered by many as the White Rose answer to Johnny Tyldesley, for in class, style, and the manner in which they scored runs they had much in common. But whereas the Lancastrian favoured the off, the Yorkist was pre-eminently a leg-side player. However, even if he was dismissed cheaply from an early buccan-eering stroke, he saved runs by the score at third man and in the long field. He seemed to divine the ball's flight from the bat; a sudden dash round the boundary and the hard-hit ball would be taken in his outstretched hand and returned very quickly in a long, low trajectory.

Straight from Cambridge, where he was captain in 1900, into the Yorkshire side, Tom Launcelot Taylor emulated Frank Mitchell in joining the county team whilst still up at University. A player of great fighting capacity in the true Yorkshire spirit, he had remark-able powers of concentration and was at his best on wet pitches. He had already been chosen by *Wisden* in 1900 as one of the five cricketers of the year, be it noted when he was the Cambridge captain and wicketkeeper. He was already in fine batting form this season with scores of 74, 114 and 106.

Jackson, Hirst, and Rhodes the Australians had met before, and some of the Cornstalks had previously made a temporary acquaintance with Schofield Haigh who, in 1896, made his mark as a bowler. A little on the fast side of medium pace, he bowled with almost a slinging action from an inordinately long final stride, dragging his right foot. The delivery could be a vicious yorker or a venomous break-back from outside the off to remove the leg stump, and he was accuracy personified; as so many of the wickets "Schof" took were bowled, he did not often need the assistance of the field. His tally from 1896 onwards to 1900 was 84, 91, 102, 79, 163, and at this time he was usually only third or fourth change. Very useful with the bat, his maiden century being as many as 159 against Notts, he was developing into a fine all-rounder. Haigh, together with his two bosom friends, Hirst and Rhodes, was to make the third of the great Yorkshire bowling triumvirate. Always a character, humorist, practical joker and the sunshine of the side, the stories of him were legion.

A young man who promised greater things was Irving Washington, now in his third season for the county, where he shared the remaining berth with Lees Whitehead. He was developing as a hard-hitting left-handed batsman and an immaculate field. Last, but by no means least, veteran stumper David Hunter made up the chosen side. Hunter was a good enough keeper for England, but as merely a tail-end – batsman Storer of Derbyshire and Dick Lilley were more highly regarded. He kept to Hirst, Rhodes, Haigh and Jackson with rare skill, and had handled fast bowler Frank Milligan (alas killed in the South African war) without fuss.

Seventy minutes late, in front of this mammoth Yorkshire throng, Trumper and Duff came down the pavilion steps cheered to the echo. The pitch was drying, and quite difficult because of the effects of the sun. As usual, Victor Trumper made the fast-playing surface look easier than it was, for he and Reg Duff started very well until the latter was clean bowled by a swerver from Hirst for 12 runs. The restart after the luncheon interval was some fifteen minutes late due to attempts by the police and ground attendants to contain the enormous crowd behind the boundary. Both teams had come onto the field to give three cheers for His Majesty the King and to sing the National Anthem, and during this noble sentiment the crowd had flooded onto the ground. The pitch was becoming more difficult than ever and the excited crowd soon witnessed a remarkable procession, commencing with Clem Hill being caught in the slips by Brown off Rhodes. The Yorkshire fielding worked superbly in support of her bowlers; Syd Gregory was taken smartly by Jackson from Hirst, and young Washington then took a really breathtaking left-hander that has never been forgotten, close to the ground with outstretched arm after a sideways dive onto his shoulder, to dismiss Joe Darling. Immediately, Monty Noble was caught in the slips by "Long John" Tunnicliffe off Jackson's bowling before he had scored, and Denton made a running catch to dismiss Armstrong. Trumper had given a fine display of 38 out of the 70 runs scored up to this point. His was to prove the highest score of the match. Fortunately for the Tourists' prestige, Hopkins made a capable knock of seventeen; then Kelly and Jones, both giving the long handle to get sorely needed runs, between them managed to lift the Australian total to 131 by 4.45 p.m. Many of the delighted spectators now dashed on to the field of play again and it took police half an hour to force them back to enable the home county to bat.

It has been questioned whether Yorkshire should have been allowed to commence their first innings as the swollen crowd was spilling over the boundary's edge, but there was little more than an hour left before stumps. With the pitch playing more awkwardly than ever, Brown and Tunnicliffe had a difficult proposition on their hands. When the score reached five, Bill Howell, taking advantage of the help the pitch gave him, had Tunnicliffe caught swiftly at third slip by Armstrong. "Lucky" Denton then hit Jones so hard in one over that the Australian captain replaced him with Noble, who lost little time in finding a length and clean bowling Brown. In what time remained Denton, now accompanied by Tom Taylor, played a characteristically flamboyant innings, almost as good as Trumper's, before his luck ran out. Noble had him caught at third man by Clem Hill. Thus at the close of this exciting day's cricket with Yorkshire 48 for 3, the game was delicately poised. The spectators, having been treated to such a marvellous spectacle, had had their money's worth. But many must have summed up their county's chances on the morrow of obtaining a first innings lead as very remote.

After more early morning rain the pitch now steamed in the sun. If yesterday it had been sticky today it was stickier, and if the weather conditions did not change it would get worse. Once more the crowd of jostling spectators ranged around the ground was immense. Immediately on the restart Howell bowled Jackson for nought; the ball was popping! Pluckily George Hirst made 12 on the dreadful turf before Bill Howell trapped him leg before and bowled Washington for five. It was a fight for every run; Howell and Noble knew the pitch was on their side. Haigh and Lord Hawke did not hold up the inevitable for long; only Rhodes determinedly made twelve to enable Yorkshire to reach as many as 107 runs. The enormous crowd was hushed. It was still before lunchtime, and Howell and Noble between them had rolled up the Yorkshire innings in no uncertain manner: 6 for 53 to the former and 4 for

55

30 to the latter. If Howell and Noble could achieve figures like these, what might Hirst and Rhodes, to say nothing of Jackson and Haigh, do on a pitch like this? Even so, the Cornstalks had every advantage – they held a 24 run lead, which would be invaluable on this wicked turf, and the county would have to bat on it last of all.

If the Australians' first innings was a surprise and the Yorkshire outing a shock for this vast concourse of partisans, they were ill-prepared for the sensation attendant upon the Tourists' second venture. With barely time for more than a couple of overs before luncheon the crowd saw the home side take the field, and the eyes of Richard Binns, who was present on that momentous day, saw Jackson saying something to Hirst, who was preparing to bowl. He conjectures it might have been, "George, we'll never have 'em again on a wicket like this!"* For both Trumper and Duff were dubiously studying the evil looking turf and doing any amount of prodding and patting with their bats.

Reggie Duff prepared to take strike to the first over from George Hirst. One can see Hirst now, in the mind's eye, bounding in to the wicket with long strides and indulging in a peculiar "hop, skip and jump" the moment before bringing that left arm twirling over. The ball would come through fairly fast and on splendid length, but it would likely swerve and come in to the batsman "like a good throw in from mid off". If it missed the wicket, Hunter would take it perfectly. Duff could hardly comprehend the first three deliveries but managed to turn the fourth ball to leg, where "Jacker", fielding close, got a hand to it, juggled, and clasped it firmly. One down for nothing!

With jutting chin and a pugnacious look to his demeanour Clement Hill strode to the crease and surveyed the changed field for the left-hander. The remaining two balls were bowled. Perhaps the crowd were a little surprised that Lord Hawke did not give the ball to Rhodes, but he was probably not wanting to risk Trumper hitting runs off his slows. So Jackson came on at the other end, medium fast, right-handed, and dead straight. From the third ball Trumper off-drove for two, and from the fifth he took a single. Now to face Hirst's second over, and the third ball Victor leg-glanced for four runs. The very next delivery George Hirst thought was the best ball he ever bowled in his life; it completely beat Trumper leaving his wicket in disarray. Seven for two! Pandemonium broke loose; the vast throng cheered and clapped to see dismissed the very batsman whom they would have loved to have seen make a hundred. Lunch was now taken by over 30,000 parched throats!

Immediately on the restart Syd Gregory got off the mark rather luckily with a hit for three off Hirst's fifth ball, only to have to face a difficult maiden from Francis Jackson. From the fourth delivery of

*Richard Binns, *Cricket in Firelight*, Selwyn Blount, p. 16.

George Hirst's third over Hill took a single to face Jackson himself, to the second ball of which "the pride of Adelaide" played hard forward and missed. He had just raised his back foot a fraction over the crease: Hunter had the bails off in a split second, a marvellously quick stumping. The spectators roared when the square leg umpire's arm shot up. Three for only thirteen; the game was slowly drifting from reality into the realm of the supernatural. None of the massed throng could have seen anything quite like it in an ordinary county game, let alone against the far-famed Australians, and as the minutes passed and wickets fell they looked at each other dumbfounded and in disbelief. But they still cheered and roared at their own county's deeds.

Meanwhile Darling was at the wicket scoring a single off "Jacker" and now had to face "George Herbert's" fourth over. The Cornstalks' skipper never saw the first and second deliveries but somehow got his bat to the third; it was a full toss and he pulled it . . . on to his wicket. Fourteen for four. Noble was as all at sea as his captain had been; he was glad when Hirst's wicket maiden was over. Gregory carefully managed a two from the second in Jackson's fourth over, and Noble, far from happy, got away from Hirst's end with a single, leaving "Little Syd" to face the rest of George's flying fury. Now Jackson again; Noble takes another run and Gregory adds two more to bring twenty up on the scoreboard. At least Syd Gregory was managing to time the ball, somehow.

It was at the commencement of George Hirst's sixth over that the hushed and watchful Yorkshire spectators went wild with delirium. Noble was facing him; George ran up to the wicket, hop, skip, jump and down ripped the ball – it clean bowled Noble. Twenty for five. Out came the lugubrious Armstrong; in came Hirst again with a ball similar to the first, Armstrong was ponderously slow, it was through him before he made his stroke and he was as cleanly bowled as his departed colleague. Twenty for six. "Could Hirst get a hat trick?" the crowd was anxiously asking one another as Albert Hopkins came in.

It was only providence, or an Act of God, that saved Hopkins. For Hirst's third ball beat him all ends up and missed the stumps by the proverbial coat of varnish. Providence stayed with him for the rest of the over; the strain on him was noticeable, but the strain on the packed mass of spectators was almost at breaking-point. Gregory eased the tension with a nicely placed ball off Jackson and they ran two.

The seventh over that Hirst bowled to Hopkins was another maiden; the crowd sucked its breath. Now "Jacker" takes the ball for his seventh over, the field settles, he runs up to the wicket, the fieldsmen creep in, but Gregory skilfully finds the gap for a single. Jackson in to Hopkins, it raps his pads, an appeal and the umpire's

57

finger goes up. Twenty-three for seven; the crowd roars! Kelly comes out with moustache bristling under his well pulled down cap. Jackson's third ball, well pitched up and dead straight, bowls him. "Can 'Jacker' get *his* hat trick?" the crowd deliriously ask each other. But no; "Jonah" got his bat to it and stopped it somehow, so Jackson comes in again with his fifth ball. Whether Ernest Jones saw it after it pitched we will never know, but it wrecked his wicket. The noise of the crowd was frenzied excitement as last man Bill Howell faced the last ball of the over. He somehow got a thick upper edge to it and the ball was in Hunter's gloved hands before the spectators could realise that the mighty Australians had been humbled for only 23 runs. It had taken just 84 balls in total to do the impossible thing, and a mere 70 minutes. Hirst and Jackson had bowled them out with the extraordinary figures of 5 wickets for 9 runs and 5 for 12, respectively. It was their second lowest score on record, for, unbelievably, the 1896 side had been routed by Pougher and J. T. Hearne bowling for M C C for just 18!

No doubt the Tourists were dumbfounded, but they most likely reasoned that with a lead of 48 runs they could manage in their turn to reduce proud Yorkshire for less than that amount. Doubtless the Yorkshire crowd was secretly afraid that on such a dreadful pitch their heroes could quite possibly fail. The drama was not yet over.

It was now Yorkshire's turn to struggle on the awful pitch, for Noble and Howell were out to wreak revenge; they bowled with every resource that they could command and the Cornstalk fielders were determined to pull the game out of the fire. Every single run of the 48 required had to be fought for. Tunnicliffe went for three, bowled by that clever ball of Howell's that was let go from a step behind the bowling crease. Brown and Denton went quickly in terms of runs, but it took a devil of a time. Taylor, playing with a very straight bat, watching the ball so carefully and making his stroke so late, managed to stay a long while; he won eleven hard-bought runs before Monty Noble bowled him. Howell had already disposed of Francis Jackson, caught behind; thus all Yorkshire's main run-getters had been removed for 41 runs. Seven to get; Hirst had now joined young left-handed Washington. While determinedly George Hirst hung grimly on, Irving Washington managed to pick the right ball. He had made five when, from the third delivery of Noble's tenth over with two runs remaining, he played a beautiful on drive to the boundary and it was all over. That stroke made history; Yorkshire had beaten the Australians. The spectators went wild, and the scene at Headingley that afternoon was indescribable confusion. Lord Hawke was a very happy man.

AUSTRALIANS 2nd INNINGS

BOWLING ANALYSIS

Overs / Balls	1	2	3	4	5	6	
Hirst 1st	(Duff)	—	—	Duff caught 0–1	(Hill)	—	
Jackson 1st	(Trumper)	—	Trumper 2 runs	—	Trumper 1 run	(Hill)	
Hirst 2nd	(Trumper)	—	Trumper 4 runs	Trumper bowled 7–2	Gregory 3 runs	(Hill)	
Jackson 2nd	(Gregory)	—	—	—	—	—	⎫
Hirst 3rd	(Hill)	—	—	Hill 1 run	(Gregory)	—	⎬ 2 byes
Jackson 3rd	(Hill)	Hill stumped 13–3	Darling 1 run	(Gregory)	—	—	⎭
Hirst 4th	(Darling)	—	Darling bowled 14–4	(Noble)	—	—	
Jackson 4th	(Gregory)	Gregory 2 runs	—	—	—	—	
Hirst 5th	Noble 1 run	(Gregory)	—	—	—	—	
Jackson 5th	(Noble)	Noble 1 run	(Gregory)	Gregory 2 runs	—	—	
Hirst 6th	Noble bowled 20–5	Armstrong bowled 20–6	(Hopkins)	—	—	—	
Jackson 6th	(Gregory)	Gregory 2 runs	—	—	—	—	
Hirst 7th	(Hopkins)	—	—	—	—	—	
Jackson 7th	Gregory 1 run	Hopkins lbw 23–7	Kelly bowled 23–8	(Jones)	Jones bowled 23–9	Howell caught 23–10	

AUSTRALIANS *v* YORKSHIRE

At Leeds, 2, 3 June.

Yorkshire won by 5 wickets.

AUSTRALIANS

V. T. Trumper c Denton b Jackson	38	b Hirst	7
R. A. Duff b Hirst	12	c Jackson b Hirst	0
C. Hill c Brown b Rhodes	7	st Hunter b Jackson	1
S. E. Gregory c Jackson b Hirst	4	not out	10
*J. Darling c Washington b Hirst	3	b Hirst	1
M. A. Noble c Tunnicliffe b Jackson	0	b Hirst	2
W. W. Armstrong c Denton b Jackson	3	b Hirst	0
A. J. Hopkins b Jackson	17	lbw, b Jackson	0
†J. J. Kelly b Hirst	23	b Jackson	0
E. Jones c Haigh b Rhodes	20	b Jackson	0
W. P. Howell not out	1	c Hunter b Jackson	0
Extras (B 1, LB 1, W 1)	3	(B 2)	2
	131		**23**

YORKSHIRE

J. T. Brown sen., b Noble	13	c Howell b Noble	9
J. Tunnicliffe c Armstrong b Howell	1	b Howell	3
D. Denton c Hill b Noble	32	c Gregory b Noble	5
Mr T. L. Taylor b Noble	22	b Noble	11
Hon. F. S. Jackson b Howell	0	c Kelly b Howell	6
G. H. Hirst lbw, b Howell	12	not out	0
I. Washington b Howell	5	not out	9
S. Haigh c Kelly b Noble	0		
*Lord Hawke c Armstrong b Howell	3		
W. Rhodes c Trumper b Howell	12		
†D. Hunter not out	0		
Extras (B 7)	7	(B 7)	7
	107	(5 wkts)	**50**

YORKSHIRE	O.	M.	R.	W.	O.	M.	R.	W.
Hirst	16.4	6	35	4	7	4	9	5
Rhodes	13	1	43	2				
Jackson	13	2	30	4	7	1	12	5
Haigh	5	1	20	0				
AUSTRALIANS								
Howell	20	4	53	6	10	3	22	2
Jones	3	0	17	0				
Noble	16.3	6	30	4	9.3	4	21	3

FALL OF WICKETS

	Aus.	Yorks.	Aus.	Yorks.
Wkt.	1st	1st	2nd	2nd
1st	31	5	0	19
2nd	42	47	7	19
3rd	56	48	13	25
4th	64	49	14	39
5th	65	69	20	41
6th	65	77	20	—
7th	76	80	23	—
8th	102	83	23	—
9th	129	107	23	—
10th	131	107	23	—

Umpires: T. Mycroft and J. Moss

An extra day off must have been very welcome to our visitors as the strain of playing cricket for six days every week would be telling on them; it was something to which they were quite unused. They were very disappointed with their current form, having batted far from well at Edgbaston and Leeds, even allowing for the state of the playing surfaces. Some of the team had not really struck form with the bat yet, and probably all, save Victor Trumper, were feeling a trifle unhappy on the consistently wet, yet varied-paced English pitches. In addition to Trumble's bowling hand and Saunders' attack of tonsilitis, Monty Noble had been feeling unwell. It was to develop into influenza, which was very prevalent in Britain at this time, and was soon to affect other members of the touring side. Furthermore, Bill Howell had received the sad news of the death of his mother, and only two days later the added shock that his father too had passed away. This cast added gloom over them all.

Their next fixture was with the County Palatine at the Old Trafford ground, and so, travelling by the Lancashire & Yorkshire Railway, they were deposited in Manchester, where Dr Rowley Pope diagnosed influenza and put Noble straight to bed. Fortunately, Hanson Carter's eye had improved sufficiently to allow him to play; Darling had an "eleven", just!

The Lancashire side in 1902 was in a state of flux. They had lost the services of their two outstanding bowlers of the Nineties, fast bowler Arthur Mold and poor Johnnie Briggs, their left-arm off-spinner, who had suffered a mental breakdown. Additionally, all-rounder Willis Cuttell had broken a bone in his hand the previous season, and that classic young batsman Reggie Spooner from Marlborough was serving in South Africa. Still there was, of course, Sydney Barnes, whom MacLaren had taken to Australia on the last tour. In addition to Johnny Tyldesley and Albert Ward, they could call on James Hallows, a good left-handed all-rounder, whose health had been indifferent of late, and Jack Sharp. Sharp, an Everton footballer, first appeared for the county in 1899 and promised to be an outstanding cricketer in all departments of the game. Former Middlesex slow left-handed bowler Sidney Webb and wicketkeeper Thomas made up the "professors" in the side. For the rest, MacLaren had to rely on any amateurs that were available – E. E. Steel, one of A. G.'s all-rounder brothers, could turn out, as could Alec Eccles, a former Oxford Blue and occasional skipper when MacLaren was absent, and a promising batsman, C. R. Hartley. Alas, it was unfortunate for Lancashire that they could play neither L. O. S. Poidevin nor fast bowler Alex Kermode against their fellow-Australians.

With the inevitable lachrymose weather at Manchester in this terrible summer, the match was severely curtailed, play being possible only on Thursday (the first day). The Australians went out to bat in an exceptionally chilly atmosphere (there was even a fire in the Old Trafford dressing-room to keep the hapless players warm), and they stayed at the wicket all day. In scoring 356 for seven down some of them managed to get a little batting practice, but only Trumper was really in form. The rest appeared nervy and played many faulty strokes; had the Lancashire bowling been stronger and

Barnes been in touch, they would have scored considerably less. Trumper, however was, as always, a treat to watch; in scoring 70 runs out of 109 in seventy minutes, he hit brilliantly all round the wicket and gave no chance. With Hill as his partner they added 79 for the second wicket in only forty minutes, but Hill made several poorish strokes and was far from his best. Neither Duff nor Gregory could achieve much, and Darling was quickly bowled by Sharp. When Hopkins was out for 31 runs, also bowled Sharp, the Tourists were but 203 for six wickets and it needed Jim Kelly, on joining Armstrong, to stem the tide. Although both of them played scratchily and gave near chances for a while, they settled down to play good cricket. Kelly drove with great power for his 75 runs, and although Armstrong was in for above two and a half hours for his 87, he played skilfully, being particularly strong to the on side. Both had made their highest scores on the tour so far and earned their "tucker".

Owing to continual rain on the remaining two days, the players were confined to the commodious pavilion where they whiled away the rain-drenched hours playing cards. By 12.30 on the third day, the playing area was so saturated that the match was finally abandoned.

Reminiscing in later years Monty Noble, in his excellent book *The Game's the Thing*,* gives an amusing account of Hugh Trumble and the sick Tourists in Manchester. Trumble, the inveterate leg-puller, had suggested to Major Ben Wardill and Major Morcombe (of Victoria) a visit to the three patients in turn, Darling, Howell and Noble, apparently sympathetically but in reality to smoke them out. With pipes burning fiercely they visited their captain, who, being a non-smoker, was far from pleased. Leaving him coughing and spluttering they repaired to Noble's room. Ordering whisky and soda to fortify themselves, they continued their fumigation process, but Noble, being a smoker, was not unduly distressed. Noble noticed Hughie Trumble had left for a few moments on some pretext and, on his return, Trumble said to Major Wardill, "It's no use, Ben, we can't smoke *him* out. Let's give Bill Howell a doing." Now Howell loathed tobacco smoke but had great faith in the effects of sulphur fumes as a cure for influenza, which he had been inhaling frequently. Trumble, on disappearing, apparently had gone straight to Bill Howell, informing him of his visitors' intentions and suggesting he got his own back by giving them the sulphur treatment instead. The party, on arriving at Bill Howell's room, walked right into the trap. Hughie locked the door from the outside and left them gasping and choking for five minutes. Vowing vengeance, the two Majors went looking for Trumble, but discreetly he had vanished.

*M. A. Noble, *The Game's the Thing*, Cassell, p. 234.

AUSTRALIANS *v* LANCASHIRE

At Manchester, 5, 6, 7 June.

Match drawn.

AUSTRALIANS

V. T. Trumper c MacLaren b Sharp	70
R. A. Duff c Barnes b Steel	6
C. Hill c Webb b Barnes	54
S. E. Gregory c Hartley b Barnes	5
*J. Darling b Sharp	9
W. W. Armstrong not out	87
A. J. Hopkins b Sharp	31
J. J. Kelly b Hallows	75
†H. Carter not out	7
E. Jones ⎫ did not bat	
W. P. Howell ⎭	
Extras (B 9, W 1, NB 2)	12

(7 wkts) 356

LANCASHIRE

*Mr A. C. MacLaren, Mr A. Eccles, Mr C. R. Hartley, Mr E. E. Steel, A. Ward, J. T. Tyldesley, J. Sharp, J. Hallows, S. Webb, S. F. Barnes, and †R. Thomas.

LANCASHIRE	O.	M.	R.	W.	FALL OF WKTS.	
						Aus.
Barnes	31	6	94	2	*Wkt.*	*1st*
Steel	22	6	57	1	1st	30
Hallows	13	2	49	1	2nd	109
Webb	8	0	42	0	3rd	128
Sharp	37	5	91	3	4th	149
Ward	6	3	11	0	5th	157
					6th	203
					7th	334
					8th	—
					9th	—
					10th	—

Umpires: T. Mycroft and J. Moss

It says much for the resilience of these young men that they were able to indulge in such pranks at a time when their fortunes were at a low ebb. For their fixture with Cambridge University, due to begin on Monday 9 June, they were reduced to nine fit men, so being forced to give Hugh Trumble's bowling hand a try-out and to asking Dr Rowley Pope to fill the remaining place in the side. He had assisted H. J. H. Scott's touring team as long ago as 1886 whilst a medical student at Edinburgh.

The University in 1902 were an attractive batting side, but had to rely too much on just two bowlers, both of whom were slow and furthermore their leading batsmen – their captain "Rockley" Wilson and honorary secretary E. M. Dowson. They badly needed a fast bowler in their attack; however, they were shaping as a much better eleven than in the previous season. Unfortunately, Sam Day, their outstanding bat, was not available for this match, but in their excellent captain, a renowned character, they had a punishing player who had scored 118 in last year's Varsity encounter, was always among the wickets and had already played for Yorkshire. When only seventeen and still at Harrow, E. M. Dowson was considered the best schoolboy bowler yet seen; he was left-handed and would have been fit to turn out for the Gentlemen. He had since then come out in his batting, and this to a certain extent had affected his bowling powers. His action was still beautiful and he concealed a fine faster ball. Even by now, he was a great bat who gloried in the straight drive, revelled in fast bowling and played back like the best professionals. R. N. R. Blaker, known to all as "Dick", was the outstanding fielder in the side; he had a tremendous throw, was a fast scorer and captained Cambridge at soccer. The young freshman K. R. B. Fry, a cousin of C. B., had made a name for himself at Cheltenham, and had played a promising innings of 127 against Leveson Gower's very strong side, and 65 when facing Yorkshire. Among the seniors in the side, C. H. M. Ebden, an Etonian, was a most reliable and consistent bat, J. Gilman of London County promised much, and F. B. Wilson, a superb slip fieldsman, was an all-round player of great natural gifts.

Surprisingly, the weather was good when the Cantabrigians opened their innings on a fair, but slow, batting pitch. It gave little help to the Tourists' bowlers, but Trumble, opening with Jones and trying out his bowling hand, had the Varsity men in trouble immediately. Ebden, going in first, played a thoroughly good innings, his defence being very sound, but nobody could stay with him for very long apart from E. M. Dowson. Trumble, making his first appearance of the tour, took the first four wickets to fall, but by the luncheon interval he was forced to retire from the match. He, too, was found to be suffering from the prevalent influenza, thus adding to the Australians' tribulations with the second Test match only three days hence. Trumper now came on to bowl at a rattling medium fast pace. The remaining Cantabrigians knew not what to do; Victor rattled the stumps four times in a row and finally had Mr Ebden stumped by Carter after a watchful 53, to sweep the Varsity under the carpet for just 108 runs. Trumper returned the surprisingly good analysis of 5 wickets for 19 runs in 8 overs and three balls.

Now it was his turn with the willow, hitting in scintillating style all round the wicket and improvising his strokes at the merest whim. Small wonder he gave a couple of very difficult chances with the game he played. Reggie Duff had batting practice for 32 runs. Come the recommencement on Tuesday morning, and Trumper carried on where he had left off, soon passing his hundred only to be missed badly at mid-on. This was the only real blemish in a swash-buckling innings played as only Trumper could. With many of his comrades still to come needing practice for the sterner game ahead, he was stumped by Winter off Dowson. Syd Gregory showed a happy return to form with a delightful knock of 72, and Armstrong played a skilful 39. With Hugh Trumble absent from the field of play, Doctor Pope scored two and remained not out at the end of the Cornstalks' frolic of 337 runs.

It seemed most unlikely that Cambridge stood much chance of clearing the deficit of 229 – even less so when Ebden was bowled by Hopkins for a duck. Hopkins opened the bowling with Jones,

AUSTRALIANS
v
CAMBRIDGE UNIVERSITY

At Cambridge, 9, 10 June.

Australians won by an innings and 183 runs.

CAMBRIDGE UNIVERSITY

Mr C. H. M. Ebden st Carter b Trumper	53	b Hopkins		0
Mr J. Gilman b Trumble	4	b Jones		9
Mr L. V. Harper c Carter b Trumble	5	not out		24
Mr E. M. Dowson lbw, b Trumble	18	b Jones		0
Mr E. F. Penn c Carter b Trumble	3	b Jones		0
Mr R. N. R. Blaker lbw, b Armstrong	6	lbw, b Hopkins		1
*Mr E. R. Wilson b Trumper	6	b Hopkins		0
Mr K. R. B. Fry b Trumper	0	b Hopkins		0
Mr F. B. Wilson b Trumper	2	b Hopkins		4
Mr L. T. Driffield b Trumper	0	b Hopkins		2
†Mr C. E. Winter not out	4	b Hopkins		0
Extras (B 2, LB 4, NB 1)	7	(LB 6)		6
	108			46

AUSTRALIANS

V. T. Trumper st Winter b Dowson	128	†H. Carter c F. B. Wilson b Dowson		7
R. A. Duff c F. B. Wilson b E. R. Wilson	32	R. J. Pope not out		2
C. Hill c Ebden b Dowson	25	E. Jones b Dowson		0
W. W. Armstrong b Dowson	39	*H. Trumble absent, ill		0
S. E. Gregory c Driffield b E. R. Wilson	72	Extras (B 12, LB 1, NB 7)		20
A. J. Hopkins c Winter b E. R. Wilson	0			
J. J. Kelly b E. R. Wilson	12			337

AUSTRALIANS	O.	M.	R.	W.	O.	M.	R.	W.
Jones	12	4	28	0	8	1	30	3
Trumble	19	6	33	4				
Armstrong	16	6	21	1				
Trumper	8.3	4	19	5				
Hopkins					8	2	10	7
CAMBRIDGE								
Dowson	40	4	146	5				
E. R. Wilson	38	5	107	4				
Driffield	11	3	24	0				
Penn	9	0	30	0				
Blaker	3	1	10	0				

Umpires: G. Porter and A. A. White

and they only needed eight overs apiece. Apart from L. V. Harper, who carried his bat from first wicket down, the Cantabrigians batted badly. By playing forward on a slow pitch to Jones and Hopkins, they gave their wickets away. Hopkins had had little chance on the tour so far at bowling, but, by varying his pace cleverly and getting quite a break on the ball, he reduced the later batsmen to a steady stream towards the pavilion. In just an hour, the Varsity had been vanquished by an innings and 183 runs; almost incredibly, Hopkins had taken 7 wickets for 10. It enabled the Tourists to enjoy a day's respite and take stock of their convalescents.

CHAPTER 6

Rain at Lord's – The Second Test

Major Ben Wardill and Joe Darling may well have been wishing they had brought more than fourteen players on tour. Bill Howell and Hugh Trumble were both far too ill with influenza to be considered. The captain himself and Monty Noble, although recovering, were far from well but were prepared to turn out. Jack Saunders, still recuperating from tonsilitis, had in addition developed eye trouble. Bravely, he too was willing to play in their straitened circumstances. Dr Pope must have been worth his weight in gold to the Tourists for his medical and personal care. It had already been suggested that, because of their enfeebled condition, the coming Test encounter should be postponed. The Australians, however, would not hear of it; they were prepared to play. The elements were as miserable as ever, it was still raining, with dark scudding clouds, and perishingly cold.

Even for a country inflicted with more poor summers than warm sunny ones, the players and followers of our national game had never experienced weather quite as bad within living memory. It had had a considerable effect on the county programme: far more matches had been curtailed and drawn owing to rain than usual, and more games had terminated in under two days because of spinners' pitches. So far it had not been a good season for batsmen. Individuals had blossomed here and there on the rain-soaked and sticky pitches, but it rendered the selectors' task a difficult one. Of those chosen at Birmingham, MacLaren, though playing little, had had a fine 112 against Leicestershire and steady knocks of 65 and 56 not out off the Gloucester attack. Jessop had performed well with 53 and 93 against Sussex, a quick 50 off Notts, an even quicker 42 (in 25 minutes) at the expense of Somerset only the day before the Test was due to start, as well as some capital bowling in the style of his best days to take 11 Middlesex wickets for 98 at Lord's in the previous week. Having only turned out five times so far this season (twice against the Australians) the Hon. F. S. Jackson had looked in fine fettle, particularly at Leyton with 101 against Essex in a rain-washed draw. This had been the first county fixture he had taken part in for two years as he had been serving with his regiment in South Africa. The continuance of the good form of the past four seasons was automatically expected of Charles Fry; surprise may well have been exhibited that he had not yet scored a hundred this season. He had often been dismissed when looking well set and, although a number of low scores appeared against his name, he had taken 68 and 70 off the full Yorkshire attack at Leeds, and for London County at The Oval against Surrey had batted splendidly for 82 and 49 not out.

As he was to be engaged in the Coronation ceremony and in welcoming certain of his fellow-countrymen for the celebrations, Ranji had been able to play little this season. Even with lack of match practice, he had showed surprisingly excellent touch at The Oval, where he had innings of 135 and 36 not out at Surrey's expense. In addition to the century in the First Test, John Tyldesley had performed another to Gloucester's disadvantage, and remained, as always, the bulwark of Lancashire's batting. Dick Lilley had had a few good knocks; Braund, Hirst and Rhodes were doing well with bat and ball, whilst Bill Lockwood continued to regard himself as an all-rounder with 102 off Worcestershire, 67 against Kent and 65 versus Warwickshire, all made when runs were in sore need.

Veteran Bobby Abel, always a tower of strength for Surrey despite his diminutive stature, was at home on the wet pitches of this summer as he had been on the dry ones of the previous three seasons. The "Surrey Crowd" had to have long memories to recall a year when he was not among the leaders in the batting averages. That he was still a Test-class batsman he forcibly reminded the selectors this season with innings of 77 versus London County, 101 against Essex at The Oval, 151 off Sussex and 150 off Essex again, this time at Leyton, in a Surrey victory. The *Punch* cartoon captioned "Abel stayed all day at the wickets" must have been full of meaning for the Essex bowlers. So much for his "bad" eyesight, "crooked" bat and supposed dislike of fast bowling!

Three other Yorkshire bats had shown themselves to be in touch; the lively David Denton, John Tunnicliffe and Mr T. L. Taylor. The last indeed looked a most polished performer, being very difficult to remove from the crease, particularly when the pitch was slow – 114 against Leicester, 106 off Derbyshire and 43 at Essex' expense at Leyton. "Pinky" Burnup had also started the season well, showing the excellent form of previous summers. He always looked full of runs and made them in the ever attractive Malvern style. At The Oval, where he always did well, he was unlucky to fall ten short of the hundred against Surrey, then with 60 off Lancashire and 63 at Worcester three days prior to the Lord's Test, Burnup showed the selectors that he merited consideration. Two of Leicestershire's professionals might also be worthy of recognition at this early period of the season: J. H. King and A. E. Knight. The latter, a particularly beautiful bat whose day was yet to come, had started well with 108 at Worcester (King made 130 in this innings) and, playing against a strong London County side just prior to the Test, he scored 70 and 145 not out with attractive, faultless strokeplay.

Under Lord Hawke the Selection Committee had their usual daunting task of choosing a representative English eleven. They finally decided upon the same players that had done duty at Edgbaston, additionally calling on Mr T. L. Taylor to present himself. This last requirement must have been extracted from his Lordship with some difficulty (remember there were already three Yorkshiremen selected) for he was always mindful of his county's chances in the Championship.

Come the morning of 12 June, the pitch was seen to be in a deplorable state in spite of careful preparation (it had been so during the two previous matches – Middlesex versus Notts and M C C against Notts) so no play was possible before lunch. The weather was cold, it was overcast and wet and less than 7,000 staiwarts paid for admission. England decided to take into the field the same eleven as at Birmingham, thus Taylor's services were not required. MacLaren won the toss and Umpires Titchmarsh and Richardson decided the pitch was fit for play at a quarter to three.

The start could be described as being as sensational as the opening of the previous Test. MacLaren faced a maiden over from Ernest Jones, and Darling, in the absence of Trumble and Howell, at a moment's whim gave the ball to Hopkins. Fry, who apparently had never seen Hopkins bowl before, made a most deplorable stroke and was easily caught by Hill at short leg. A horrified spectator was moved to remark, "Hill could have caught it in his mouth." None for one! Would it be another disastrous England start? Ranjitsinhji came to the wicket and, in Hopkins' next over, to the consternation of all present, was bowled off his pad by a simple straight ball to which the bowler had applied considerable "finger-work". Two English wickets down for none; a saddened hush had descended on the cold, cheerless spectators. Their gloom matched and mirrored the climatic conditions exactly. MacLaren, runless and facing the fast bowler, was now joined by Jackson, and immediately rain sent the players scurrying for the shelter of the pavilion.

Fortunately it did not last long, but before the runs started to come "Jacker" was nearly caught at slip. As Darling changed his bowlers to attempt to unsettle them, Jackson and MacLaren began to score. The Yorkshire amateur looked good and made some admirable shots – as the scoreboard read 19 he had made 15 of them. England had now been batting for half an hour and down came the rain again. It was more persistent this time and it seemed unlikely that play would recommence that day.

Fry recalls how many of the players had gone back to their hotels and had to be telephoned for when it was decided that the match could restart at about five o'clock. The pitch was playing quite dead, so it was difficult for the batsmen to get the ball away, and the light was poor; even so, the two amateurs fought for their runs with rare skill. MacLaren played superbly, being exceptionally strong off the back foot, and although he gave a palpable chance to Darling in the slips off Trumper when he had reached 34, he dealt magnificently with some of Jones' fast rising balls on the leg side. He never seemed to be in the slightest difficulty. Jackson, however, at times seemed less sure: two or three hits luckily for him did not go to hand, and on 45 he could have been caught by Saunders if the latter had moved in to the ball instead of throwing himself forward. Surviving these he took every opportunity to score. Their determined stand and fight-back from the dreadful start had a warming effect on the chilled and patient spectators. So when at the close the scoreboard read 102 runs for 2 wickets, the England pair were enthusiastically cheered as they came off. The host country was in a strong position, the morrow hopefully promised great things and the pitch would undoubtedly get more difficult by the time the Cornstalks went in to bat; perhaps it would be Hirst and Rhodes all over again!

Sadly, it was not to be – the arch enemy of our hopes and fears fell in torrents all the following day. Come Saturday morning Lord's was waterlogged and it was immediately obvious that play would not be possible. Thus, by a quarter past eleven o'clock, the game which had promised so much had to be abandoned. There had been just one and three-quarter hours of play. The second Test match had disappointingly gone the way of the first.

> With Fry and Ranji out for nought
> The latter bowled, the former caught,
> Then Jacker in with Archie Mac
> Played up well and fought back.
> Till 102 at close of play,
> They promised more the following day.
> Alack for England, all in vain,
> Their hopes were "drownded" in more rain.

ENGLAND v AUSTRALIA

(2nd TEST)
At Lord's, 12, 13, 14 June.
Match drawn.

ENGLAND

*Mr A. C. MacLaren not out	47
Mr C. B. Fry c Hill b Hopkins	0
K. S. Ranjitsinhji b Hopkins	0
Hon. F. S. Jackson not out	55
(2 wkts)	102

Did not bat: J. T. Tyldesley, †A. A. Lilley, G. H. Hirst, Mr G. L. Jessop, L. C. Braund, W. H. Lockwood and W. Rhodes.

AUSTRALIA

V. T. Trumper, R. A. Duff, A. J. Hopkins, C. Hill, S. E. Gregory, *J. Darling, M. A. Noble, W. W. Armstrong, †J. J. Kelly, E. Jones and J. V. Saunders.

AUSTRALIA	O.	M.	R.	W.	FALL OF	
Jones	11	4	31	0	WICKETS	
Hopkins	9	3	18	2	*Eng.*	
Saunders	3	0	15	0	*1st innings*	
Trumper	8	1	33	0	1st	0
Armstrong	5	0	5	0	2nd	0
Noble	2	2	0	0		

Umpires: V. A. Titchmarsh and C. E. Richardson

71

CHAPTER 7

By all the "flaming" gods of June

The Australians thought our June weather was "flaming" all right!
But they were in London, staying at the Inns of Court Hotel, and
there was much to see and do by way of evening entertainment,
even if it was cold and wet. Beerbohm Tree and Ellen Terry were at
Her Majesty's Theatre with their production of *The Merry Wives of
Windsor*. Mr George Hawtrey's new comedy *Lord of His House*
starring Miss Nina Boucicault had opened at the Comedy Theatre,
but the big attraction of the London stage was the appearance of
Madame Sarah Bernhardt in a series of roles at the Garrick. Some
of the Tourists went to see her in *Francesca Da Rimini*.

His Majesty the King, also affected by the miserable weather,
suffered a severe chill and an attack of lumbago, so being unable to
review his troops at Aldershot on the 16th. It was on this day that
the Australians were due to encounter "An England Eleven", and
the venue was to be the attractive Saffrons ground at Eastbourne.
The side was a scratch combination of individuals ranging from
Test-class performers like Jessop and Abel to the second-class
County all-rounder George Thompson of Northants. It was filled
out with the military Mr W. Troup and Harry Wrathall, two
Gloucester batsmen, hefty six-footer Mr V. F. S. Crawford and
Captain H. S. Bush, both hard hitters from Surrey, Bill Bestwick
the Derbyshire fast bowler, and William Storer, the wicketkeeper-
batsman from the same county. Finally, two Worcestershire players
were included: Ted Arnold, now fully fit, a young fast-medium
bowler of great promise who could also bat, and the distinctly pacey
G. A. Wilson. Many good players, though it was rather an ill-
balanced side.

The invalids, no longer "crook", being fully restored to health
meant that the Australians were able to field their full strength
team; Trumble, Howell and Noble, as well as Darling, were included. The inevitable rain delayed the commencement and no

play was possible until after lunch when the Australians opened on a slow, wet pitch. Trumper (31) and Hill (46) were the only batsmen at ease under the prevailing conditions in the face of Bestwick's and Wilson's attack. The only other man to reach double figures was Gregory with 19, and the last 8 wickets fell for 62 runs. In view of the state of the pitch, 154 was a decent score.

The pitch suited Trumble admirably; spinning the ball cleverly he had the "English Eleven" in trouble: only Abel played him with confidence. At stumps the scratch side were 5 down for only 29 runs. Next morning the pitch was more awkward than ever. Abel and Arnold fell to Trumble; they had slumped to 46 for 7. Now came a change over the game; from the moment Jessop and Crawford came together the batting sparkled. In the next forty minutes 90 runs were added. For the one and only time in his life the mighty Jessopus was out-paced; Vivian Francis Shergold Crawford, who admittedly had more of the bowling, made some effortless big hits, twice driving Trumble smack out of the ground for six. On that pitch they lived dangerously and in the end Hugh Trumble had them both, to finish with the excellent analysis of 8 for 58. Out of the "England Eleven" total of 138 (of which 7 were extras), 120 runs had come from the combined efforts of only three bats – Crawford, Jessop and Abel.

After Hill and Gregory retrieved the bad start of the Cornstalks' second venture the inevitable watery elements sent them in at 3.30 p.m. By the time they were able to continue their innings on the Wednesday morning unexpected bright sunshine made the pitch extremely treacherous. For after Syd Gregory (71) and Clem Hill (32) had added 64 in forty minutes the previous day, only Hopkins and Kelly with 23 runs apiece could stay for long. Thompson bowled splendidly and, by varying his pace, took 8 wickets for 88 runs. The ball was coming off the turf at all angles; even Storer could not keep the byes down.

The scratch "England Eleven" would not last long under these circumstances, which again suited Trumble perfectly, so, assisted by Howell, he proceeded to dismiss them very cheaply in under two hours. Any chance of the Eleven to make a fight of it went when Jessop hit across the ball and sliced it to Duff, and Crawford followed with a skier to Hopkins. No doubt this was a bowlers' match, thus Hugh Trumble made a welcome return to the Australian fold with a match total of 14 wickets for 84 runs. It showed just how much his absence from the side had weakened their attack.

For the remainder of the week they contended with Derbyshire at Derby on, needless to say, another wet pitch. The Peak County was not quite at full strength, for Arnold Warren, one of their fast bowlers, was passed over, and Ernest "Nudger" Needham, Sheffield United's celebrated "Prince of Half Backs", was not

AUSTRALIANS
v
AN ENGLAND ELEVEN

At Eastbourne, 16, 17, 18 June.
Australians won by 131 runs.

AUSTRALIANS

V. T. Trumper b Bestwick	31	b Thompson	7
R. A. Duff lbw, b Wilson	1	c Bush b Thompson	5
C. Hill c Thompson b Bestwick	46	run out	32
S. E. Gregory c Crawford b Bestwick	19	b Thompson	71
*J. Darling b Bestwick	6	b Wilson	1
W. W. Armstrong b Wilson	8	c Arnold b Thompson	6
M. A. Noble b Wilson	5	b Thompson	0
A. J. Hopkins b Wilson	6	c Storer b Thompson	23
†J. J. Kelly c Bush b Arnold	7	b Thompson	23
H. Trumble not out	8	lbw, b Thompson	0
W. P. Howell b Arnold	7	not out	0
Extras (B 3, LB 5, NB 2)	10	(B 7, LB 7, NB 3)	17
	154		**185**

AN ENGLAND ELEVEN

R. Abel c Howell b Trumble	32	run out	1
H. Wrathall c Darling b Howell	1	b Trumble	0
G. J. Thompson c Gregory b Trumble	1	run out	2
Mr W. Troup b Trumble	0	not out	10
Capt. H. S. Bush b Trumble	0	b Trumble	5
†W. Storer st Kelly b Armstrong	1	c Howell b Trumble	14
E. Arnold b Trumble	8	c Kelly b Howell	15
Mr G. L. Jessop c Trumper b Trumble	31	c Duff b Trumble	3
Mr V. F. S. Crawford c Hopkins b Trumble	57	c Hopkins b Trumble	7
G. A. Wilson not out	0	c Duff b Trumble	3
W. Bestwick b Trumble	0	lbw, b Howell	2
Extras (B 6, LB 1)	7	(B 6, LB 2)	8
	138		**70**

ENG. ELEVEN	O.	M.	R.	W.	O.	M.	R.	W.
Wilson	15	5	34	4	18	4	53	1
Arnold	16.5	3	56	2	3	1	2	0
Bestwick	14	3	30	4	5	0	25	0
Thompson	9	3	24	0	25.1	6	88	8
AUSTRALIANS								
Trumble	20.3	7	58	8	19	6	26	6
Howell	13	5	39	1	11.4	1	20	2
Armstrong	5	1	18	1	2	1	1	0
Noble	2	0	16	0	5	0	15	0

Umpires: A. A. White and G. Bean

available. However, the West Indian batsman Mr C. A. Ollivierre, who did not fully qualify for the county until late in July, was allowed to assist the home side. Storer was played for his batting alone, and young Humphries, his deputy, acted as stumper. The county were fairly strong in batting, the captain, Mr A. E. Lawton, being a renowned hitter, and the veteran player Mr L. G. Wright and the younger Mr Maynard Ashcroft were blossoming into the runs this season.

Jack Saunders returned to the side, Noble was being rested, and Carter came in for Kelly. The county elected to bat and, in the face of Saunders and Howell, managed to obtain 152 runs, thanks to Storer's sterling 36 and "Bertie" Lawton's capital knock of 50 with his heavy bat. Derbyshire's captain scored his runs out of 67 added in 40 minutes having hit the initial 22 runs off only two overs! Saunders and Howell took 4 wickets apiece and Armstrong had the valuable wickets of Ashcroft and Storer.

Hopkins opened with Trumper, and he did so quite effectively. After the latter was caught behind, Hill suffered the unusual fate of being bowled out twice by Bestwick. The first delivery which bowled him was a no-ball and immediately afterwards he was bowled again – this time by a legitimate one! From 2 down for 20, Darling came to the rescue, and with Hopkins added 113 runs very quickly. The Cornstalks' captain, who had been out of touch, made his 65 runs in a healthy manner at a run a minute before being bowled by Ollivierre. They ended the day four runs ahead with six wickets left.

Friday unfortunately was a complete blank owing to still more rain, therefore on Saturday morning they were ordered to get runs or get out. Although most of the Derbyshire side had a turn with the ball, Bestwick, who always bowled his best with Warren at the other end, had 6 wickets for 82 out of the Australians' total of 218.

The county's second innings on a drying pitch was little more than a procession. They could do little or nothing with Saunders and Trumble, so after an hour and a half they left the Tourists with but 13 runs to get. After reversing their batting order, these were obtained with eight wickets to spare.

Travelling by train to Bradford for their return match with Yorkshire at Park Avenue, due to start on 23 June, the Tourists were out for revenge after their humbling at Headingley. As H M King Edward VII's coronation was due to take place the following Thursday, 26 June, both Lord Hawke and the Hon. F. S. Jackson had already gone to London, and this reduced Yorkshire's chances whilst the Australians were at full strength. The Yorkshiremen were led by Mr T. L. Taylor, and the two vacant places were taken by the veteran all-rounder Ted Wainwright and Lees Whitehead. After weekend rain and a little sunshine the pitch was going to be difficult – it would suit the spinners. Rhodes would be in his element, but so would Trumble and Saunders!

Joe Darling had the luck of the toss and before another large Yorkshire crowd sent Trumper and Hopkins to the wickets. They were both back with only 3 runs on the board! Would this be Headingley all over again? Hill and Darling soon dispelled any such

AUSTRALIANS *v* DERBYSHIRE

At Derby, 19, 20, 21 June.
Australians won by 8 wickets.

DERBYSHIRE

Batsman	1st	2nd dismissal	2nd
Mr L. G. Wright c Howell b Saunders	2	c Carter b Saunders	2?
Mr C. A. Ollivierre c Carter b Saunders	15	c sub. b Trumble	1?
W. Storer b Armstrong	36	b Saunders	(
Mr E. M. Ashcroft b Armstrong	14	b Saunders	
W. Chatterton b Howell	14	b Trumble	1?
*Mr A. E. Lawton b Howell	50	c Trumble b Saunders	2?
†J. Humphries c Hill b Howell	0	b Trumble	
J. Hulme c Gregory b Saunders	12	c and b Saunders	?
Mr T. Forester b Howell	2	run out	
Buxton not out	4	st Carter b Saunders	
W. Bestwick c Gregory b Saunders	0	not out	
Extras (B 1, LB 2)	3	(B 2)	?
	152		**7?**

AUSTRALIANS

Batsman	1st	2nd dismissal	2nd
V. T. Trumper c Humphries b Bestwick	10		
A. J. Hopkins b Bestwick	68		
C. Hill b Bestwick	1		
*J. Darling b Ollivierre	65		
S. E. Gregory c Humphries b Ashcroft	1		
W. W. Armstrong b Hulme	25		
R. A. Duff not out	26	not out	?
H. Trumble b Bestwick	1		
†H. Carter b Hulme	7	not out	?
W. P. Howell b Bestwick	11	c and b Lawton	?
J. Saunders b Bestwick	1	c Ollivierre b Ashcroft	?
Extras (LB 1, NB 1)	2		
	218	**(2 wkts)**	**1?**

AUSTRALIANS	O.	M.	R.	W.	O.	M.	R.	W.
Trumble	16	6	37	0	12	3	36	3
Saunders	18.5	3	69	4	12	2	40	6
Hopkins	9	4	24	0				
Armstrong	10	4	11	2				
Howell	6	3	8	4				
DERBYSHIRE								
Hulme	21	3	57	2				
Bestwick	26.2	3	82	6				
Forester	4	0	19	0				
Lawton	3	0	12	0	1	0	2	1
Buxton	3	0	20	0				
Ollivierre	5	0	17	1				
Ashcroft	3	1	9	1	2	1	3	1
Wright					1.1	0	8	0

FALL OF WICKETS

Wkt.	Derby 1st	Aus. 1st	Derby 2nd	Aus 2nd
1st	5	17	23	
2nd	20	20	31	?
3rd	64	133	31	-
4th	67	142	48	-
5th	134	161	50	-
6th	134	183	66	-
7th	134	194	67	-
8th	140	203	77	-
9th	152	216	77	-
10th	152	218	78	-

Umpires: J. West and J. Moss

idea for within 35 minutes they had hit Hirst and Rhodes hard for 74 runs. Perhaps Taylor kept Rhodes on too long for Darling was knocking him about. Although it was not realised at the time, this stand was to determine the result. Nobody else could do much with the accurate bowling except Reg Duff, who hung on grimly at one end to remain 11 not out when Saunders' wicket was spreadeagled by Haigh. The mighty Australians had only managed 106 runs. Rhodes had 5 for 49 and "Schof" Haigh 4 for 18.

Now how would they fare with Trumble and Saunders? Tunnicliffe fell immediately, Brown and Denton carried the score to 27 and then were both caught. Taylor stayed for 11 runs whilst his middle order batting collapsed hopelessly from Trumble's and Saunders' onslaught. The Cornstalks' fielding was matchless, so utterly determined were they to get Yorkshire out quickly and cheaply. Eight wickets down for 49 runs; nobody could stave off the inevitable. Whitehead and Hunter, the last pair, desperately chanced their arms and managed to raise their side's total to a still meagre 77. Trumble at 6 for 17 had been much less expensive than Rhodes.

With a lead of 29 the visitors went in a second time that day; the initial wickets fell, Trumper was out of form. It was Syd Gregory, often called "Little Tich", who played the big innings this time. He was still in possession at the close of play when Australia were only 70 for 6 wickets, or 99 runs ahead. It was still very much a bowlers' pitch.

With the ground being no easier next morning, the Tourists added a mere 17 runs, leaving Gregory not out with 42 hard earned runs to his credit. Rhodes, whose imperceptible variations of flight and length were difficult to get away, had 4 for 22 and Haigh 5 for 49. Both had taken 9 match wickets.

To obtain 117 runs to win against Trumble and Saunders on this pitch seemed remote even to the most optimistic Yorkshire fanatic. They never looked like getting them from the start. Hughie Trumble mesmerised them and the wickets tumbled. Hirst and Irving Washington held up the rattle of stumps for a while, the young left-hander playing with rare confidence, but Trumble had them in the end. Yorkshire slumped to defeat by 44 runs before half past three on the second day. Trumble's 12 wickets in the match had cost him only 44 runs. This superlative bowler was the Australians' real match winner, and they were glad to have him back. Surprisingly, no time had been lost by rain.

During the course of the foregoing match, to a concerned and astonished public, it was announced that, owing to a sudden deterioration in the King's health, the Coronation ceremony and festivities would have to be cancelled. The offical bulletin signed by five royal doctors stated that His Majesty was suffering from perityphlitis and surgery was immediately necessary. That same day, the 24th, Sir Frederick Treves successfully operated on the Monarch. It had been arranged that the Australians were to go up to London to witness the Coronation; so now, in its stead, a fixture was hastily organised at Bradford against yet another "England Eleven". It was due to commence on 26 June (the original Coronation Day),

AUSTRALIANS *v* YORKSHIRE

At Bradford, 23, 24 June.
Australians won by 44 runs.

AUSTRALIANS

V. T. Trumper c Hirst b Rhodes	3	c Hunter b Rhodes	5
A. J. Hopkins b Hirst	0	b Haigh	10
C. Hill c Wainwright b Rhodes	34	c Taylor b Hirst	8
*J. Darling c Hunter b Haigh	40	c Rhodes b Haigh	
S. E. Gregory lbw, b Rhodes	6	not out	49
R. A. Duff not out	11	b Haigh	4
M. A. Noble c and b Rhodes	0	c and b Rhodes	
†J. J. Kelly c Tunnicliffe b Rhodes	0	b Rhodes	7
H. Trumble b Haigh	0	c Hunter b Rhodes	0
W. P. Howell c Washington b Haigh	3	b Haigh	
J. V. Saunders b Haigh	4	b Haigh	
Extras (B 1, LB 4)	5	(LB 3, NB 1)	4
	106		**87**

YORKSHIRE

J. T. Brown c Darling b Trumble	14	b Trumble	5
J. Tunnicliffe b Trumble	0	c Trumble b Saunders	7
D. Denton c Hill b Saunders	13	b Trumble	6
*Mr T. L. Taylor lbw, b Trumble	11	b Trumble	0
G. H. Hirst c Noble b Saunders	5	b Howell	14
I. Washington c Gregory b Trumble	3	c Hopkins b Trumble	22
E. Wainwright c Trumper b Saunders	4	lbw, b Trumble	2
S. Haigh b Trumble	0	c Hill b Saunders	3
W. Rhodes b Saunders	0	run out	5
L. Whitehead c Saunders b Trumble	11	not out	8
†D. Hunter not out	14	lbw, b Trumble	0
Extras (B 2)	2	(B 4)	4
	77		**79**

YORKSHIRE	O	M	R	W	O	M	R	W
Hirst	6	1	34	1	4	1	12	1
Rhodes	11	2	49	5	18	8	22	4
Haigh	7.3	2	18	4	20.4	6	49	5
AUSTRALIANS								
Saunders	15	1	58	4	10	1	26	2
Trumble	14.2	6	17	6	17.1	6	27	6
Howell					7	2	15	1

FALL OF WICKETS

Wkt.	Aus. 1st	Yorks. 1st	Aus. 2nd	Yorks 2nd
1st	3	0	2	14
2nd	3	27	12	14
3rd	77	38	23	14
4th	86	43	43	15
5th	91	47	59	37
6th	91	48	60	40
7th	91	48	86	49
8th	92	49	86	56
9th	100	60	87	67
10th	106	77	87	79

Umpires: W. Wright and A. Pike

and it was again rather a scratch combination. It was captained by twenty-year-old Mr Reggie Crawford, the Leicestershire brother, who brought with him batsman Albert Knight, and all-rounders J. H. King, left-hander, and H. Whitehead from that shire. Two capital professional bats from Warwickshire in the diminutive Willie Quaife and S. P. Kinneir were engaged at short notice. In the Warwickshire versus Lancashire engagement just concluded at Old

Trafford, these two had had a successful match. Quaife had played a masterly innings of 106 on a difficult pitch, and Kinneir in the second venture was unfortunate to fall two short of the century mark in a fine knock. Both had materially assisted in their county's win. Harry Wrathall, the hard-hitting Gloucester opener, was obtained once again and travelled up from Bristol (where he had witnessed his captain, Jessop, vigorously punishing the Worcester bowling to the tune of 126 in 120 minutes and capturing 7 wickets for 77). The young Kent professional James Seymour's services were offered, and he had to come from Bournemouth! To fill out the remaining places at such short notice, the authorities had recourse to three Bradford Club players. It must have been the only occasion that they ever took the field under such a high sounding title as "An England Eleven". They were Messrs. Knutton, Sowden and Bairstow.

In view of the nearness of the third Test match, Darling decided not to overwork Trumble, Gregory and Kelly, so Ernie Jones, Armstrong and Carter filled the vacancies. The morning was fine and another large crowd took the unexpected opportunity of an extra viewing of the Australians. With the spin of the coin in their favour, they lost little time in getting to the business at hand, or rather Trumper did! Monty Noble, who had so far had rather a thin time with the willow, went in first with Victor. His fortunes, alas, remained unchanged – he left for a single. Clem Hill fared no better, and Darling himself bagged the first half of a pair. The pitch was good but it was the Bradford bowler J. Knutton who foxed them; he bowled all three. Quickly Knutton added a fourth scalp in getting Hopkins caught for 10. Thus, the Tourists were in the surprising position of four down for 35 runs. Trumper, who had not been among the runs in his last few innings, was batting with all his old assuredness from the start. Now joined by Reggie Duff, who had not previously displayed his best form, together they set about the bowling in no uncertain fashion. The pair of them came good to the tune of 191 runs added in little more than 90 minutes. Before Victor started, somebody had told him that he had nearly completed his 1,000 runs for the tour; it interested him but little – he was more concerned at his recent lack of form. His punishment of the bowlers, changed with great regularity, was as extreme as it was delightfully elegant. His century was completed in little more than even time, and swart Reg Duff was virtually keeping pace with him, run for run. This pair of handsome batsmen gave the large crowd more than their money's worth, for Trumper's graceful cutting, driving and pulling delighted them, and Duff's hostile and brilliant driving enthralled them. Innings to treasure in the mind's eye for a lifetime. When he had made 113 Victor carelessly mistimed Knutton and paid the penalty; they had raised the score to 226. With Warwick

Armstrong now for company, Duff completed his century and faultlessly batted on. After reaching 182 (all but 50 of them made in fours), he too succumbed to Knutton. The tail wagged a little, thus the Australians topped the 400 mark. Knutton could be well pleased with himself for he had taken all the wickets save one for 100 runs, and seven others had taken a turn with the leather.

The Englishmen's first knock was given a good start by Wrathall (33), who coped with Jones and Noble well enough after "Jonah" had sent back Kinneir and Seymour in his opening spell. Now came Quaife, seeing the ball as large and clear as he had done at Old Trafford. When he was disposed of for 68 good runs, King and Whitehead came together and seemed to take root; it was not so much in terms of runs scored but more the time they took up at the crease. Outclassed, the Bradford tail did not prosper long. Thus, the English Eleven closed for 240 and were invited to follow on.

By the third morning when the Eleven's second attempt was ailing, Crawford, promoting himself in the batting order, proceeded to play a captain's innings. For the sixth wicket, with J. H. King as a sleeping partner, 53 runs were added before the latter was run out. Crawford continued his splendid hitting, and in less than two hours reached 90 (sixteen fours) out of 137 before the South Australian fast bowler bowled him. Little further resistance was offered and the Tourists needed 42 runs to win. These were comfortably obtained for the loss of Darling, Noble and Hopkins. Joe Darling had "bagged a pair", falling victim to Knutton for a second time. The visitors thus ended with a seven-wicket victory and the sun continued to shine.

Now for a little relaxation and light relief from the strenuous and unaccustomed work of playing the county sides day in and day out, the Cornstalks travelled north of the border to Edinburgh to visit that fair and ancient burgh and engage in play with "The Gentlemen of Scotland" for two days. It was something of an occasion for Scottish stalwarts of the game – Australian touring teams did not always venture that far north – and some 7,000 of them eagerly turned up on Monday 30 June, quite the largest concourse for a cricket match in Scotland.

The match was to prove a lighthearted affair, and although the Scotsmen were not up to county standard, they played some good cricket. Trumper, Trumble and Howell were being rested for their coming labours in the third Test match, and their places were taken by Gregory, Jones and Carter, who did duty behind the stumps. Although Darling won the toss and the pitch was perfect, he most generously allowed the home side to bat. Against the bowling of Jones and Noble they made a moderate start, but Mr J. Anderson (Perthshire) played them with the skill of a good county bat and made an excellent 33 before he was caught off Hopkins. Likewise, Mr C. M. Campbell (Edinburgh Academicals) stayed for a careful

THE ELEVENTH AUSTRALIAN TOURING TEAM
Back Row: J. J. Kelly, J. V. Saunders, H. Trumble, W. W. Armstrong, M. A. Noble,
W. P. Howell, Major B. Wardill (Manager)
Middle Row: C. Hill, R. A. Duff, J. Darling (Captain), V. T. Trumper, E. Jones
Front Row: A. J. Y. Hopkins, H. Carter, S. E. Gregory
(*Marylebone Cricket Club*)

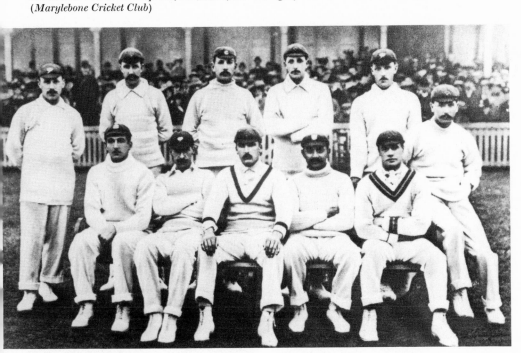

THE ENGLAND ELEVEN AT BIRMINGHAM
Back Row: G. H. Hirst, A. A. Lilley, W. H. Lockwood, L. C. Braund, W. Rhodes, J. T.
Tyldesley
Front Row: C. B. Fry, F. S. Jackson, A. C. MacLaren (Captain), K. S. Ranjitsinhji, G. L. Jessop
(*Marylebone Cricket Club*)

Victor Trumper

(E. Hawkins & Co.)

(The George Beldam Collection)

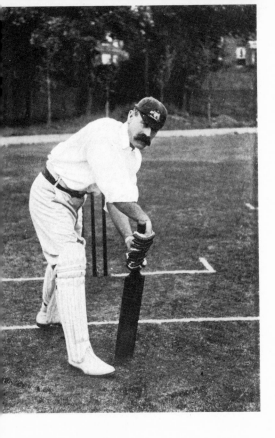

J. Darling
(*E. Hawkins & Co.*)

C. Hill
(*The George Beldam Collection*)

R. A. Duff
(*The George Beldam Collection*)

M. A. Noble
(*The George Beldam Collection*)

H. Trumble
(*Marylebone Cricket Club*)

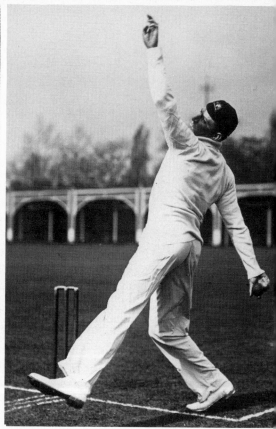

W. W. Armstrong
(*The George Beldam Collection*)

AUSTRALIANS
v
AN ENGLAND ELEVEN

At Bradford, 26, 27, 28 June.

Australians won by 7 wickets.

AUSTRALIANS

V. T. Trumper b Knutton	113		
M. A. Noble b Knutton	1	b King	1
C. Hill b Knutton	1		
*J. Darling b Knutton	0	c Crawford b Knutton	0
A. J. Hopkins c sub. b Knutton	10	c Wrathall b King	11
R. A. Duff b Knutton	182	not out	11
W. W. Armstrong c Crawford b Knutton	38	not out	14
†H. Carter b Knutton	2		
E. Jones not out	19		
W. P. Howell b Wrathall	16		
J. Saunders b Knutton	5		
Extras (B 10, LB 1, W 2, NB 2)	15	(B 5)	5
	402	**(3 wkts)**	**42**

AN ENGLAND ELEVEN

H. Wrathall c Carter b Noble	33	c Trumper b Noble	23
S. P. Kinneir b Jones	4	b Jones	18
J. Seymour b Jones	1	c Darling b Noble	19
W. G. Quaife c Howell b Hopkins	68	c Armstrong b Saunders	4
A. E. Knight c and b Saunders	12	b Saunders	8
J. H. King run out	47	b Saunders	13
H. Whitehead c Trumble b Saunders	43	c Saunders b Howell	0
*Mr R. T. Crawford c Jones b Noble	2	b Jones	90
Sowden b Saunders	9	c Carter b Saunders	8
J. Knutton b Noble	8	c Armstrong b Noble	5
†Bairstow not out	0	not out	10
Extras (B 9, W 3, NB 1)	13	(B 2, LB 1, NB 2)	5
	240		**203**

ENG. ELEVEN	O.	M.	R.	W.	O.	M.	R.	W.
Knutton	35.2	10	100	9	10	3	17	1
Kinneir	7	0	41	0				
Quaife	9	0	59	0				
Crawford	5	0	29	0				
Whitehead	10	1	50	0				
Seymour	2	0	16	0				
Sowden	8	0	48	0				
Wrathall	10	1	44	1				
King					10	5	20	2
AUSTRALIANS								
Jones	26	7	76	2	12.3	4	20	2
Noble	15.3	5	34	3	17	4	67	3
Hill	6	1	18	0				
Saunders	11	8	13	3	17	0	66	4
Howell	11	6	18	0	1	0	7	1
Hopkins	11	5	31	1	16	4	29	0
Armstrong	9	2	37	0	4	0	9	0

Umpires: W. Wright and A. Pike

20, but after lunch Jones and Hopkins shared the remaining six wickets equally for the addition of only 38 more runs. The Scots were all out for a total of 109.

The Tourists' opening pair Noble and Duff proceeded to play entertainingly bright cricket; 117 runs came from their bats in the first hour. This was a gratifying return to form with the willow for

AUSTRALIANS
v
AN ELEVEN OF SCOTLAND

At Edinburgh, 30 June, 1 July.

Australians won by an innings and 105 runs.

SCOTLAND

Mr J. Anderson c Darling b Hopkins	33	c Carter b Duff	24
Mr W. R. Sharp b Noble	4	c Hill b Armstrong	9
Mr L. G. D. Hole c Carter b Jones	14	c Carter b Armstrong	0
Mr C. M. Campbell run out	20	b Duff	2
Mr R. H. Johnston b Hopkins	4	not out	30
Mr A. W. Duncan b Hopkins	7	c Noble b Kelly	11
Mr G. W. Jupp c Gregory b Jones	21	b Duff	0
Mr H. J. Stevenson c Duff b Hopkins	0	c Armstrong b Kelly	2
Pepall b Jones	5	c sub. b Hill	0
Mr A. Downs not out	1	c Armstrong b Hill	1
Mr W. A. N. Hunter b Jones	0	c Saunders b Hill	7
		Extras (B 3, LB 1, NB 1)	5
	109		**91**

AUSTRALIANS

M. A. Noble b Campbell	59	J. J. Kelly run out	0
R. A. Duff c Downs b Stevenson	98	†H. Carter c Jupp b Pepall	0
C. Hill b Campbell	21	E. Jones c Johnston b Stevenson	15
*J. Darling c Campbell b Hunter	1	J. V. Saunders c Johnston b Pepall	2
S. E. Gregory b Stevenson	40	Extras (B 2, LB 11)	13
A. J. Hopkins not out	47		
W. Armstrong b Pepall	9		**305**

AUSTRALIANS	O.	M.	R.	W.	O.	M.	R.	W.
Jones	17	4	33	4				
Noble	10	2	25	1	3	0	6	0
Saunders	3	0	7	0				
Hopkins	9	1	36	4				
Duff	1	0	8	0	8	3	17	3
Hill					9	2	30	3
Kelly					4	0	13	2
Armstrong					9	4	13	2
Carter					1	0	7	0

SCOTLAND ELEVEN	O.	M.	R.	W.
Pepall	17	5	63	3
Hunter	8	0	52	1
Stevenson	22	2	81	3
Campbell	12	0	69	2
Jupp	7	0	27	0

Umpires: T. Sellars and G. Howell

Monty Noble, his 59 runs being by far his highest score of the tour so far. Duff continued his purple patch from Bradford, and was most unluckily caught at the wicket for 98 off the lob bowler Mr H. J. Stevenson (Edinburgh Academicals) to be fourth out at 197. Gregory and Hopkins continued to make light of the Scots bowlers and the day closed with 4 wickets in hand and 283 runs on the board.

The next morning saw the Cornstalks' total reach 305, leaving Hopkins not out with 47 to his credit. Thus the Scottish gentlemen went to the wickets again 196 runs behind on a bright, sunny Edinburgh day, but alas, there had been much rain in the night and the pitch was decidedly treacherous. In such circumstances their chances were small so Joe Darling, in a most sporting manner, called upon some lesser known trundlers in the side. Reg Duff sent down eight overs of his slow off-breaks and captured three wickets, including the invaluable one of Mr J. Anderson, who did so well in the first innings. "Mother" Kelly turned over his arm and took two wickets in humorous fashion, whilst "Kruger" Hill, although hit for thirty runs in his nine overs, was quite amused at his captures. As the wickets fell, the match became one of lighthearted cricket, even "Sammy" Carter took off his pads and had one over. By mid-afternoon the affair was all over, the Scotsmen being removed for only 91 runs, leaving Mr R. H. Johnston of the Grange Club with 30 not out, in excess of one-third of the runs from the bat. The Visitors enjoyed themselves hugely with some light relief, and won by an innings and 105 runs. They now had the rest of the day free and on the morrow would travel south to Sheffield in good heart.

CHAPTER 8
Smokestack Sheffield – The Third Test

It must have occasioned surprise amongst the fraternity of county cricketers, if not the cricketing public, when Sheffield was chosen as one of the Test match grounds in 1902. Honoured with the third encounter, Bramall Lane was hardly a suitable venue. Its pitch was sometimes described as fiery, but its real problem was the light conditions. Gilbert Jessop wrote, "If there is one ground in England less suitable for matches of so great an importance than Sheffield, then I have yet to know it. Even when the sun shines its bravest from cloudless skies and stokers of furnaces have refrained from depositing just that one more shovelfull for the benefit of the visiting team, the light is still only moderate; but when the day is dull, and the atmosphere heavy with smoke, then does batsmanship become more a matter of luck than judgement."* Other players have been equally scathing, and it was a cricketers' joke that from the middle on a dull day the gas lamps could be seen burning within the pavilion. The experiment of a Test match in the stainless steel city was, one may hasten to add, never repeated.

The Australians, largely unaware of this, had only one real problem – whom to leave out to make room for Hugh Trumble? To keep their batting strength it meant that that great trier, the ever reliable Bill Howell, had to be dropped from the side. An alternative might have been Jack Saunders, but he was a left-handed bowler who would be of great value under any conditions, so Howell had to stand down along with Jones and Carter.

Lord Hawke and his colleagues obviously intended to pin their faith in the near victorious team they had chosen for Edgbaston and Lord's with the exception of Charles Fry, who had been quite out of touch so far this season. It is quite likely that Fry asked his fellow-selectors to stand him down from the team. In his stead they picked the veteran Bobby Abel, enjoying an Indian Summer at the age

*G. L. Jessop, *A Cricketer's Log*, Hodder & Stoughton, pp. 185–6.

of forty-four and who, alone with Trumper, had already reached 1,000 runs this season. Although "The Guv'nor" was capable of getting runs his inclusion would rather unbalance the fielding. For many years now he had stood in the slips, and England already possessed the finest trio available in MacLaren, Ranji and Braund – who were all due to play.

As the state of the weather was in doubt – in 1902 it could not have been otherwise – Schofield Haigh was added to the eleven names. It would depend upon the conditions of the ground on the morning of the match as to preference being given to either Haigh or Lockwood. The first upset occurred when Ranjitsinhji strained a leg muscle two days beforehand during the Sussex and Essex match at Leyton. It was a pity, for the Prince had batted magnificently for 230 runs. Fry was persuaded by the selectors to take his place. So the selection rested until the morning of the match.

Thursday 3 July dawned fair, and when the rival captains inspected the pitch it appeared to be neither fiery nor even fast and lively; it looked like being a good batting surface. For reasons best known to himself MacLaren had, prior to this, before nine o'clock, telegraphed to Old Trafford to contact Sydney Barnes – he wanted him in Sheffield! "Archie Mac", acting on one of his intuitions, chose, rightly or wrongly, to play Barnes. One assumes he had consulted his selectors! Now Barnes was not one hundred per cent fit: the knee that had let him down in Australia the previous winter was still troubling him and had curtailed his bowling already this season. MacLaren, as his county captain, would have been well acquainted with this. Also the pitch, as it turned out, was not ideally suited to him for he needed it fast and lively in those days to be most effective.

When Joe Darling won the toss and Trumper and Duff walked to the wickets, the large Yorkshire crowd was quite unaware of MacLaren's intentions for Haigh accompanied the other England players into the field. By the time Barnes arrived the match had already begun. Whilst he was changing a loud roar announced the dismissal of the lordly Victor Trumper. Braund had bowled him for one run. Barnes was now ready, so he prepared to follow out Clement Hill, the next man in. Hill was cheered to the echo, but, as Barnes wrote afterwards, "I followed and for the life of me couldn't understand why the spectators booed when I appeared. It proved to be because Schofield Haigh was coming off the field after fielding substitute until I arrived. When he had gone out on the field with the others at the start of the match it had been assumed that he was playing and his disappearance was a big disappointment to the Yorkshire crowd."*

Trumper had fallen to the last ball of Braund's over. Hirst, who

*L. Duckworth, *S. F. Barnes – Master Bowler*, Hutchinson, p. 53.

had opened the bowling, bowled again to Duff. Slowly at first Reg Duff picked his runs, then, together with Hill, they put on 36 before MacLaren tossed the ball to Barnes instead of Braund. The crowd immediately became hostile again, booing with increased vehemence, and Syd Barnes commenced to bowl amid the cater-wauling. With his stubborn character he may have been spurred on by this outburst and perhaps Duff's concentration might have wavered. Immediately he had the batsman missed by Rhodes, then he found the top edge of Duff's bat, who was caught behind. From the very next delivery "Barney" had Darling caught in the slips by Braund, playing back at that deceptive leg-break to the left-hander. Three down for thirty-nine, and two wickets in his first over! The spectators were perplexed, they were not sure how to react – but they applauded. From now on during the remainder of the Australians' first innings the vociferous section of the crowd transferred their hostility to MacLaren.

Sydney Barnes continued to bowl with venom; he was described as being irresistible. Backed by fine fielding, especially by Jessop at extra cover, he made runs hard to come by. Only Montague Alfred Noble played him with confidence: his excellently made 47 in seventy minutes was the highlight of the innings, first with Gregory as partner and then with Hopkins while 75 runs were added. It needed the wiles of Rhodes to remove him aided by Braund in the slips, who soon afterwards made his third catch to assist in the downfall of Hopkins. Kelly was bowled for a duck to give Barnes his sixth victim and Australia were 8 wickets down for 137. This should have been the end, but Armstrong stonewalled – his first six runs took forty minutes – whilst Hughie Trumble put bat to ball to raise the total to 194.

The Englishmen could be very pleased with themselves for getting the opposition out so cheaply. Barnes with 6 wickets for 49 had carried all before him, and Len Braund, as well as bowling Trumper, had taken four superlative catches including one off his own bowling. The England fielding had been keenly anticipative and only one chance had gone begging. Jessopus had cramped the scoring on the off side; no batsman would run if the ball went anywhere near him.

So far the day had been a bright one and the light had been reasonably good – for Sheffield. It still continued so at mid-afternoon on the commencement of England's first innings. Abel accompanied MacLaren to the wickets and they immediately set about the bowling. The pitch was playing well, it did not help either Trumble or Saunders in any way, and runs were coming at the rate of one a minute. Fifty appeared on the scoreboard in as many minutes, to the spectators' satisfaction. MacLaren's strokeplay was faultless, impeccable and conceived in the grand manner, whilst

Bobby Abel, his blade not always quite straight, punished anything slightly short of a length.

After having used Trumper unsuccessfully, Darling decided to put Noble on; he soon slowed the run-rate. Imperceptibly at first the light began to fade which, combined with Noble's accurate off-spin, mixed with the occasional out-swerver and artfully concealed variation of pace, forced England on to the defensive. He soon clean bowled MacLaren at 61. Having closed one end right up he meted out similar treatment to the "Guv'nor" when the score had reached 86. The sky around the Bramall Lane ground was now noticeably darker, but Tyldesley was playing watchfully, assisted by Jackson. They could have complained about the light but they batted on. The hands of the pavilion clock pointed to six o'clock and the hundred came up. England were in a healthy position, only 94 runs behind with 8 wickets in hand; the spectators were contented, for those northern stalwarts, Tyldesley and Jackson, were in possession.

From out of the gloom Noble bowled to Johnny Tyldesley; did John Thomas see it? The ball spun from his bat into the slips where Armstrong saw it and made no mistake. Now Saunders came up to the wicket with his slanting run left-handed into Jackson. This run-up could be puzzling to batsmen, particularly if they were not used to him. "Jacker" played him in the air into the covers. Syd Gregory accepted the gift. Surprisingly, the batsmen still did not complain about the light. Fry later commented, "The Sheffield smokestacks were in fine form and the light was otherwise grim."[*] Nevertheless he faced Saunders – "The light was atrocious when I was stumped, I literally saw no ball at all to play at." 102 runs for 5 wickets! Lilley and Braund at last appealed and the umpires, Jim Phillips and W. Richards, upheld them; so at 6.15 the players trooped into the pavilion from under the murky Sheffield sky. Lilley said, "In the evening, while we were at the wickets, the light was very bad, and altogether the conditions were heavily handicapping us."[†]

Therefore, at the end of the first day, during which fifteen wickets fell, England had unnecessarily lost at least three good bats in the smoke-laden Sheffield atmosphere. Even so, their position was reasonably sound with half the side remaining.

In the night it rained, heavily enough for a time, and followed by sunshine on Friday morning it turned the pitch into a difficult proposition for the rest of the England batsmen. With the turf "caking", Saunders and Noble, both turning the ball abruptly, between them ran through the remainder, only Jessop reaching double figures. Thus the favourable position evaporated in the

*C. B. Fry, *Life Worth Living*, Eyre & Spottiswoode, p. 232.
†A. A. Lilley, *Twenty-Four Years of Cricket*, Mills & Boon, p. 121.

morning sun. The overnight loss of three good wickets was now keenly felt, for the remaining five had gone down for the paltry sum of 43 runs. Noble's brilliant bowling realised 5 wickets for 51, and Saunders' leg-breaks from the pavilion end secured 5 for 50. Jessop, however, was convinced, now even more than ever, of the illegality of his action. (Saunders' action had been questioned by many in the recent Antipodean tour.)

Darling had the heavy roller put on the pitch to take some of the spite out of it, but even so it was still playing far from easy when Australia, with a valuable lead of 49, went in again at five minutes past twelve o'clock. If the spectators had hopes of another collapse at the hands of Hirst, Rhodes and Barnes, they were very soon dispelled by Victor Trumper. The state of the pitch made no difference to him, and he proceeded to play an innings of superlative brilliance. Jessop, from his vantage-point at extra cover, watched him with wonder and admiration, "for throughout, though the ball turned quickly at times, there was never a false stroke".* He described Trumper's artistry as astounding. Of the first 20 runs on the board Victor had made 19 in almost as many minutes, jumping out to drive the ball time and again, or laying back to cut. Duff had watched this fine exhibition whilst being virtually a sleeping partner, for he had contributed but one run, when he was tempted by Rhodes to have a go himself; Hirst caught him. It was now 12.25 as Hill joined Trumper at the crease. In the next twenty minutes Victor reached his 50 and the score was 62. This was exciting cricket, and the large crowd marvelled at Trumper's ability to do just what he liked with the England bowlers. MacLaren rang the bowling changes but they all came alike to Victor: "He simply cut, drove and pulled the bowling about, gave a display of aggressive brilliance in batsmanship the like of which had rarely been seen in this country or any other."† In another ten minutes he reached 62 – the telegraph read 80 and the innings was but fifty minutes old; he was scoring at a rate of 74 runs an hour. The fine English bowling had been completely demoralised on a pitch that was giving them considerable help. Even a genius may commit the slightest error: Trumper pulled a good length ball of Jackson's finer than he intended, which should have gone for another four, and Dick Lilley leapt clairvoyantly to short leg to make a splendid catch. The crowd roared, but they were sorry to see the hero depart; there was only one Victor Trumper. Generously, Victor congratulated Lilley on the fine catch that dismissed him – it was typical of the man. Trumper's innings had given the Australian batsmen that extra confidence in showing how good bowling could be hit, and although Hill was a trifle uncertain at the start of his innings, he commenced to bat with assurance.

*G. L. Jessop, *A Cricketer's Log*, Hodder & Stoughton, p. 187.
†Richard Binns, *Cricket in Firelight*, Selwyn Blount, p. 154.

During this magnificent performance the light had deteriorated, and although the sun still shone it was little more than a glimmer through the smoky Sheffield atmosphere. Joe Darling – "sitting on a pair" – now faced Barnes in the next over and played the same stroke to the same ball as he had in the previous innings. Braund brilliantly caught him in the slips once more and the Cornstalk captain had the unhappy experience of "two duck's eggs". Three down for 80 and again the crowd cheered. Barnes, it may be noted, was being troubled by his knee again and could no longer put everything into his bowling. Clem Hill now pasted Jackson for 14 runs in one over, and at lunch had advanced his score to 45. Having taken over Trumper's mantle, he was proceeding to demoralise the bowling in just as assured a manner. Australia at luncheon were 3 for 115; it had taken only 95 minutes.

Resuming where he had left off, the left-hander smacked Hirst three times to the fence in one over and carefully farmed the bowling to allow Syd Gregory to play himself in. For the fourth wicket they put on 107 runs from a flagging England attack in just 67 minutes. When Gregory was smartly thrown out by Fry at third man for 29 immaculate runs, Hill had reached 93; a few minutes later he cut Jackson to the boundary to reach his well-earned hundred. He had been at the crease for 115 minutes, and the light was described as poor. Dick Lilley, in a better position than most, described this effort: "Under the adverse conditions it was one of those displays that are only occasionally seen, and only possible at all by a first-class bat."* Fry and Jessop were equally full of praise. The pugnacious left-hander had given two rather hard chances in reaching his century: he could have been caught low down to slip's left hand off Barnes at 74, and off Rhodes three runs later when long off was considered "lucky" to get a hand to it. These slight blemishes could be easily overlooked as "the pride of Adelaide" continued to farm the bowling for Noble to get his eye in. He could not repeat his first innings performance, however, and was bowled by Jackson for eight. Five wickets for 214, but Hill was still going strong! After doing his best to assist Hopkins, who gave a sharp chance to Braund when 3, Hill was brilliantly caught eleven runs later high up at second slip by MacLaren for 119. It had taken 145 minutes and he had hit 16 fours in this sound, tactical innings.

Now it was Hopkins' turn to take on the role of attacker and, with Armstrong's assistance, he piled on the runs. Soon Australia's lead was 320, when at last it must have occurred to the England captain that he still had Rhodes. He said afterwards that Jackson suddenly had made two balls nip back very quickly bowling from the pavilion end (this was the end that Saunders, also a left-hander, had previously exploited so successfully). Possibly, Wilfred Rhodes should

*A. A. Lilley, *Twenty-Four Years of Cricket*, Mills & Boon, p. 121.

have been brought on sooner; he clean bowled Armstrong with a ball that the batsman left alone, and had Kelly caught by Hirst at cover. Just 12 more runs were added to Australia's total after Rhodes came back, and they were all scored from the other end! With 19 balls he polished off the last four wickets; Trumble and Saunders were both clean bowled without another run being taken from him. Australia were all out for 289 – it had taken them less than four hours – so England were faced with the uphill task of trying to obtain 339 to win on a pitch showing signs of considerable wear.

There was still an hour and a half left for play that day, but the sky was darkening steadily and rain seemed imminent. Australia were undoubtedly on top; in the prevailing conditions they would obviously attempt to ram home their advantage. With batsmen wearied in the field they would not unreasonably hope for some quick wickets. Much to the surprise of the gathered throng in the gloom of the arena, it was not MacLaren who came out of the gate with Bobby Abel to commence England's second venture. Gilbert Jessop strode determinedly towards the middle. A turn up for the books indeed! In his delightful biography *A Cricketer's Log* Jessop explains the reason for his opening the innings. He had offered to go in first because the player deputed to do so was fatigued and there might be rain about. England needed to keep her wickets intact and, if possible, obtain some quick runs. MacLaren, always a great believer in Jessop, readily agreed, the idea probably appealed to him, "Otherwise I might have been told, with that urbanity of manner which my captain so constantly displayed, that it were more seemly for little boys to be seen than to be heard – or words to that effect."*

The idea worked, but not before "the Surrey Guv'nor" was given out to a doubtful decision. In playing back to a quickly turning ball of Noble's, after watching it like a hawk onto his bat, Abel steered it towards the slips a couple of inches above the ground. Hill caught it low down and only he appealed. Other fieldsmen thought it a "bump ball", as did Abel himself. He hesitated at the wicket, but the umpire's index finger was raised. One down for 14 as a disappointed Abel walked to the pavilion. Jessop was, for him, playing a careful game, but was scoring off every possible ball he could. The spectators' applause greeted his every stroke and cheers greeted each run scored, and the runs were beginning to flow from his bat. He hit the ball very hard and if a fielder managed to interpose a hand it left his fingers tingling. John Tyldesley was content to leave the hitting to Jessopus; anybody who batted with him had to. But J. T. was backing up well, ready to run whenever possible; there was perfect understanding between them. Jessop crouched at the wicket, his hands rapidly clamping and unclamping low down on

*G. L. Jessop, *A Cricketer's Log*, Hodder & Stoughton, p. 188.

the bat's handle as the bowler ran up to deliver, then jumped down the pitch to the good length ball to make it hittable. He was severe on Saunders this way – he cared not whether that bowler's action was possibly illegal. Armstrong, and Noble too, came in for some rough handling as Jessop found the gaps in the field. He was scoring above a run a minute. When Darling put more men on the leg side after some fierce pulls, Jessopus daringly, but safely, ran out and cut from outside the leg stump. This was enterprising batsmanship and the crowd loved it. In forty-five minutes he had cracked 50 sparkling runs without a semblance of a chance, and this on a wearing pitch and in very bad light! It was now so dark that they had to draw stumps at about ten minutes to six, with Jessop not out 53 and England 73 for one. The home-going spectators, having cheered "The Croucher" in, were a good deal happier than they had been an hour before, for England's position was far healthier than they had dared hope.

Suspecting that the pitch had been rolled early on the previous day contrary to the rules, Darling thought it possible that the groundstaff might do so again. Saturday morning saw him, together with Jim Kelly (an acknowledged expert), attempting to catch them in the act. They saw nothing but were convinced the turf had been rolled illegally for a second time. When Archie MacLaren arrived they confided their fears and took him out to inspect the pitch. MacLaren agreed with them, but they could do nothing.

The threatening rain had not materialised. It was bright and fair as Jessop and Tyldesley, to thunderous applause, took guard afresh. The crowded spectators speculated on the possibilities: 266 runs still needed to win – could they possibly get them? If "The Croucher" carried on in yesterday's vein, who knew what might happen?

The pitch, as well as being decidedly worn, as the batsmen found as soon as the first ball was bowled, was playing faster than before. Two more runs to Jessop off Trumble, and then came the lucky breakthrough for Australia. Trumble in again, and Jessopus went right down on one knee to "mow" him round to square leg, a stroke he always thought a paying one, particularly to off-break bowlers on a sticky pitch. But he missed and the ball, according to Fry, "hit him in the middle of his chest on the lower shirt button; he was trying to hit a straight ball to square leg from the position of a doormat".* Given out LBW, "the umpire later apologised to him for what he realised had been a bad decision"† (remember, the ball had to pitch in a straight line between bowler's wicket and striker's wicket). Even so, being technically not out after having been given out and removed from the firing line did not help England in her

*C. B. Fry, *Life Worth Living*, Eyre & Spottiswoode, p. 232.
†G. Brodribb, *The Croucher*, London Magazine Editions, p. 6.

moment of need. This was the vital wicket: the Tourists were jubilant as the crowd's favourite departed at 75 for 2. For the spectators the light had gone out of the match.

It was Hugh Trumble, the leg-pulling humorist, who broke the back of the English innings, for the injury to his thumb on the previous day caused him to grip the ball in a slightly different manner, which resulted in him turning the ball a trifle from the leg instead of from the off as the batsmen expected. Although MacLaren stood resolute, after nine more runs Trumble clean bowled Tyldesley and, with a further fourteen added, Fry was leg before to him. MacLaren watched helplessly from the bowler's end. Three wickets had fallen for 25 runs and twenty-five minutes had elapsed; it was still before noon. Now came the fight to try to save the match as Jackson partnered his captain. Whilst "Jacker" played second fiddle, "Archie Mac" fought a captain's innings, hitting everything possible on that wearing pitch, keeping Trumble at bay and pasting Saunders and Noble. For nearly an hour they kept their ends up, and the runs still came faster than one a minute. Impervious to England's near hopeless situation, MacLaren's proud bat flashed down on the cunning ball to crack it through the field. During one over from Saunders he dispatched him three times to the rails. His 50 appeared on the scoreboard, and soon afterwards the partnership was worth 53 runs.

At this point Joe Darling decided to switch his bowlers. It must have occurred to him, as in the previous innings it had belatedly became apparent to MacLaren, that the badly worn patch at the end opposite the pavilion would suit Noble ideally, whereas he was being unsuccessfully used at the other end. Either end would be suitable for Trumble's finger spin. The changeover immediately achieved results, for Monty Noble found the spot and broke back from it in an unplayable manner. Jackson played and missed, the ball kicking up sharply and glancing off his chest onto the stumps. It was 12.30 and England were 162 for 5. Three runs later, MacLaren, on 63, mistimed his stroke to Noble's sizzling ball. Trumper dived forward from short leg to take the catch and end this splendidly challenging innings. The agony for England was nearly over; only a deluge could save them now.

Lilley tried his best to counter the wiles of Monty Noble and the guile of Trumble. With the telegraph showing 174, Noble clean bowled the English wicketkeeper with a good paced delivery which whipped back in a puzzling manner. "It was a ball," Lilley said, "that no batsman need be ashamed of losing his wicket to."[*] The following ball came through low-pitched on the off stump and completely beat George Hirst, knocking his leg stump out of the ground. It was only a matter of time; could they last out until lunch?

[*] A. A. Lilley, *Twenty-Four Years Of Cricket*, Mills & Boon, p. 121.

Braund and Rhodes managed to add another twelve runs until Len Braund over-eagerly tried to square-cut Noble. It was easily taken by Armstrong at point. A few minutes later, with the clock pointing to 1.15 and the scoreboard showing 195, Trumble bowled Barnes – the agony was over. The delighted Australians had won by the splendid margin of 143 runs. Noble had taken 6 wickets for 52 in this second innings, or, since he changed to bowling from the pavilion

ENGLAND *v* AUSTRALIA

(3rd TEST)
At Sheffield, 3, 4, 5 July.
Australia won by 143 runs.

AUSTRALIA

V. T. Trumper b Braund	1	c Lilley b Jackson	62
R. A. Duff c Lilley b Barnes	25	c Hirst b Rhodes	1
C. Hill c Rhodes b Barnes	18	c MacLaren b Jackson	119
*J. Darling c Braund b Barnes	0	c Braund b Barnes	0
S. E. Gregory c Abel b Barnes	11	run out	29
M. A. Noble c Braund b Rhodes	47	b Jackson	8
A. J. Hopkins c Braund b Barnes	27	not out	40
W. W. Armstrong c & b Braund	25	b Rhodes	26
†J. J. Kelly b Barnes	0	c Hirst b Rhodes	0
H. Trumble c & b Jackson	32	b Rhodes	0
J. V. Saunders not out	0	b Rhodes	1
Extras (B 3, LB 5)	8	(LB 3)	3
	194		**289**

ENGLAND

*Mr A. C. MacLaren b Noble	31	(4) c Trumper b Noble	63
R. Abel b Noble	38	c Hill b Noble	8
J. T. Tyldesley c Armstrong b Noble	22	b Trumble	14
Hon. F. S. Jackson c Gregory b Saunders	3	(6) b Noble	14
Mr C. B. Fry st Kelly b Saunders	1	lbw, b Trumble	4
†A. A. Lilley b Noble	8	(7) b Noble	9
L. C. Braund st Kelly b Saunders	0	(8) c Armstrong b Noble	9
G. H. Hirst c Trumble b Saunders	8	(9) b Noble	0
Mr G. L. Jessop c Saunders b Noble	12	(1) lbw, b Trumble	55
W. Rhodes not out	7	not out	7
S. F. Barnes c Darling b Saunders	7	b Trumble	5
Extras (B 4, LB 3, NB 1)	8	(B 4, LB 1, W 1, NB 1)	7
	145		**195**

ENGLAND	O.	M.	R.	W.	O.	M.	R.	W.
Hirst	15	1	59	0	10	1	40	0
Braund	13	4	34	2	12	0	58	0
Barnes	20	9	49	6	12	4	50	1
Jackson	5.1	1	11	1	17	2	60	3
Rhodes	13	3	33	1	17.1	3	63	5
Jessop					4	0	15	0
AUSTRALIA								
Trumble	18	10	21	0	21.5	3	49	4
Saunders	15.3	4	50	5	12	0	68	0
Trumper	4	1	8	0	6	0	19	0
Noble	19	6	51	5	21	4	52	6
Armstrong	5	2	7	0				

FALL OF WICKETS

Wkt.	Aus. 1st	Eng. 1st	Aus. 2nd	Eng. 2nd
1st	3	61	20	14
2nd	39	86	80	75
3rd	39	101	80	84
4th	52	101	187	98
5th	73	102	214	162
6th	127	106	225	165
7th	137	110	277	174
8th	137	130	287	174
9th	194	131	287	186
10th	194	145	289	195

Umpires: J. Phillips and W. Richards

end, 5 wickets in 12 overs for just 22 runs. In all, he exhibited the fine figures of 11 for 103. Trumble bowled no less admirably with 4 for 49, and it was he who initiated England's downfall in the first half hour.

Undoubtedly, the side who had played the best cricket had won. It is true that England experienced the worst of the wicket and the light but, as Fry, Jessop and Lilley all agree, they were thoroughly outplayed and the Australians' victory was well deserved. Many felt that MacLaren had been in error in choosing Barnes in preference to Lockwood or Haigh. The pitch did not suit Barnes in spite of his success in the first innings, and there was that suspect knee which prevented him from bowling at his best later on. MacLaren defended his choice by saying that the effect of the heavy roller in the second innings made Barnes' bowling practically harmless. Both Jessop and Lilley thought that a fast bowler should have been played – in particular Lockwood, who was also a very capable bat. The biggest blunder, however, was the choice of Sheffield.

CHAPTER 9
The Midland Tour

Just as the Australians were winning the third Test match, the most gratifying news was made public that the King was now out of danger. At least his cricket-following subjects could be mollified somewhat for England's disaster at Sheffield.

The Cornstalks were due to appear at Birmingham again on the following Monday, 7 July, this time to do battle with the county of Warwickshire. Prior to this fixture they had been invited to stay at Warwick Castle over the weekend as guests of the Earl and Countess of Warwick, and were much impressed by its treasures. The Honorary Secretary of the County Club, Mr W. Ansell (in his final season at the helm of Warwickshire's affairs), had the honour of welcoming the Tourists. It reflected considerably on Mr Ansell's untiring efforts that the county had been raised to first-class status in 1894, and to his eternal credit that Edgbaston had become one of the finest cricket grounds in the country.

Of the original side only W. G. Quaife, Sydney Santall, Dick Lilley and Jack Devey played regularly. Mr H. W. Bainbridge, although still joint captain, had turned out only on six occasions in the previous season, but in honour of the Tourists was making his fourth appearance of the year. "Bags" Bainbridge, an engaging personality, was held in considerable affection by his side. He was one of the best county captains and most popular cricketers of his day, always having a kind word for the young visitor – professional and amateur alike. The county eleven he led into the field after winning the toss was a strong one.

The Australians rested Trumble and Kelly from the Test side, bringing in Ernie Jones and Carter as stumper. They took the field on Edgbaston's rather lush billiard-table sward as Jack Devey, Aston Villa's forward of international fame, prepared to open the Midland county's innings with the graceful left-hander Septimus Kinneir. This pair got Warwickshire off to a good start, being quite comfortable against the opening attack of Jones and Noble on the slow paced pitch. Devey, a dashing bat who had scored as many as 246 and finished thirteenth in the averages last season, was the first to go, being caught by Duff off Saunders for 21 as soon as the bowling was changed. The joint captain Mr T. S. Fishwick, a most polished bat, did not stay long before falling to Jones. Next man in was Edgbaston's own hero, the diminutive Willie Quaife – known to all as "little W. G." – the perfect textbook batsman. Here was a wonderful player who had made a close study of the science of the game, and, although not a particularly fast scorer, he was quickly off the mark, using his feet perfectly to Saunders and Noble.

The score had mounted to 79 and both Kinneir and Quaife were playing with confidence. Darling decided to try Armstrong, who, on striking a length immediately, made the ball do strange things. First Quaife on 21 was caught behind off a ball from Jones that got up, and, very soon after, Kinneir, with a handsomely made 38, was deceived by the burly Armstrong. The England wicketkeeper Augustus Lilley, not having had too happy a season with the bat, was soon snapped up at point by Trumper to give Armstrong his second wicket. "Bags" Bainbridge was immediately bowled and Charlesworth, a fine all-round-the-wicket hitter, in attempting to hit Armstrong to the boundary, missed and was as clean bowled as his captain had been. The Warwickshire innings was soon over; Armstrong had proved most puzzling. He had taken six wickets for only 13 runs and the County had slumped to 124 all out.

Now came the treat the Edgbaston *habitués* were looking forward to hopefully. On an easy paced pitch Trumper and Duff did what they liked with the slow-medium left-hand bowling of Sam Hargreave and the pace (deadened by the pitch somewhat) of Frank Field. They both hit hard. It needed a bowling change, the bringing on of Moorhouse, to trap Duff into error for 16. Trumper delighted the eye with many of his entrancing strokes, being par- ticularly heavy on the cheery and optimistic Field, whose deter- mination was finally rewarded with Trumper's wicket when he had pillaged 45 runs in less than even time. Soon afterwards, although handicapped by muscle strain, Field claimed the equally vital wicket of Clem Hill for 16 when T. S. Fishwick, one of the best slip fielders the county ever had in those days, took a splendid catch.

The runs continued to come. Hargreave, who had taken over 100 wickets last season, toiled lucklessly on and Sydney Santall, a fine medium-pacer who commanded an impeccable length, strove with as little success against Darling and Gregory. At the close the Cornstalks were 158 runs with seven wickets intact.

Syd Gregory, of about the same stature as cover point Willie Quaife and often amusingly referred to as "Little Titch", played a magnificent knock of 83. He enjoyed a stand of 97 with Joe Darling before the hard-worked Santall bowled the latter for 37, and continued with Noble until, at last, Sam Hargreave had the reward of both their wickets. So far, Hargreave had been one of the most successful bowlers of the season, and MacLaren thought highly of him. Before the Australians' innings ended eight bowlers had been tried, including Quaife's slow leg-breaks. Nevertheless, Hopkins showed continued form for 33 and Hanson Carter gave a good idea of his abilities with the willow for 31 well hit runs before Charlesworth bowled him in his solitary over. The Tourists were all out for 316.

Commencing their second venture 192 runs behind, the Midland county had so far been quite outplayed. They soon lost Kinneir to Jones. Kinneir was not at home on a slow pitch, although on the dry ones of 1901 he had averaged 52.07 with four hundreds and was always a joy to watch. But Fishwick played up well, timing the ball with confidence, his cutting and driving being features of an excellent innings of 68. He was partnered first by Devey, one of the best bats in the side, whose sound innings was terminated by Noble, and later by Quaife. The latter, always a delightful performer even when scoring slowly, was seen to advantage with some quality hitting. When the day's play ended, however, the home side were only ten runs ahead with five wickets down.

The weather now took a hand and robbed the Tourists of a certain victory. After they had taken two more wickets for 23 runs in forty minutes of playing time on Wednesday morning, the seeming ever-present enemy – rain – came down again. It proved heavy enough to cause the match to be abandoned. But the Australians could be quite satisfied with themselves.

And so the Cornstalks made their way the following day to Worcester for the second encounter of their Midland tour. The lovely Severn-girt ground, with the cathedral in the background, well favoured light conditions, superb pitch and fast outfield, was always a pleasure to play on. The county team of Worcestershire were the "new boys" of first-class cricket, having been admitted to the highest level as recently as 1899, largely due to the hard work of the county Secretary Mr P. H. Foley and the cricketing abilities of the elder sons of the Reverend Henry Foster, a housemaster at Malvern College. The contemporary newpapers, with a flair, even in those days, for the romantic, had christened them "Fostershire".

The eldest brother H. K. Foster came straight from the Varsity side at Oxford to captain the county. A product of Malvern and coached by Charles Toppin on the splendid school pitches, as were all his brothers after him, he was an exemplar of the public school amateur batsman of the golden age. Possessor of natural gifts for the game, he was a beautiful off-side player renowned for his off driving, particularly along the ground, and crackling square cuts. He had been taught that the ball was to be hit! In 1895 during the

AUSTRALIANS v WARWICKSHIRE

At Birmingham, 7, 8, 9 July.
Match drawn.

WARWICKSHIRE

J. Devey c Duff b Saunders	21	c and b Noble	34
S. P. Kinneir c Saunders b Armstrong	38	b Jones	9
Mr T. S. Fishwick c Hill b Jones	10	c Trumper b Jones	68
W. G. Quaife c Carter b Jones	21	c Carter b Hopkins	39
†A. A. Lilley c Trumper b Armstrong	7	c Saunders b Armstrong	22
C. Charlesworth b Armstrong	9	b Jones	14
*Mr H. W. Bainbridge b Armstrong	2	not out	15
S. Santall b Jones	2	c Darling b Jones	11
Moorhouse not out	5	not out	2
S. Hargreave b Armstrong	6		
F. E. Field b Armstrong	0		
Extras (B 1, LB 2)	3	(B 4, LB 5, NB 2)	11
	124	**(7 wkts)**	**225**

AUSTRALIANS

V. T. Trumper b Field	45	W. W. Armstrong not out	14
R. A. Duff c Hargreave b Moorhouse	16	†H. Carter b Charlesworth	31
C. Hill c Fishwick b Field	18	E. Jones run out	1
*J. Darling b Santall	37	J. V. Saunders b Hargreave	0
S. E. Gregory b Hargreave	83	Extras (B 12, LB 2, W 1)	15
M. A. Noble lbw, b Hargreave	23		
A. J. Hopkins c Field b Hargreave	33		**316**

AUSTRALIANS	O.	M.	R.	W.	O.	M.	R.	W.
Jones	16	2	52	3	19	4	66	4
Noble	11	2	32	0	9	0	47	1
Saunders	9	2	24	1	16	5	28	0
Armstrong	9.2	4	13	6	20	7	35	1
Hopkins					12	5	30	1
Gregory					1	0	8	0

WARWICKSHIRE	O.	M.	R.	W.
Hargreave	32	6	81	4
Field	26	2	119	2
Moorhouse	10	4	26	1
Santall	11	2	27	1
Quaife	6	0	21	0
Devey	1	0	12	0
Kinneir	2	0	10	0
Charlesworth	1	0	5	1

FALL OF WICKETS

Wkt.	Warw. 1st	Aus. 1st	Warw. 2nd
1st	41	44	10
2nd	62	84	98
3rd	80	85	128
4th	98	182	167
5th	98	224	185
6th	101	233	202
7th	112	268	222
8th	116	312	—
9th	124	313	—
10th	124	316	—

Umpires: W. Wright and J. Carlin

inter-Varsity match, his second innings of 121 runs out of 159 in just over two hours on a worn pitch in a back-to-the-wall attempt to stave off defeat was highly regarded. He was a rackets player, too, as also were his brothers, and had won the England championship. Furthermore, H. K. was a shrewd captain, gifted with leadership and a charming personality.

The next brother, W. L., a year younger, had played for the county in their opening seasons before joining the army, and, although a little less brilliant, he proved a steady scoring and reliable bat. But the third brother, Reginald Erskine, popularly known as "Tip", blossomed in the 1900 season into one of the outstanding bats of the era. Previously at school and at Oxford, he had not been considered up to the standard of his elder brothers, but now he began to play in a style which, as it developed, became at once so fluent and elegant that it elevated him on to a plane of his own. Whilst in his last year at the University, as their captain, he made 950 runs at an average of 77.50 and, in the season as a whole, his record was 1,807 runs for 51.62 with seven centuries. In 1901 his aggregate was 2,128 runs for 50.66, with six scores over a hundred. Owing to business commitments, however, he could not play at all regularly in 1902. Held in high esteem by all who saw him play, Jessop thought him a brilliant bat and Colonel Philip Trevor considered him "one of the dazzling personalities of the cricket field . . . He belonged to the 'could-do-anything-if-he-tried' brigade."[*] Some idea of this beautiful player can be gleaned from the George Beldam photographs. Furthermore, he was one of the finest anticipative slip fielders the game has known. He was a remarkable all-round sportsman, for as well as being a rackets player of considerable skill, "Tip" Foster was a sufficiently outstanding soccer player to be chosen as inside forward six times for England between 1900 and 1902. On the last occasion, in the 1902 soccer season against Wales, he captained ten professionals. C. B. Fry knew him intimately as a fellow Corinthian, and says of him, "He had a fine dexterity of foot and controlled the ball, caressed and persuaded it with an almost manual cunning. His feet had, as it were, the Oxford accent."[†]

Malvern School was producing a rich harvest of young cricketers about this time: "Pinky" Burnup, now with Kent; Sam Day; W. H. B. Evans, at present at Oxford but soon to be an illustrious member of the Worcestershire eleven; in addition to the seven Fosters. But two more old Malvernians were in the current side to play the Tourists. W. W. Lowe, a Cambridge double blue, could be classed as an all-rounder. He could certainly bat, an attractively made century against Gloucester in the previous year had proved that, and he could, for a few overs, bowl very fast indeed. As centre forward for his university side, he had played soccer with distinction. But the unusual old boy was G. H. Simpson-Hayward, the lob bowler. At school he had batted well and bowled fast overarm, though while at university he discovered he could spin the ball in a most remarkable manner with an underarm delivery. The last of the lob bowlers, he was certainly its finest exponent. "Simmer" had a unique grip: the ball was held only by the top of the thumb and the index finger and he was able to impart to it a most surprising variety

[*]Colonel Philip Trevor, *Cricket & Cricketers*, Chapman Hall, p. 87.
[†]C. B. Fry, *Life Worth Living*, Eyre & Spottiswoode, p. 271.

of spin by flicking his fingers. According to Jessop, the ball would "fizz off the pitch in a most bewildering fashion".* With the same apparent action he could, at will, change from a leg-break to an off-break. He "caused discomposure among batsmen loath to leave their crease. One of his most dangerous deliveries was the ball sent down without a break, which frequently resulted in LBW. Rumour had it, that he cunningly disguised it by flicking his fingers of the other hand."†

The county side was leavened by a goodly selection of professors. Opening batsman F. L. Bowley was probably the next best bat outside the Foster family. Fred Bowley's reputation as a run-getter was no mean one, for he generally got them when they were most needed. His cricket reflected the charm and ease of his own good nature. In partnering him to the wicket, yet another Fred and yet another soccer player – Fred Wheldon of Aston Villa and England fame – brought some of the same skill to cricket that he had shown as inside left for the Villa in their great period. He had been a member of that club's side in 1897, when they won both the League and the Cup.

The young professional whom the county club had great hopes in for the future was a lean, tall, angular fellow who promised to be an excellent all-rounder. In E. G. Arnold they had come by a very good medium-fast right-hand bowler who could bat and was very knowledgeable about the game. Using his six-foot height for a high delivery, he could make the good length ball bounce and had excellent control of pace and flight. Ted Arnold's day was yet to come when he would worry even the best batsmen, but he already showed splendid all-round abilities.

All the members of the eleven could be described in the broadest terms as all-rounders for G. A. Wilson could bat, but it was as a fast bowler that he earned his place in the side. He was owner of a rather curious round-arm delivery which imparted a curl in the air to his bowling. This natural late swerve from the leg often kept low after pitching, so on a fast or fiery pitch he could be a distinctly difficult proposition. The wet surfaces of the current season had, however, nullified much of his fire. Another good run-getter when occasion demanded was the new county wicketkeeper G. Gaukrodger; and Albert Bird, formerly with neighbouring Warwickshire, rendered excellent service with ball and bat. Finally, burly Dick Burrows, whose large moustache made him appear older than he was, was not having a very successful summer. Possessor of great reserves of stamina and a bowler of greater pace than one would imagine, which could be sustained for hours on end, he often made the ball get up awkwardly, but could also be erratic in length and direction.

*G. L. Jessop, *A Cricketer's Log*, Hodder & Stoughton, pp. 237–8.
†Ibid. pp. 237–8, abridged.

In the previous year he had bowled Archie MacLaren with a snorter which broke the wicket and hurled one of the bails a distance of 64 yards 6 inches. When Dick began to bowl no batsman knew exactly what he would do; however, this plucky bowler's greatest days were yet to come in the autumn of his career.

Against this considerable array of talent, the Tourists' Selection Committee had decided to give a well-earned rest to Trumper and Kelly, and as Hugh Trumble's thumb was still troublesome he too stood down. With three of their outstanding players being rested it gave an added chance to the County. So on the morning of 10 July, with the Worcester pitch still damp from the deluge of the previous day, the luck of the toss had a distinct advantage to the Australians. This became more apparent after luncheon when, between showers, the sun at last made its appearance; thus the pitch subsequently became quite difficult. To everyone's surprise the weather turned quite hot and humid, though doubtless the Visitors were gratified to feel the warmth on their backs and be able at last to shed their long-sleeved sweaters.

The Cornstalks had started in fine fettle; the pitch playing slowly spoiled any attempts by Wilson and Arnold to extract life from the wet turf. Reg Duff, first with Hopkins, then with Hill and finally with Noble, put bat to ball, pushing the score along at a steady rate. Duff played a beautiful game and was never really troubled for his superb 90 runs, but it was Monty Noble who stole the limelight. By now, in and out between sunshine and showers, he played a splendid forcing game, his 56 runs coming in little over an hour's playing time, before being snapped up in the slips by "Tip" Foster.

It was now four o'clock. So far only four wickets had fallen for 200 runs, when the ministrations of the warm sunshine really began to be felt. In the next hour the rest were outed for the addition of 74, mostly coming from hard-hit drives by Ernie Jones and the careful grafting of Armstrong. Bird could feel very satisfied with his bag of 6 for 69, and Burrows, latterly cutting his pace, did well with 3 for 42.

The County lost wickets from the start – Bowley, Wheldon and both the Fosters were caught on the sticky turf. On the following morning in similar conditions 24 runs were still needed to save the follow-on with but 3 wickets remaining. At this point they were saved by their new wicketkeeper Gaukrodger, who showed his skill with the blade in baffling conditions. That Worcester's total finally reached as many as 202 was due to his resolute batting aided and abetted by long-handled hitting from Dick Burrows.

Some splendid bowling on the part of Bird, Wilson and Simpson-Hayward quickly reduced the Tourists to 3 down for 54 at the start of their second innings. The pitch was still very tricky and "Simmer", although he was hit by Clem Hill and Gregory, confused the Visitors no end. They were not used to lobs at all. Coming down the pitch to hit an expected off-break Hill was completely bamboozled and stumped. So ended a valiant knock of 50 on Clem Hill's part which did much to restore his side's ailing fortunes. Not many runs had been added before Mr Simpson-Hayward clean bowled Darling with a similar ball. With Armstrong playing a tight game at one end and Gregory scoring whenever he could, the Australians eventually left the home side 272 runs to obtain.

They never looked like getting them. Jones and Armstrong bowled 36 overs and 4 balls without a change, and, backed by the brilliant fielding that had become synonymous with the Tourists, demoralised poor Worcestershire completely. The County could only muster 97 runs, Bowley alone playing with any confidence. For Ernie Jones with 6 wickets for 53, and Warwick Armstrong 4 for 34, it had been a triumph. As the Tourists enjoyed their dinner that Saturday evening, they were able to congratulate themselves on another well-deserved victory.

The Saturday had been a day of excitement: Lord Kitchener and General French, the heroes of the hour, had been acclaimed by enthusiastic crowds in the London streets as they drove from Paddington on their return from South Africa. Came the Sunday, the Tourists journeyed down to Bristol to meet Gloucestershire, once "the shire of the Graces". Now only E. M., "The Coroner", remained as the semi-autocratic County Secretary. The Cestrians had fallen on leaner days since their golden seventies; it all seemed so long ago. If only all their best amateurs could have been available for most of the season, they could have given a good account of themselves, but alas, for varying reasons, this was never possible. Even so, their bowling would have still been a little thin for Gilbert Jessop could now no longer bowl as fast as he had done until two years ago, and they had no one else. It was as a fielding side that they really shone. W. G. had always insisted on good fielding from his players, and since taking over the captaincy in 1900, Jessop had made Gloster into the finest county side in the field. A dearth of good bowlers meant they had to save runs and, with the supreme example set by their brilliant and agile captain, they became out-standing, always being a joy to behold.

Unfortunately, Charles Townsend, the wonder-boy bowler of 1893, could no longer play regularly – business claimed him. For with his all-round talents, the best left-hand bat in England and an outstanding right-arm leg-break bowler, allied to Jessop's hurricane batting, they could have provided a solid basis round which to build a team. If C. O. H. Sewell, Frank Bateman Champain and W. H. Hale, all first-rate bats and fielders, had been more freely available a considerable difference to the county's lowly position in the Championship table would have been possible. As it was, during the 1902 season Mr Harry Beloe, the Chairman of the County

AUSTRALIANS
v
WORCESTERSHIRE

At Worcester, 10, 11, 12 July.
Australians won by 174 runs.

AUSTRALIANS

R. A. Duff b Wilson	90	c R. E. Foster b Wilson	30
A. J. Hopkins c Gaukrodger b Bird	23	b Bird	16
C. Hill b Burrows	29	st Gaukrodger b Simpson-Hayward	50
M. A. Noble c R. E. Foster b Bird	56	c Gaukrodger b Bird	1
S. E. Gregory c Bowley b Bird	11	c Gaukrodger b Wilson	45
*J. Darling b Bird	0	b Simpson-Hayward	9
W. W. Armstrong not out	23	b Arnold	21
†H. Carter b Bird	1	not out	0
E. Jones b Bird	30	c Burrows b Wilson	2
W. P. Howell b Burrows	0	c Wheldon b Simpson-Hayward	8
J. V. Saunders b Burrows	1	c R. Foster b Wilson	5
Extras (B 5, LB 2, W 3)	10	(B 5, LB 3, W 4)	12
	274		**199**

WORCESTERSHIRE

F. L. Bowley c Armstrong b Howell	0	c Hopkins b Armstrong	35
F. Wheldon c Darling b Jones	5	b Jones	1
E. G. Arnold b Noble	38	b Armstrong	3
Mr R. E. Foster b Jones	8	lbw, b Armstrong	0
*Mr H. K. Foster c Gregory b Noble	6	b Armstrong	9
Mr W. W. Lowe b Noble	14	c Duff b Jones	11
Mr G. H. Simpson-Hayward b Armstrong	25	c Gregory b Jones	15
G. A. Wilson c Hopkins b Noble	0	c Gregory b Jones	0
†G. Gaukrodger c Duff b Hopkins	59	c Duff b Jones	9
A. Bird b Armstrong	2	b Jones	1
R. Burrows not out	20	not out	3
Extras (B 16, LB 9)	25	(B 8, NB 2)	10
	202		**97**

WORCS.	O.	M.	R.	W.	O.	M.	R.	W.
Wilson	24	4	91	1	12	1	35	4
Arnold	17	3	62	0	5	0	19	1
Bird	18	3	69	6	10	1	40	2
Burrows	15.2	3	42	3	3	0	23	0
Simpson-Hayward					14.1	0	70	3
AUSTRALIANS								
Howell	23	8	61	1				
Armstrong	16	5	28	2	18	4	34	4
Jones	17	3	46	2	18.4	3	53	6
Noble	9	2	34	4				
Hopkins	2.3	0	8	1				

Umpires: W. Richards and C. E. Richardson

Committee, and Mr Jessop had to call on the services of some twenty-nine players.

For the Australian fixture, which attracted a large contingent of Bristolians to the County ground, the Cestrian shire were somewhat stretched to put a representative eleven into the field. Jessop was most unfortunately suffering from a strain but pluckily he turned out; he did not want to miss leading his own county against the "friendly foe" he had met so often. Jessop was a cricketing phenomenon, the like of which had never been seen before or since. He was a most remarkable hitter who scored his runs at the rate of about 80 an hour, or about twice as fast as most of the amateur batsmen of the day. Bowlers despaired of bowling to him, and captains despaired of setting a field to him when he was on the kill. With an eagle eye and so fleet of foot, with powerful forearms and wrists, he would run down the pitch to bowlers, fast or slow, destroy their length, cut or pull them off the middle stump, or drive them clean over the ring. Had he not already, in his short career as a batsman, passed the hundred mark seven times within the hour – twice off the powerful Yorkshire attack – the fastest being in a mere forty minutes? Since 1897 he had so far lambasted twenty centuries, and whilst at the wicket he dominated the run-getting completely. On one occasion at Bristol, he had scored 66 runs out of 66 added in just twenty-eight minutes. Small wonder, then, that Gilbert Laird Jessop was such an idol of the cricketing public, and as great a crowd-puller as W. G. Grace had been. Already known as "The Croucher" from his stance, the "Electric Battery", the "Human Dynamo" and a host of similar names all savouring dynamic energy, "Plum" Warner christened him simply "Jessopus". It placed him amongst cricket's immortals, whilst the American Ralph D. Paine eulogised him as "the Human Catapult"!

Alas for Gloucester, Charles Townsend, whom W. G. always called "Challey", was unable to play, neither were Frank Bateman Champain nor young Hale. The resources would be thin! Monday 14 July dawned fair and warm and it promised to be another hot day. As neither Trumble nor Saunders were fully fit Darling had little choice in the composition of his team. Presumably the commencement must have been delayed for some unapparent reason, for only about five hours' playing time was recorded, and the home county expended over three and a half of these in obtaining the paltry sum of 155. Mr W. Troup and Harry Wrathall, on going in for the first wicket, were very slow in getting started. The former, who had captained the county for the remainder of the 1899 season after W. G. had left, was a stocky little Indian Army Officer with a cast-iron defence. He was inclined to be slow to score, but would occasionally hit "like a horse kicking" if the off side was too close for his liking. Wrathall, another stocky moustachioed individual, was a good professional opener who liked to hit hard and had an appetite for runs. But they came all too slowly against the excellent opening attack of Jones and Armstrong. With 24 to his credit, Wrathall went to Bill Howell after a bowling change. Now came L. D. Brownlee, the son of W. Methven Brownlee, the old friend and biographer of

W. G. He was little more successful in penetrating the Cornstalk field than the openers had been. On Troup's departure Langdon joined him; they withstood the varied attack of pace and spin for another hour but they could not get runs. Jessop tried to change all that, but he only stayed for two overs and 13 runs before missing one from Armstrong and getting himself stumped. C. O. H. Sewell fared no better in attempting to push the score along. He was a brilliant stroke-player in the classic mould and one of the finest cutters in the game but lacked patience, and a rash stroke led to his quick demise. If the last pair, Paish and Roberts, had not put bat to ball the Cestrian total would not have reached anything like 155. "Jonah" had taken 3 for 56 and Warwick Armstrong's leg-spinners had accounted for 4 wickets at 51 runs. The pitch was a good one throughout and could not be held to account for Gloucester's inept display. They had collapsed like the Campanile of St Mark's in Venice earlier that day; only much more slowly!

By the time the Australians came out only an hour remained until the drawing of stumps, but such was the magnificent display of strokemaking that Trumper and Duff reached 111 runs in that time. At one point, Victor scored 27 runs off two overs; he batted in his most brilliant vein. To score at this rate against the outstanding Gloucestershire fielders – particularly Jessop at extra cover, Brownlee (cover), W. S. A. Brown (mid off) and Sewell (third man) on the off side, Wrathall at long on, Paish, Troup and Roberts in the slips – must have called for superb placement on Trumper's part. Fred Roberts, Paish and Huggins bore the brunt of this aggressive batting. Jessop's strained side prevented him from putting himself on, for no doubt he would have liked to have done so. Roberts was a medium-pace left-hander; he had been fast when he first played for the county as long ago as 1887, and was one of the earliest to learn to swing the ball. He was a very capable bowler, and was still very much in form with a tally of 118 wickets in the previous year. Paish, too, had previously had his hundred wickets, but was a slow left-hander of considerable spin and quite unperturbed when hit. Unfortunately, some umpires were already beginning to question his action. The only pace available came from the medium-fast deliveries of Huggins. Possessor of a fluent action, he came off the turf sharply and swung the ball appreciably. Capable of finger spin, and with an unplayable one in his armoury, he tended to tire himself through "swinging" too much to the detriment of his powers. Already this season at Hove against Sussex he had taken his 7–17, which Jessop considered one of the finest performances he had seen from a bowler of his type.

The next day, Trumper continued to hit in Jessopian style until he was first out at 134. He had made 92 of these and was unlucky to fall to a splendid catch of Jessop's within sight of his century: his first error of judgement, but this innings of Trumper's set the tone and pace of what was to follow. Reg Duff carried on with a fine display of strokes for 62 runs. The Tourists were now 184 for 2, and Clem Hill, who had been partnering Duff, endured an uncomfortable period against the left-handers. He had played and missed quite a few times – quite unlike his usual self. With Monty Noble assisting him his composure returned, but it was Noble who came good from the moment he came in, and he scored all round the wicket. No matter how well the Cestrians fielded, this pair found the gaps. The atmosphere became torrid and the temperature soared up to nearly 90 degrees. In 140 minutes of grand hitting 205 runs were put on the board. Noble reached his admirable hundred, for the first time on the tour, only to be clean bowled.

Three down for 389. The Gloucestershire attack had now quite wilted. W. S. A. Brown, another left-hander – but of medium pace – for all his confidence and cheerfulness had been punished but never lost his length. Brownlee, Wrathall and even Langdon were given a few overs, but still the runs came. With the removal of Hill for 123, Hopkins flayed the weary bowlers, reaching his own century in even time before Joe Darling applied the closure. The Cornstalks had amassed 545 runs for 5 declared.

During this day of sudden summer, batsmen all over the country were enjoying themselves at the expense of hot and tired bowlers. For London County at Crystal Palace against M C C, the father-figure of Gloucestershire and cricket, W. G., was making yet another century – his 123rd. The "Old Man" was joined in this enterprise by L. O. S. Poidevin (the N S W player), who was doing likewise. Had the Tourists been a batsman or two short Poidevin would have been a highly useful substitute. At Hastings, too, in the Sussex versus Surrey match, Ranjitsinhji was piling up 234 and Fry amassing 159 in a total of 705 for 8 declared. By way of reply, Abel pillaged 179, Hayward 144 and Captain Bush 122 in making 552.

Little need be said about Gloucester's second innings. Being 390 runs behind their position was a daunting one, especially as the pitch had by now become worn. Jones and Howell took immediate advantage of it to break the back of the innings, and, as soon as the former had disposed of Mr Jessop, the Australian captain was able to let his men relax somewhat. Sewell and Board delayed the inevitable with a watchful stand, but Armstrong's leg-breaks tempted them both to hit out rashly. The act of finality occurred when Darling handed the ball to Reg Duff and Clem Hill in turn to dispose of the tail. They were thus able to rejoice in a mammoth victory over the "shire of the Graces" to the extent of an innings and 222 runs. So, with a week remaining and two more fixtures to play before the fourth Test match, the touring party was in excellent form and spirits.

AUSTRALIANS
v
GLOUCESTERSHIRE

At Bristol, 14, 15, 16 July.

Australians won by an innings and 222 runs.

GLOUCESTERSHIRE

Mr W. Troup b Hopkins	23	c Kelly b Jones 0
H. Wrathall c Noble b Howell	24	b Howell 5
Mr L. D. Brownlee c Jones b Armstrong	21	b Jones 1
T. Langdon b Jones	14	b Howell 23
*Mr G. L. Jessop st Kelly b Armstrong	13	b Jones 21
Mr C. O. H. Sewell b Jones	6	c Hill b Armstrong 35
†J. H. Board c Howell b Jones	0	c Hopkins b Armstrong 36
Mr W. S. A. Brown lbw, b Armstrong	6	c Trumper b Armstrong 6
J. H. Huggins c Noble b Armstrong	6	c Noble b Duff 17
A. Paish not out	18	not out 10
F. G. Roberts c Kelly b Howell	17	c Duff b Hill 3
Extras (B 1, LB 5, W 1)	7	(B 4, LB 3, W 4) 11
	155	**168**

AUSTRALIANS

V. T. Trumper c Jessop b Roberts 92	Extras (B 2, LB 7, W 3, NB 3) 15
R. A. Duff b Brownlee 62	
C. Hill c Board b Wrathall 123	(5 wkts dec.) 545
M. A. Noble b Wrathall 100	S. E. Gregory ⎫
A. J. Hopkins not out 105	†J. Kelly ⎬ did not bat.
W. W. Armstrong b Brown 35	E. Jones ⎪
*J. Darling not out 13	W. P. Howell ⎭

AUSTRALIANS	O.	M.	R.	W.	O.	M.	R.	W.
Jones	32	12	56	3	...13	2	67	3
Armstrong	33	11	51	4	...10	4	13	3
Howell	12	5	28	2	...14	2	42	2
Hopkins	10	5	13	1	...6	1	22	0
Duff					...5	0	9	1
Hill					...2.5	1	4	1

GLOUCESTERSHIRE				
Roberts	27	7	78	1
Paish	31	1	144	0
Huggins	36	3	137	0
Brown	20	3	68	1
Brownlee	4	0	21	1
Langdon	5	0	33	0
Wrathall	9	2	49	2

Umpires: V. A. Titchmarsh and G. Bean

CHAPTER 10

Somerset, Surrey and Rain

The Tourists' pleasures after the day's play were simple enough. They always dined together as a team; this was important for a sense of comradeship and team spirit. Sometimes, of course, they were the guests of their county hosts or notabilities connected with the game, when they were joined by amateurs, and sometimes the senior pros. Occasionally, however, they would be invited to a splendid function at one of the large houses, but, if left to their own devices, a small group might visit a local theatre or music-hall. Often enough they were quite content to gather in the smoking-room of their hotel for a sing-song round the piano. Monty Noble was invariably the leader in this entertainment, for he possessed a fine baritone voice; and when he could be encouraged sufficiently to do so, Victor Trumper would play the piano. Vic, of course, was never a seeker of the limelight, and although on the friendliest of terms with all of his team-mates and relaxed in their company, he still had to be encouraged to partake of anything smacking of self-esteem.

Having journeyed on to Taunton the party were warmly greeted by the Somerset captain and secretary, Sam Woods. He was an expatriate Australian who, since his schooldays at Brighton, had stayed on in England and qualified for Somerset. "Sammy" was one of the characters of cricket, and stories about his doings both off and on the field were legion. This genial giant was described by Charles Fry as a perfect specimen of manhood. He had lost little of his boyish sense of fun or his Australasian lightheartedness, and from a cricket point of view he was the complete all-rounder. Allied to these attributes the "cove" had become as Somerset as cider.

At the beautiful little county ground in Dene Park, the Tourists met Somerset on Thursday 17 July for what promised to be quite an interesting and enjoyable fixture. Somerset were much stronger, particularly in bowling, than their Cestrian neighbours. Although Sam Woods, one of the great fast bowlers of the nineties, did not bowl so much nowadays, there were the thunderbolts of George Gill. The mainstay was the fast-medium leg-spin of Len Braund of England fame, who had brought the art of right-hand leg-break bowling to a formerly undreamed-of perfection. In Robson they possessed a lively, fastish right-hander who could also bat, and the persistently accurate slow left hand of Cranfield completed the Somerset regular attack. That it could be formidable on its day, even Yorkshire knew to their cost. Up North they were known as the "Giant Killers"!

With the luck of the toss favouring the home side, they had the good fortune to bat on a splendid pitch where Mr Lionel Palairet and Leonard Braund gave the county a very fine start. Regardless of the bowling changes and first-class fielding, the runs came at a goodly rate, 88 of them in seventy minutes, before "Coo" Palairet made his only mistake in hitting Saunders into Gregory's hands when he had made 44. A welcome return to his excellent play of the previous season. Braund shortly afterwards fell to the same bowler for 52 well-earned runs. Lewis batted steadily, but neither Robson nor Sammy Woods were able to withstand the renewed onslaught by a refreshed Ernest Jones. Now at this stage of the innings entered the Somerset new boy Harry Martyn, the fearless Oxford wicketkeeping Blue, who, being as fearless a bat, proceeded to knock the Australians' bowling about just as if it were commonplace club stuff. His 52 runs made in brilliant style came very quickly: indeed, he twice hit the ball out of the ground and on each occasion was awarded six runs for the feat. In the hour and a half following luncheon eight wickets fell for the addition of 158, which showed that the Somerset men were far from being overawed by the renown of their august visitors, and had indeed taken 109 off Saunders' 22 overs and 87 at the expense of "Jonah" on a pitch that suited him admirably. The county were all out for 274, but it might well have been more.

They were soon able to feel even more pleased when the lordly Victor Trumper went for 5, and they further enjoyed the added success of Joe Darling's wicket, who had promoted himself into Clem Hill's place, but Reg Duff and Monty Noble set about their bowling in earnest. Now came some vigorous and splendid hitting from the pair of them and the scoreboard clicked round at a furious pace. At last Noble was trapped into a caught and bowled by the patient Braund for 53, and immediately Syd Gregory went for a duck. Hopkins, who had a little luck, settled down to play second fiddle to the regal Duff, who carried on serenely at the rate of a run a minute. A beautifully polished innings without the shadow of an error finally came to an end after three hours when he gave a sharp

109

return catch to Gill. Deafening applause greeted Reg Duff's walk to the pavilion after this magnificent feast of 183 runs to which he had treated everyone; he was well applauded by the fielding side. His wicket, the fifth, had fallen at 319, and with Hopkins batting very confidently another large total seemed inevitable, but Albert Hopkins soon fell after completing his fifty and the remainder were accounted for very quickly by Braund and Gill. It was surprising on such a good batting pitch for the Cornstalks to have slumped to 348 all out. Gill's persistence had been rewarded with 5 wickets for 80 runs on another warm day in the field.

With the western shire at the wickets again Palairet immediately went onto the attack, Jones coming in for some severe punishment at his hands. Twelve came off the first over and ten were taken from the third. Seeing the ball splendidly, he brought into play so many of his graceful strokes, repeating his success of the previous day; his initial 51 runs came out of 69 in forty minutes from the start. This most sublime of polished strokeplayers, who had been third in averages last year and had previously figured four times in the first twenty, had soon lost three partners. When his captain, the redoubtable Sammy Woods, joined him a delightful small stand ensued with the latter gradually taking over the punishing role. Within sight of his century, Palairet was unluckily clean bowled by a perspiring Jones, and then Sam Woods was leg before to Hopkins at the end of the day. The score now stood at 159 for five and the County were only 85 runs on.

When play recommenced on the Saturday morning, with the pitch still playing true, it soon became obvious from the vigorous batting of Martyn and Gill that Somerset intended to give the Cornstalks a large total of runs to chase. However, the feature of the day was the elegant strokemaking of twenty-one-year-old Mr P. R. Johnson, a New Zealander by birth and a Cambridge Blue, whose father had played in the 1850s. The Tourists had high praise for this graceful young batsman's magnificent innings of 62. He looked, every inch of him from his upturned brim panama hat to his immaculately whitened boots, the classic amateur bat. Jones' express deliveries were off-driven with superb timing and power of which even Lionel Palairet would not have been ashamed. That Somerset even batted well down to number ten could be observed when their veteran wicketkeeper Mr A. E. Newton banged delightfully about him for 21 runs and remained undefeated at the end. This second venture of the County's was a most creditable effort of 315 runs. Hopkins had been the most successful bowler for the Visitors with 3 wickets for 46, whereas "Jonah's" 4 wickets had cost him 104 runs.

The sky was now overcast and the atmosphere quite heavy when the Australians faced the total of 242 to win. They had just commenced the task when, with the score at 16 in the fourth over,

Trumper's wicket fell and the rain came down. It proved to be heavy and prolonged enough to rule out any more play in the match. As the time was now about ten minutes past four the Cornstalks would have needed to score at a rate of 88 runs an hour. Had this enjoyable and satisfying match been played to a finish, it would most likely have been drawn, so Somerset and Sammy Woods could feel pleasure at their creditable efforts.

AUSTRALIANS *v* SOMERSET

At Taunton, 17, 18, 19 July.

Match drawn.

SOMERSET

Mr L. C. H. Palairet c Gregory b Saunders	44	b Jones	90
L. C. Braund c Trumble b Saunders	52	b Jones	6
A. Lewis c Kelly b Saunders	38	run out	11
E. Robson c Noble b Jones	13	b Hopkins	4
*Mr S. M. J. Woods c Kelly b Jones	9	lbw, b Hopkins	30
Mr H. Martyn b Trumble	52	c Hopkins b Jones	25
G. Gill lbw, b Saunders	10	c Hopkins b Trumble	27
Mr P. R. Johnson b Jones	0	c Saunders b Hopkins	62
Hardy c Trumper b Saunders	20	c and b Trumper	17
†Mr A. E. Newton b Armstrong	20	not out	21
B. Cranfield not out	2	b Jones	5
Extras (B 7, LB 3, W 4)	14	(B 13, LB 4)	17
	274		**315**

AUSTRALIANS

V. T. Trumper c Hardy b Gill	5	lbw, b Gill	5
R. A. Duff c and b Gill	183	not out	11
*J. Darling c Palairet b Robson	20		
M. A. Noble c and b Braund	53		
S. E. Gregory c Newton b Gill	0		
A. J. Hopkins c Braund b Palairet	52		
W. W. Armstrong b Gill	15		
†J. J. Kelly b Gill	7		
H. Trumble b Braund	1		
E. Jones b Braund	1		
J. V. Saunders not out	2		
Extras (LB 4, W 2, NB 3)	9		
	348	**(1 wkt)**	**16**

AUSTRALIANS	*O.*	*M.*	*R.*	*W.*		*O.*	*M.*	*R.*	*W.*
Jones	23	3	87	3	...	25.2	2	104	4
Armstrong	13.5	3	37	1	...	13	6	18	0
Trumble	14	5	27	5	...	33	12	59	1
Saunders	22	4	109	5	...	15	3	52	0
Hopkins					...	15	2	46	3
Trumper					...	3	0	19	1
SOMERSET									
Cranfield	10	0	65	0	...	2	0	11	0
Gill	24	4	80	5	...	1.3	0	5	1
Robson	14	3	56	1					
Braund	23.2	4	80	3					
Palairet	7	0	37	1					
Hardy	3	1	21	0					

Umpires: V. A. Titchmarsh and G. Bean

Before the fourth Test match at Manchester later in the week, the Australians still had to meet Surrey for a second time. This meant journeying up to London on the Sunday so that they were in readiness to engage the South Londoners at Kennington Oval on the following day, Monday 21 July. With the prospects of a strong Surrey side against them, when Darling in all probability would have liked to have rested certain key players, they were to have little respite before them. It must be remembered that the Australians were quite unused to six days a week cricket for months on end, and it was a tribute to their resilience and strength of character and purpose that they continued to play such keen and attractive cricket without ever appearing jaded.

Their previous meeting with Surrey had been in mid-May and resulted in an innings victory for the Tourists. The composition of the eleven they were to meet, on about as cold and cheerless a July morning as could be imagined, would be considered a little less strong than that which they had vanquished two months before. V. F. S. Crawford was not able to appear but his place was capably filled by "Shrimp" Leveson Gower. As neither E. M. Dowson nor A. Baker were available, Walter Lees and H. Clode, two Surrey Colts who spent much time in the second eleven, had their opportunity to play against the Tourists. Lees commanded a medium pace and had been developing into a very steady bowler with an occasional break-back that went with the arm. His flight was deceptive in that he came through the air much faster than the batsman expected. However, his great years still lay ahead of him.

In view of the nearness of the fourth Test, Joe Darling decided to save his prime offensive weapon – Hugh Trumble. Kelly, too, for obvious reasons, was rested, as was Ernie Jones, whose services might well be required at Old Trafford if the pitch looked likely to favour his expresses. Thus, with a certain edge missing from their bowling department, the Australians took to the field after Darling's third consecutive loss of the toss.

With the pitch never easy, the old firm of Abel and Hayward settled themselves in and proceeded to pick their runs. Playing back and scoring where they could, having to fight for their runs as the Cornstalks were alert and as keen as mustard in the field, they made no mistake until Tom Hayward hit one of Saunders' deliveries hard to Noble at point. "The Guv'nor", however, batted serenely on, never seeming in the least difficulty, and many averred they had never seen him play better. His judgement of which balls to leave alone and which to hit showed what an outstandingly skilful player he was. Hayes came and went for a nicely played 37, Lockwood for 16, and veteran Bill Brockwell for an excellent 39. Surrey were now four down for 241; then Trumper, coming on for a second spell, deceived Bobby Abel when the latter had reached 104. Up to this

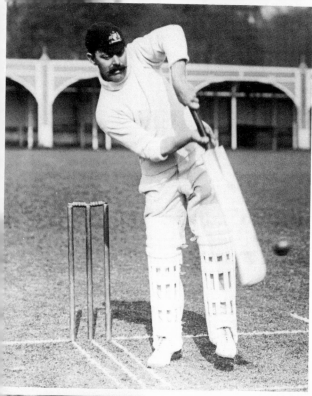

S. E. Gregory
(*The George Beldam Collection*)

J. J. Kelly
(*Marylebone Cricket Club*)

A. J. Y. Hopkins
(*The George Beldam Collection*)

A. C. MacLaren
(*E. Hawkins & Co.*)

F. S. Jackson
(*The George Beldam Collection*)

G. L. Jessop
(*The George Beldam Collection*)

J. T. Tyldesley
(*Marylebone Cricket Club*)

L. C. Braund
(*Marylebone Cricket Club*)

G. H. Hirst
(*The George Beldam Collection*)

W. Rhodes
(*The George Beldam Collection*)

Trumper cutting at Lockwood in the final Test at the Oval
(*The George Beldam Collection*)

The end of the Oval Test
(*The George Beldam Collection*)

point the Tourists' bowling, although accurate and tight, had little penetrative edge and Carter, behind the stumps, had surprisingly let through quite a number of byes. As ever, Howell pounded away at one end – he had taken two wickets so far. A trier if ever there was one, he was not called "Billy the Plugger" for nothing. He immediately bowled the Surrey captain Digby Jephson.

From the cold and windy Monday it rained overnight, and on Tuesday morning it was still raining. Play could not be resumed until 4 o'clock in the afternoon, when the remainder of the Surrey wickets tumbled. They were all out for 296, leaving Leveson Gower without a partner for 26 runs. Bill Howell had earned his 5 wickets for 80.

With the pitch fast drying in the wind Trumper and Duff made a capital start in difficult conditions. They went for the runs in tremendous style, and those of the "Surrey Crowd" who were present at The Oval that day enjoyed a rare treat. Taking advantage of Lockwood not being able to obtain a foothold, the Australian opening pair plundered the bowling of Clode, Lees, Brockwell and Richardson. Trumper reached his 50 in forty-five minutes. To quote Percy Cross Standing, "His masterful decision and skill in going back and making faultless bowling of convenient length to pull, quite baffled the attack."* Together they hit up 142 runs in an hour and a quarter before Duff was caught in the slips off Lockwood for 57. The latter had at last been able to bowl and secured Duff's wicket almost immediately. Trumper, by beautiful batsmanship, increased his own score to 85 in the last over of the day when he too fell to a clever catch behind off Lockwood. The Surrey and England fast bowler had shown that he was in excellent mettle for, in bowling 20 balls, he had collected both these prize wickets for 15 runs.

On the last day it was Clem Hill who made the running, supported first by Armstrong and then by his captain. Darling had come in to face a crisis, for the Australians' total had slumped from 142 for one to six down for 197. Lockwood did no more bowling after the four balls of his unfinished over of the previous evening. The pitch was still wet, but perhaps Jephson was sparing him for the Test match on the morrow. Hill and Darling, two left-handers together, continued to play magnificent and faultless cricket, and the former was unlucky to put a leg in front when but ten short of his century. The Cornstalk innings closed with a lead of 17, with young Clode being the most successful bowler with 4 wickets for 65 runs.

As time was by now well advanced, it seemed doubtful that Surrey would complete their second innings, especially as Tom Hayward and Hayes were batting very well on what was still a difficult pitch. The patient Tom, playing back, using a dead bat or not making a stroke at all, reached 48 before he fell to the deception

*P. C. Standing, *Cricket of Today*, T. C. & E. C. Jack, Vol 2, p. 154.

of Armstrong. But it was Saunders who became the angel of destruction for, in nine overs, five of which were maidens, and one ball, he took the remaining six wickets for only nine runs. The collapse was as total as it was complete for 111.

It had already been agreed to finish the match early to allow the Tourists time to travel to Manchester that evening, so, with only a

AUSTRALIANS *v* SURREY

At Kennington Oval, 21, 22, 23 July.
Match drawn.

SURREY

R. Abel c Noble b Trumper	104	c and b Howell	5
T. Hayward c Noble b Saunders	26	c Hill b Armstrong	48
E. G. Hayes lbw, b Armstrong	37	c Armstrong b Noble	22
W. H. Lockwood c Armstrong b Howell	16	c Darling b Saunders	18
W. Brockwell b Howell	39	st Carter b Armstrong	6
Mr H. D. G. Leveson Gower not out	26	c Noble b Saunders	0
*Mr D. L. A. Jephson b Howell	0	c Armstrong b Saunders	7
W. Lees c Trumper b Saunders	6	c Duff b Saunders	0
H. Clode b Saunders	9	c Duff b Saunders	3
†A. Stedman c Armstrong b Howell	6	not out	0
T. Richardson b Howell	2	c Duff b Saunders	0
Extras (B 22, LB 2, NB 1)	25	(B 1, NB 1)	2
	296		**111**

AUSTRALIANS

V. T. Trumper c Stedman b Lockwood	85		
R. A. Duff c Abel b Lockwood	57		
†H. Carter c Hayes b Clode	0		
W. W. Armstrong c Richardson b Brockwell	21	not out	1
C. Hill lbw, b Clode	90		
M. A. Noble lbw, b Lees	0		
S. E. Gregory c Hayes b Lees	0		
*J. Darling b Richardson	32		
A. Hopkins c Leveson Gower b Clode	6		
W. P. Howell not out	6	c Leveson Gower b Clode	2
J. V. Saunders c Leveson Gower b Clode	0	not out	8
Extras (B 16)	16		
	313	(1 wkt)	**11**

AUSTRALIANS	O.	M.	R.	W.	O.	M.	R.	W.
Howell	28	70	80	5	11	4	34	1
Saunders	34	10	82	3	9.1	5	9	6
Armstrong	34	13	49	1	11	2	34	2
Trumper	14	3	23	1				
Hopkins	5	2	21	0				
Noble	6	2	16	0	12	4	32	1
SURREY								
Clode	16	2	65	4	3	1	5	1
Lees	20	1	93	2				
Brockwell	12	0	56	1				
Richardson	12	0	65	1	3	1	6	0
Lockwood	4	0	18	2				

Umpires: W. Hearn and W. A. J. West

quarter of an hour's play possible, Darling sent in his last pair, Howell and Saunders. Only 95 runs remained outstanding and had time been played out in full they should have obtained them easily enough. As it was, stumps were drawn with the Tourists 84 runs short. Nevertheless it was a moral victory for the Australians, who departed for the North with the highest hopes and full of confidence at having the added advantage of being one game up in the rubber.

CHAPTER 11

Victor Victorious – The Fourth Test

After England's defeat at Sheffield, the Selectors were in a quandary. The opinions of the sporting press, and indeed the cricketing public, were many and varied; they all had their own favourites. The choice was far from simple – England's chance of squaring the rubber was at stake. Charles Fry, a member of the Selection Committee, had failed on each occasion with the bat and had not been making runs this season in his accustomed manner. Gaining his place at Sheffield only by Ranjitsinhji's injury, he was ready enough to agree to Ranji's reinstatement at his own expense. The meetings of the Committee were interminably long and covered many days. Should they include Jack Mason of Kent or Lionel Palairet of Somerset; should they persist with Bobby Abel or play his colleague and opening partner Tom Hayward? They had all performed well recently and must be considered on their respective merits. How about Jessop? Archie MacLaren always wanted him for his fielding; he had batted superbly at Sheffield, and his recent performance at Lord's of 8 Middlesex wickets for 58 runs was a reminder that he could still bowl when the occasion demanded.

How about bowlers? Rhodes would be a certainty with his left-arm spinners, so would Jackson as the all-round man of the side. Hirst, of course, the great swerve bowler and a most reliable bat in a crisis, must be considered, although he had been fairly expensive at Sheffield. Whom to use as the fast bowler: Lockwood or Syd Barnes? Or, if conditions were wet (it being dry and sunny at the time of the meetings), there was Schofield Haigh of Yorkshire, who had been twelfth man at Sheffield. Now Lord Hawke, at the thought of the loss of his four best bowlers in the Yorkshire side with the possibility of one of them only being twelfth man again, felt far from pleased at the prospect and said so. He was willing to forgo three men, but not four, which, for all the vituperation that has been heaped on his Lordship's head since, was reasonable. Many uncharitable things have been said over this incident, and about Lord Hawke's parochial outlook in putting Yorkshire before England, but placed in his position one wonders how many other county captains would have acted differently. He may not have been the best possible candidate for Chairman, he may well have temporised and taken too much notice of what he thought was public opinion and perhaps allowed it to sway his judgement, but in this instance at least the position he took was hardly unreasonable.

Fry disagreed, but the others must have acquiesced. Then, according to Fry, somebody mentioned the name of Fred Tate. Now Tate, a good steady medium-paced bowler, was having his best season and at the moment was top of the county bowling averages. It was not surprising that his name should be put forward. Fry gave his opinion on his county colleague, saying that Tate could only field at slip, and although a careful slip in the Sussex side he thought him not up to Test match standards. Additionally, as well as Tate was currently bowling he was at his most effective on fast, dry pitches. Evidently, in spite of Fry's opinion – quite a fair one – the remainder of the Committee, with misgivings, agreed to Tate's inclusion.

For the fast bowling attack Lockwood was reinstated; he had been chosen at Sheffield but left out on the morning of the match. Of Sydney Barnes we hear no further word; could it be that the Selection Committee, particularly the Chairman, were pardonably annoyed at MacLaren's apparently high-handed method of choosing Barnes all by himself for the Third Test, and for this reason passed him over? It must also be remembered that Barnes did not appear to be the outstandingly dangerous performer in 1902 that he became some nine years later.

The eleven names chosen were: MacLaren, Palairet, Abel, Tyldesley, Ranjitsinhji, Jackson, Braund, Lilley, Lockwood, Hirst and Rhodes. Surprisingly, perhaps, it had not occurred to the Committee to select the near successful team of the First Test. In Manchester it had been a rainy day on Tuesday, on Wednesday Tate's name was added to the list, and there was more rain that night. An outcry from the sporting pages of the press made quite clear the deficiencies of the side and castigated the Selectors roundly. In one regard this was certainly true, for that august body seemed to have overlooked its fielding capabilities. Abel, Lockwood and Tate were only suitable for the slips, and England already had three of its finest incumbents present in MacLaren, Braund and Ranji. The outfield would be thin; it was ill-balanced. Consternation reigned at the omission of Jessop; and Barnes had his many supporters, as did Schofield Haigh.

Came the morning of Thursday 24 July – it had rained again. So, on making his final decision the England captain, possibly feeling piqued at the composition of the team in which he had been denied Haigh, Jessop and Barnes, reportedly said, "Martin [Hawke] chose Fred Tate for a wet wicket and it will rain!" Thus Tate, whom MacLaren felt had been foisted upon him, was frivolously chosen and George Hirst, the more likely wet-pitch bowler, left out. In the event Archie Mac may well have reflected bitterly on his whim, for a less strong side than had represented England in the previous three Tests had been further weakened both in batting and in the field.

Joe Darling's selection problems presented him with no difficulty. The pitch was wet and, although the sun shone fitfully, the likelihood was there would be more rain. He could safely leave out Jones and Howell. Naturally, Carter would not be played as Kelly was quite fit. Trumble, Saunders and Noble should be able to exploit the prevailing conditions, but much would depend on the luck of the toss. The pitch was very soft and would play slowly and easily, so runs were there to be had cheaply enough. But they must be obtained quickly, for with the effect of the sun and wind there would be trouble in store later on. It fell to Darling's good fortune to call correctly and he naturally elected to bat.

MacLaren came back into the England dressing-room and cheerfully announced, "It's all right, boys, they're batting; the sun's coming out; we've only to keep 'em quiet till lunch, and then . . . "*
As a prophecy, or guesswork, it proved to be wildly inaccurate in this game of fluctuating fortunes. But, he mused, as well as the pitch being wet, the outfield was sodden and sluggish, even muddy in places; certain fours on a dry ground would be twos at most, or maybe only singles. "The pitch will be sticky after lunch," continued MacLaren, "then we'll bowl 'em out as quick as they come in. If the Australians are only 80 or so at the interval we've won the match, and the rubber. So keep Victor quiet, at all costs!"†

When, seven minutes late, the England side followed Archie MacLaren onto the field, the huge crowd with many Yorkshiremen in its midst looked anxiously at the players emerging. "Jacker; Rhodes; what's Tate doing there; and where's George 'Erbert?" That Hirst had been left out at the last minute in favour of Tate: "What on earth was the England captain thinking of; had he lost his senses?" The consequences could only be dire and many northern hearts were filled with foreboding. A small twelve-year-old boy in the crowd, with his face pressed against the railings watching his first Test match, saw Trumper and Duff come out of the pavilion. Trumper was his idol, he wanted him to score a century, but, as a Mancunian and a patriotic lad, he naturally wanted England to win. So, in his dilemma, young Neville Cardus prayed in the most accommodating terms he could think of: "Please, God, let Victor

*A. A. Thomson, *Hirst and Rhodes*, Epworth Press, p. 44.
†N. Cardus, *Autobiography*, Collins, p. 181.

Trumper score a century today for Australia against England – out of a total of 137 all out.''* As we shall see, the small boy's prayer was to be answered . . . in part!

The pitch was far too slippery to open with Lockwood, so MacLaren decided to pin his faith on Rhodes and Jackson with the field set deep to save the fours. He told his bowlers to pitch them short on the off so that Trumper would have to come and fetch them. Rhodes would not have been too keen on these tactics – he remembered trying a similar experiment at Bradford with Jessop two years before and it still rankled! Rhodes opened to Victor Trumper, who leapt out and cover-drove him. In again and up a fraction, and again Trumper drove him, a little squarer, just above the sodden turf. MacLaren altered his field slightly, bringing a man across from the leg side, so Trumper jumped out and pulled the ball through the open gap. The duel was on. In Wilfred Rhodes' next over Trumper twice drove him high over the sightscreen behind the bowler straight into the practice ground. They were only counted as fours then! The crowd applauded, this was great stuff; their appreciation was genuine enough, even though it was Australia. Jackson was faring little better at the other end. Duff was hitting him hard on the rise, and made a slashing cut that not even Johnny Tyldesley at third man saw; then Victor hooked him hard.

MacLaren, all the while adjusting his field, brought on Fred Tate in place of "Jacker": Duff slashed him and Trumper pulled him right from the middle stump round to square leg. The scoreboard was ticking over furiously as the runs came in a steady stream: twos and singles mainly inside the deeply set field, then, when Archie MacLaren brought a man in, bang would go a four streaking from the middle of Trumper's bat through the vacant gap. After half an hour there was 50 on the board. Braund took over and Victor pulled and cut him to reach his own 50 in 52 minutes when the telegraph read 92 for 0. The England captain was still scheming how to stop the runs coming. Rhodes was brought back, bowling now as he wanted to, pitching them up to just beat the bat, but still the brilliant Trumper pranced out and pulled and drove. The 100 was up in fifty-seven minutes. This was keeping Victor quiet! Such a remarkable display of batting had the spectators entranced, there was an unreality about it all, that this young man could so devastate the cream of England's bowling. According to Richard Binns, "The shorter they bowled the more energetically he hooked them; the fuller their pitch the more deftly he drove and pulled. It was impossible to bowl a length that he could not by his speed and certainty in judgement and execution convert into whatever *he* decided it should be."†

*Ibid, p. 169.
†R. Binns, *Cricket in Firelight*, Selwyn & Blount, p. 162.

Trumper never for a moment appeared to be in the slightest of difficulties — everything served up to him was at his complete command. Reg Duff, too, was batting brilliantly, but it was hardly surprising that he tended to be overshadowed by his more dashing companion. At 129 MacLaren at last brought on Lockwood; Trumper reached 80 and Duff, now facing the fast bowler, was immediately caught behind by Lilley standing well back. One down for 135 in only seventy-eight minutes of play. This remarkable opening partnership, to which Duff had contributed 54, the highest that Australia had made in a Test match, had been scored at a rate of 103 runs an hour — a record if ever there was one!

With the left-hander Clem Hill joining the fray Victor Trumper continued to hit, but, as many were singles, the run-rate dropped a little because of the field continually having to change over, and, furthermore, the drying pitch was beginning to help the bowlers. Then, five minutes before the luncheon interval, after only 108 minutes play, Trumper superbly pulled and hooked Lockwood for two fours to reach his century. The telegraph showed 168 runs for 1 wicket; this was Trumper's answer to MacLaren's vainglorious attempt to keep him quiet. Pandemonium broke loose in the crowd as they cheered the pale and slightly embarrassed young man in the middle: a century before lunch on the opening day of a Test match had never been thought possible. As Lilley, the wicketkeeper, congratulated him, Vic replied with a smile, "Thanks very much, Dick, but I've had a bit of luck." The innings had been completely chanceless, and was his sixth hundred of the tour. By lunchtime Trumper was 103 not out and Australia's total the astonishing figure of 173 runs for 1 wicket! The members in the pavilion rose to him and a crowded Old Trafford buzzed with excitement.

The first half of young Cardus' prayer had been answered, and he was conscious that he had witnessed history being made. Recalling Trumper's innings, he wrote, "He was the most gallant and handsome batsman of them all; he possessed a certain chivalrous manner, a generous courtly poise. But his swift and apparent daring, the audacity of his prancing footwork, were governed by a technique of rare accuracy and range. Victor was no mere batsman of impulsive genius; he hit the ball with the middle of his bat's blade — even when he pulled from the middle stump round to square leg."*

With all the hearty congratulations he received during luncheon, Trumper may well have been unsettled. The interval, too, was to assist the England bowlers in another way: the fitful sun and the chill breeze were doing their work on the drying pitch to give it added life and devil. Victor scored a single and faced Rhodes. The ball was now turning and he played each delivery with care. Off the fifth ball of the over he stepped across and back cut, but

*N. Cardus, *Autobiography*, Collins, p. 182.

as the ball spun from the turf he cut it later than intended. Lilley's right hand shot out and caught him low down. 175 for two and a brilliant innings was brought to a close. Victor's 104 had taken only 115 minutes, so overall he had scored at the rate of 56 runs an hour; despite this, not a ghost of a chance had he given. With fourteen fours, many from powerful pulls and hooks, and in the audacious manner and circumstance in which it was performed, this was one of the finest innings that he had played.

As Clem Hill carefully picked his runs Noble did his best to counter the guile of Rhodes. It was becoming difficult to score off him, and in Rhodes' third over after lunch Monty Noble hit back a return which the bowler succeeded in holding almost on the turf. He was given out. Thinking it was a bump ball Noble appealed, but the umpire was adamant. 179 for 3. Gregory fared little better: after collecting three runs he too fell in Rhodes' fourth over since the interval, caught at the wicket by Dick Lilley. This was the third wicket for each of them, bowler and wicketkeeper. 183 for 4! A great change had come over the game since luncheon – 10 runs had been added for the loss of three wickets, all taken by the effectiveness of the Yorkshireman's sharp away-spin now the pitch was helping him.

Joe Darling had to stop the rot. The pitch was becoming more spiteful, and it was up to him to try and knock Rhodes off because his left-arm break-away was less troublesome to a left-hander like himself than it would be to his remaining right-handed bats. To Darling they were off-breaks, but Wilfred Rhodes had previously been worrying Joe with a ball he swung with his arm. It was Trumper who advised his captain how Rhodes held the ball for that particular delivery. "I'll hit him out of the ground" – and he cracked Rhodes a mammoth soaring drive clean out of Old Trafford. Six runs! Keeping up his onslaught in an endeavour to discourage the spinner's impeccable length, Darling twice more drove him over the ring – only fours this time. But Australia's captain again gave the long handle to emulate his former feat with another hit right out of the ground for six. During this duel, Clem Hill had been far from idle at the other end – the runs were still coming, he had reached 50, even though he was having to fight for them. In an effort to break this successful stand Archie MacLaren decided to bring back Lockwood into the fray. It was to be a satisfactory move for England. With Lockwood bowling at full pace and the ball rising shoulder high, Hill, in attempting a lofted drive, mistimed his stroke and presented the ever alert Rhodes with an easy catch at mid-off. This was a misfortune for Australia, and probably Hill felt he should kick himself, but he had made 65 valuable runs and held his castle intact whilst his captain bludgeoned the enemy's prime attack. 256 for 5. Hopkins came and went in the same over, pluckily caught by Palairet running in to short leg, without addition to the score. Armstrong joined his captain, who was still attacking Rhodes, and did his best to hold up one end, but after he had made 5 runs his stumps were uprooted by a Lockwood snorter. 288 for 7.

MacLaren knew he was now through to the soft underbelly. There only remained the defiant Darling, who had reached 51 ferociously hit runs. Undaunted by the Australian captain's assault upon him, Rhodes continued to feel for his spot on the turf. In once more, with the scoreboard showing 292, his spinning finger tricked Joe Darling at last. Attempting another big drive, Darling mistimed his stroke and sent the ball ballooning through the air into MacLaren's eager hands at mid-off. Doubtless this wicket, his fourth, gave Wilfred great satisfaction. Fortune, which had smiled on Australia before lunch to the tune of 173 for one, had, with the sticky drying turf under the now warm sunshine, come to England's assistance to reduce what once looked to be a heavy score to eight down for 292 runs. Rapidly now Lockwood disposed of Trumble, caught in the slips by Fred Tate, and Saunders, bowled. The crowded ring, happy and delighted to see Australia all out for as little as 299, felt that England had fought back to a winning position. MacLaren thought so too as he congratulated Lockwood on a fine performance of 5 wickets for only 8 runs in his last spell and inning's figures of 6 for 48. Rhodes had done sterling work, too, and, without wavering under pressure, his 4 wickets for 104 was a better effort than it seemed in cold print on the scorecard.

It was now 5 o'clock and Trumble and Saunders, during their short sojourn at the wickets, were delighted at the prospect of bowling on a "sticky dog". The warming sun of the last hour had been doing devilish work – they could not get on it quickly enough. By 5.15 the English openers, Palairet and Abel, emerged. They found themselves in difficulties immediately. With the field set close in and the ball literally popping, defence of the wicket was paramount. Trumble's subtle variations of pace and flight were difficult enough to counter, but it was Saunders' slanting run up with the hand hidden until the last moment that they found confusing. Saunders struck first: he found the top edge of Abel's bat – the ball flew to Armstrong in the slips. 12 for 1. One run later Lionel Palairet, playing his first innings in a Test match, mistimed Saunders, cocking the ball up to Noble at point. A bad start for England, but worse was to follow. MacLaren imperiously strode to the wicket to join his compatriot Tyldesley; the crowded spectators' hopes rose.

Archie Mac was off the mark with a single; he now settled to take strike from Trumble. Playing forward to drive in the classical MacLaren mould, he missed and was bowled! 14 for 3. The Australians were overjoyed, and gloom descended on the crowded arena. Gone was the vociferous shouting that had earlier greeted the fall of each Australian wicket; the crowd was silent now, sullen almost, as the English captain haughtily disappeared from view. Ranji came to join Tyldesley, who was picking his runs with caution. With the score at 30 and the innings thirty-five minutes old, Ranjitsinhji, who had never looked happy, put a leg in front to Trumble. So the fourth wicket fell and the gloom deepened.

The Australian fielders, mustard keen and on their toes, clustered round the bat as Stanley Jackson took guard. He played himself in slowly, using the utmost caution against the turning ball. Darling saw no reason to change his bowlers – Saunders and Trumble had the English batsmen in turmoil and they were getting wickets. Fourteen runs came in the next fifteen minutes when Tyldesley, facing the left-armed Saunders, cut uppishly and was caught by Hopkins at third man. Five down for 44 runs in three-quarters of an hour. Depression round the ring was complete. England's chances had slumped to a new low.

Jackson was on 7 when Leonard Braund joined him, and this pair somehow, and with difficulty, survived until the drawing of stumps. Braund, seeming the more confident of the two, made 13, and "Jacker" added a further 9 to his score. Thus at the close England were 5 down for 70 runs. The Tourists could be well pleased with their efforts: the match was firmly in their grasp, five of the greatest reputations had gone, and they could see the glow of victory before them.

A clear night and fine weather on the Friday made life somewhat easier for the not-out batsmen. Gone were yesterday's sticky conditions (the turf had bonded more firmly and was playing faster), but runs still proved hard to get. Australia's fielding was as smart and alive as ever and the bowling as penetrative, for Trumble and Saunders could still get a break on the ball. Jackson and Braund, with an uphill task before them, set about pulling the match back out of the fire. By slow, sure cricket, treating each delivery with care, they determinedly and skilfully defended, scoring a hard-fought-for run whenever they could. Little was heard from the crowded spectators except the concerted gasp of apprehension when there was a near miss, as when Jackson, now on 41, hit a sharp return to Saunders and was very nearly caught and bowled. Applause broke the silence when "Jacker" reached his well-earned 50; it had taken him one-and-three-quarter hours. Slowly they were pulling the game round by the kind of cricket the Northerners were used to at a Roses match – but there was much more at stake here.

With a trickle of twos and singles, then a four, Jackson was hitting anything a little loose with a flourish. Darling knew he must break this stand, so Hugh Trumble and Saunders, although still difficult to play, were rested. Noble and Armstrong relieved their colleagues, and the grim game continued. Braund, in a heady rush, got hold of Armstrong and punished him four times to the ring through the seven-man leg-side field in as many overs. As the morning session was ticking away on the pavilion clock, the hundred partnership came and went. Braund reached his 50, applause breaking through the concerted silence which reigned whilst each and every ball was bowled. When 58, he gave the crowd palpitations with a wretched stroke just as it was beginning to feel easier as the magnificent backs-to-the-wall partnership unfolded. With only five minutes to the luncheon interval, the telegraph credited England with 185 runs: Jackson 77 and Braund 65. Noble came up to the wicket, the field crouched, and out came the ball from his hand: an outswinger going a little wide of the off stump. But Noble's flight was troubling Braund – in stepping out to drive nearly square, he turned it onto his wicket. They had added 141 runs for the 6th wicket and it had taken two-and-three-quarter hours. At the interval England were 6 for 186, and Stanley Jackson was not out 78.

Dick Lilley did not stay long after the 200 had been posted; he, too, was fooled by Noble's puzzling flight three runs later. Bill Lockwood, a somewhat brusque fellow, came in and soon had seven runs to his name. Jackson edged into the nervous nineties. When 92 he cut Noble – Duff, at short third man, only half stopped it. It was Lockwood's call. "Jacker" hesitated then started to run. Duff by this time was fumbling with the ball. Jackson stopped and started off once more as Duff prepared to throw to Kelly behind the stumps. Lockwood, now over half way down the pitch, was almost level with the amateur; it was clear to him there would be a run out. Gallantly he kept on running, past Jackson, so sacrificing his wicket. For this sporting gesture he received a grand ovation from the ring; it redounded greatly to his credit, but England were 8 down for 214.

Now partnered by Rhodes, a fellow-Yorkshireman, Jackson reached his hundred with a single. The cheering that broke out was tumultuous; it was heartfelt relief. This was Stanley Jackson's third century in a Test match and, under the exceptional circumstances in which it was made, was probably his finest; it had taken him three-and-three-quarter hours. Wilfred Rhodes knew exactly what to do – keep his end up! With a century behind him, the Hon. F. S. began to hit at everything and England's supporters lustily cheered every run. "Jacker" was pulling the match out of the fire for them. Although a refreshed Trumble had been brought back on, his skilful hitting and sure placement of the ball through the field was remarkable. But shortly Trumble out-foxed the wily Wilfred into a return catch at 235, so leaving Mr Jackson to be partnered by Fred Tate, the last man in. Tate kept his bat in the blockhole, leaving Mr Jackson to do the scoring. Still hitting out bravely, the amateur, now 123, was missed badly by Gregory, of all people, at cover point from Noble's bowling. He was tiring: the concentration of batting for four-and-a-quarter hours under such conditions was enormous. But the end was nigh. He was still hitting and, at 3.35 p.m., he drove Trumble powerfully for what seemed another boundary; but Duff, racing round the outfield, took a grand catch at full speed. The innings was over and, thanks particularly to Jackson, England were still in the hunt. With 262 to their credit they were but a slender 37 runs behind on the first innings. No wonder the large assemblage of all present were feeling much happier than they had that morning; they could scarcely believe the recovery.

It must have been readily apparent to both players and spectators that the first hour of Australia's second innings would probably settle the result of the match. If only Trumper's wicket could be claimed quickly to prevent his decimation of the bowling again, for heaven knows what he might do in the mood of yesterday! Then, too, Duff, Hill and Darling would need to be sent back before settling themselves in. It seemed almost an impossibility.

But the seemingly impossible was about to occur. Shortly after four o'clock on a good fast pitch when Australia had seven runs on the board with Trumper and Duff looking confident and full of runs – it happened! Lockwood was bowling to four slip fielders, very fast indeed. Trumper attempted to cut a fast away-going ball outside his off stump, which an eager Len Braund, with surprising agility, got his hands to – only for it to bounce out again. The shout of approval had died in the spectators' throats when next they saw Braund throw the ball aloft. Cheering themselves hoarse, very few present possessed a quick enough eye to have witnessed it. Seven for one and Trumper, the greatest prize of all, was gone. Now Lockwood's tail was up; this was just the kind of success to incite him to do greater things. Two runs later, in his next over, Duff also tried to cut him; but the ball broke back and the pace was so great that it flew from the edge of the poor deluded Duff's bat onto the stumps – the ball had been unplayable. The crowd was beside itself as Gregory came in to join Hill, who had yet to get off the mark, and somehow got a single. Clem Hill now faced Lockwood. Deceived by extreme pace and break-back, the ball was through him to take his off stump out of the ground before he knew what had happened. Frenzied, delirious excitement greeted this – three of Australia's greatest guns gone for only ten runs. The cheering crowd could hardly believe what it had witnessed – but there it was on the scoreboard. Mental calculations were made. Australia were only 47 runs ahead with seven wickets in hand. Lockwood's inspired opening spell had indeed swung the match quite remarkably in England's favour.

Joe Darling had already decided at the fall of Duff's wicket to send in Gregory to hold one end steady, but with the loss of Hill he felt that he should go in himself and play the left-hander's forcing game, and keep Noble back to close up the game entirely should he fail. These were sound tactics. Joe was a man for a crisis if ever there was one – cool, unruffled and unflappable, he knew the result of this Test match rested in his own hands. Together they doggedly added six runs, the last of which little Syd Gregory had played wide of mid-off from the fifth ball of Len Braund's over. This brought Darling to face Braund's last delivery.

As the field was changing over for the left-hander, Braund said to MacLaren, "Can I have Mr Palairet across to square leg?" (Palairet always fielded there for Braund in the Somerset side, and he knew how Braund's leg-break curved when a left-hander hit it.) Archie MacLaren now made his second fatal error. Rather imperiously, he replied, "What, do you want me to ask Lionel Palairet to run right across Old Trafford for one ball? Send Fred Tate out there."* And so he did. Now "Chubby" Tate only ever fielded in the slips, and he was quite lost at deep square leg. Did MacLaren at this moment reflect on Fry's words at the Selection committee meeting? Still, it was only for one ball!

Down it came and Joe Darling, intending to put it out of the ground, carted it high with the spin; but Joe had mistimed slightly and the ball was lofted out in the direction of Tate on the square leg boundary. In its high flight from the bat it curved in the air with the spin and, on reaching its apogee, descended in a parabolic arc. The excited spectators, certain of a catch, were already mentally making it 16 for 4 as Fred Tate moved to his right in doubtful apprehension; but with the ball still curling away he frantically tried to get back, got his left hand to the spinning red missile, but it dropped to the ground. A horrified groan from the ring was heard far beyond the bounds of Old Trafford – this missed catch was probably going to matter.

Heaving a heartfelt sigh of relief at the let-off, Joe Darling went for the runs. He hit Lockwood, and in Braund's next over satisfactorily brought off the big leg hit he had tried for previously – this time right over the ropes. MacLaren next brought on Rhodes and the Australian captain set about him to destroy his length. Gregory, too, was hitting out and the runs were coming in a steady flow. They had been together for an hour now and had added 54 runs for the fourth wicket, or another 48 since the "let off". Lockwood was tiring, and MacLaren, realising that Tate was probably suffering from his dropped catch, put him on to bowl; it was a successful manoeuvre. Fred Tate broke the flourishing partnership by trapping Gregory leg before. Four wickets for 64 runs (instead of 16) and Gregory's share was 24.

Joe Darling proceeded confidently onwards in his duel with Rhodes, still hammering him, until he was deceived by flight and

*J. Arlott, *Rothman's Jubilee of Cricket*, Arthur Barker Ltd, p. 55.

spin and another would-be big hit was taken at long-on by Palairet. Five for 74, thus Darling had collared 37 runs – 31 of which might not have been made. The Old Trafford throng gave a delighted cheer to see the back of Darling; "It won't be long now," they thought.

Bringing back a refreshed Lockwood was a good move by Archie MacLaren: straight away he had Hopkins caught in the slips by a now more cheerful Tate, and Monty Noble caught by Lilley standing back. Seven for 77; they could not last much longer. Armstrong was bowled by Rhodes at 79, but Kelly and Trumble managed to hold out until the drawing of stumps when Australia's meagre total was 8 wickets for 85 runs. So in dramatic circumstances after a day of thrills and shocks, the Tourists, after starting the day in an unassailable position, found themselves sliding to a possible defeat. They were only 122 runs on with two wickets to fall. Lockwood had been the architect of their downfall. He had broken the back of their innings before they had started, on a good batting pitch, and had come back later to almost polish them off. With such superlative figures of 5 wickets for 28 runs, the importance of a fast bowler was never more admirably shown. So the *aficionados* of English cricket present at Old Trafford that day went home certain that England would win on the morrow.

In the words of Gilbert Jessop, "Manchester did not gain the title of 'the Watering-Pot of England' without good reason,"* for that night the heavens opened. For some five or six hours the rain poured down; it was surprising that the pitch was even playable by midday. It was obvious that the pitch would be affected but nobody was quite certain how; time alone would tell.

A portentous omen was the Australians' inability to get runs – albeit tailenders, they only managed a single for the loss of the remaining two wickets. "Chubby" Tate and Rhodes were the successful bowlers and it took them only a quarter of an hour. As Australia had finally made 86, this meant that England had to obtain 124 runs to win. It seemed an inconsiderable total, and many of the crowd were certain that only a few English bats would be needed for the task; but some were of a more cautious turn of mind. Perhaps the pitch might get worse with sunshine added, or it might even rain again.

At twenty minutes to one o'clock MacLaren and Palairet came out to open the last innings. As Trumble and Noble commenced bowling everybody appeared over-anxious: England's opening pair to get runs as quickly as they possibly could and the bowlers and fielders to get wickets. The English captain and his partner displayed a nervousness in their actions quite out of keeping with their usual manner – they were palpably on edge. During Noble's second

*G. L. Jessop, *A Cricketer's Log*, Hodder & Stoughton, p. 192.

over "Archie Mac" played and missed, Kelly was beaten for four byes. The runs were slow to come from the bat and somehow they got to 24 between them, but the odd ball was beginning to pop up. Seeing this, Darling brought on Jack Saunders in place of Noble. There was nearly a run out: Gregory's shy at the stumps only just missed – a close shave for MacLaren. In the next over, off Saunders, "Tich" Gregory dived at short leg with the ball from Palairet's bat just missing his outstretched fingers. It was painfully apparent that the pitch was becoming more difficult, and in the fifty minutes to the lunch interval they made 36 runs.

During the luncheon recess Archie MacLaren, whether from rashness or confidence at the thought of only 88 runs to win, visited the Australians at their lunch table. "Ah Joe," he said to Darling, "I think we've got you this time." "Oh! have you," replied the Cornstalks' captain, "why, we've only to get two or three of you out and the rest will shiver with fright."* Had he temporarily forgotten that the Australians were never more dangerous than when they appeared to be beaten?

Eight more runs were added after the restart in two overs – the spectators were feeling easier at this – when Palairet, facing the last ball of Saunders' over, played too late and his off stump was uprooted. 44 for 1. John Tyldesley joined his captain but had a narrow escape straight away; Gregory nearly caught him at short leg. Fortunately for England this did not upset his composure; MacLaren, too, looked more his old self. They attempted a hitting game. Although these were desperate measures on this dangerous pitch to the likes of Trumble and Saunders, they nearly succeeded. In no time John Thomas had 16 on the scoreboard and his captain had added 8. Sixty-eight runs scored, only 56 needed. But brave Johnny Tyldesley over-confidently cut Saunders and was well taken by Armstrong at extra slip.

As Ranji came out the sky was noticeably darkening, with heavy rain clouds building up to the north-west. Observing this, MacLaren decided to force the pace thinking the rain might deprive his team of their rightful spoils, and imperiously he off-drove Trumble for four. With nothing succeeding like success, he rashly tried to hit Trumble clean over the ropes. But the ball was more pitched up, the big hit did not carry and Duff, fielding deep, took the catch easily. Three down for 72. Hugh Trumble had been bowling his off-breaks from round the wicket, and the Tourists' fielding was tenacity itself. The "Surrey Guv'nor" – Bobby Abel – trotted out only to give everyone present heart failure when Saunders nearly caught him at mid-on under a glowering sky. Four runs were added, all from Bobby's bat, when a shower drove the players in for a quarter of an hour. The rain must have eased the pitch a trifle, but the sky was as threatening

*M. A. Noble, *The Game's the Thing*, Cassell & Co, p. 225.

as ever, and Abel, having been instructed to hit out, successfully made a couple of healthy looking twos on the leg side from Saunders' bowling. He followed this with two cracking drives off Trumble for four apiece, one of which sailed into the crowd out of Clem Hill's reach at long-on. But could this last? – it was not the little Surrey man's natural game.

Meanwhile, Ranji at the other end, with only four runs to his name, was batting in the manner of a man totally out of touch, unable to judge either the pace of the pitch or interpret the break-back. To keep the Indian prince from scoring Darling placed two or three extra men on the leg side – Syd Gregory at "silly" fine leg and himself at "silly" square – then one or other of them would move as the bowler's arm came over. Ranji never knew where they were, and, with an attack on his leg stump and pads, it put him off his game. Clem Hill, observing the Indian bat so timidly, became convinced that the Australians could win. He soon fell to Trumble LBW, on the third appeal in one over; 4 down for 92. The throng, hushed at Ranji's dismissal, nevertheless felt, with only 32 runs wanted and six wickets in hand, confident in England's eventual victory. Bobby Abel was still hitting but, at 97, attempting to drive Trumble, he missed the ball completely and was clean bowled – five down.

If the Australians' fielding had been tenacious in not giving away a ghost of a chance it now became galvanic, so determined were they to get the remaining English wickets. Trumble and Saunders bowled as they never bowled before, hardly erring or wavering in length or direction. Braund had joined an uncertain Jackson, and, getting a lucky snick off Saunders that he knew little about, sent up the 100 with a three between the wicketkeeper and first slip. The strain on the spectators was quite noticeable. The anxious cheer that erupted was as much one of acute concern, then they immediately lapsed into a pained silence. Seven more runs were slowly added: the bowling was tight, the fieldsmen gave no quarter. Only 17 more runs needed now, when Hugh Trumble, of all bowlers, sent down a full toss. It deserved to be hit over the ropes. "Jacker", over eager, hit the ball hard intending to place it between mid-off and cover. But Syd Gregory, predicting its flight, leapt to his right and brilliantly plucked the ball from the air. A disconsolate Jackson walked away downcast and annoyed with himself. The Australians were more confident than ever, and the ring was silent.

Trumble started his next over: Len Braund played forward and lifted his back foot for a fraction of a second only to have his wicket broken by a supremely alert Kelly. Seven down for 109, and a still silent ring felt near panic at the state of things occurring in the middle. Lockwood, who had not added to the score since he came in, took a big lunge in an attempted drive at Trumble only to hear his wicket shatter behind him. Eight had fallen now and the scoreboard still showed 109. The sky still brooded dark as if in mourning for the recent departed and the fifteen outstanding runs needed to win.

With one run, the undefeated Lilley was now joined by Rhodes, who middled the ball well from the start, and the confidence he must have felt comforted the nervous and worried around the ropes. A cheer rent the air as he swept Saunders, a ball pitched outside the off stump, clean over the long-on boundary. Lilley now scored a single (nearly running himself out) and then a two. With 116 showing clear on the telegraph they were slowly getting nearer to the coveted 124. Eight runs to win. The Australians, determined to stop those runs by all fair human agency, crouched lower in their allotted positions with faces betraying nothing save concentration. Lilley, still facing Trumble, with his sap rising, walloped the ball – a hard skimming pull shot right round to square leg. The breathless spectators cheered a certain fourer. Alas for England, the soaring ball was held a trifle in its course by the wind and Clem Hill, fielding on the boundary in front of the pavilion, started off in an all-out effort to save the boundary. Running at top speed for twenty-five yards, he threw himself in a dive at the missile, astonishing everyone by holding it in one hand and somersaulting twice before realising he had brought off the catch of a lifetime. As Dick Lilley walked past Hill on his way to the pavilion, he said, "Oh Clem, what a bally fluke!" The overjoyed Hill, for appearance's sake, felt he had to reply – "Never on your life!" But, he relates, "The English wicket-keeper knew the truth and spoke it."* The stunned crowd was disbelieving; that certain four had been caught and the scoreboard ominously read nine down for 116.

Before a deathly silent crowd, with last man Fred Tate coming out, the rain, which had long been threatening, started to fall. The umpires debated for a few moments whether to suspend play or finish the game, which must have been an agony for Tate as he was becalmed in the middle. But it was heavy enough for them to remove the bails so the players ran for shelter. It was just past four o'clock.

With the downpour adding to the spectators' depression, the fearful wait for the players in their dressing-rooms was even more oppressive. While Rhodes appeared calm enough, poor "Chubby" Tate had to endure the acute tension of waiting forty minutes with his pads on and receiving advice from his companions. Many of them, for their part, felt remorse at having thrown their wickets away. The rain stopped, so at a quarter to five Tate found himself walking out to bat for a second time. Rhodes had the strike (he and Lilley had crossed before Hill's miraculous catch), playing out the

*G. Brodribb, *Maurice Tate*, London Magazine Editions, p. 8.

130

remaining four balls of Trumble's over. Although he was trying his hardest to get a single to keep the bowling the predatory Australian field denied him. Their plan to get Tate had worked.

In front of the grim and silent Australian fielders, on a very wet pitch, Fred Tate prepared to face his ordeal. Darling arranged the field with scrupulous care to add to the batsman's nerves, and Saunders stooped and rubbed the greasy ball in a pile of sawdust before slowly walking back to his mark. In he came with his usual slanting run up, the field crept closer, and the ball swung away to leg. Tate somehow touched it, with what part of his bat he knew not, but it shot through the legs of the too eager fielders, speeding on its way to the fine-leg boundary. The batsmen ran a single and crossed for a second: the crowd rose hoarse-voiced and shouted in excitement. Armstrong heaved himself after it in an effort to save the four. Gaining on the ball as it neared the boundary the desperate Armstrong tried in vain to scoop it with his foot. The Australians watched with bated breath the race to reach the ball. Seeing the England last pair were starting their third run they hoped against hope the ball would cross the boundary – they wanted to keep Tate at the striker's end, for he was their chance.

Only four runs needed to win now. Tate blocked the next ball, and a sigh of relief was the heartfelt outlet from the tense spectators. Somehow, too, he coped with the third delivery; only three balls left to the over and then it would be up to Rhodes: he'd get them. Tate settled in his blockhole once more, the bowler went to the sawdust pile again and the field set themselves ready. Now Saunders ran in with his left arm extended parallel to his body, signifying to his comrades "a fast one coming". It pitched straight and came on through as poor Fred Tate played forward, too late. The ball, keeping low, sent the leg stump somersaulting. The massed crowd sat horrified and silent at the spectacle and even the Australians were momentarily bemused, not fully aware that they had won by just three runs. Suddenly they leapt in the air excitedly, shaking hands as they sprinted for their dressing-room.

The spectators were devastated at the final turn of events. They could hardly believe what had happened, that England had lost by three runs when at lunchtime they seemed so sure of victory. To finally crown their discomfiture, as they made their way from the ground the rain began to torrent down once more. Archie MacLaren was a very disappointed man, but being a great sportsman he immediately sought out the victorious Australians and sincerely congratulated them. This sensational win had earned them the rubber by virtue of having now won two Tests with one left to play. Thus the mythical "Ashes" remained in their hands.

The fourth Test match has come down to posterity as the one "Fred Tate lost for England". Why was a scapegoat needed for our unexpected defeat in such a remarkable cricket match? It is a pity to lumber a man for two incidents in hundreds which occurred during those three days. It should not be forgotten that he was chosen for his bowling and could only field at slip. In these two departments he was reasonably successful, whereas his "errors" were in the outfield and at batting. Equally, should not MacLaren's

ENGLAND *v* AUSTRALIA

(4th TEST)

At Manchester, 24, 25, 26 July.

Australia won by 3 runs.

AUSTRALIA

V. T. Trumper c Lilley b Rhodes	104	c Braund b Lockwood	4
R. A. Duff c Lilley b Lockwood	54	b Lockwood	3
C. Hill c Rhodes b Lockwood	65	b Lockwood	0
M. A. Noble c and b Rhodes	2	(6) c Lilley b Lockwood	4
S. E. Gregory c Lilley b Rhodes	3	lbw, b Tate	24
*J. Darling c MacLaren b Rhodes	51	(4) c Palairet b Rhodes	37
A. J. Hopkins c Palairet b Lockwood	0	c Tate b Lockwood	2
W. W. Armstrong b Lockwood	5	b Rhodes	3
†J. J. Kelly not out	4	not out	2
H. Trumble c Tate b Lockwood	0	lbw, b Tate	4
J. V. Saunders b Lockwood	3	c Tyldesley b Rhodes	0
Extras (B 5, LB 2, W 1)	8	(B 1, LB 1, NB 1)	3
	299		**86**

ENGLAND

Mr L. C. H. Palairet c Noble b Saunders	6	b Saunders	17
R. Abel c Armstrong b Saunders	6	(5) b Trumble	21
J. T. Tyldesley c Hopkins b Saunders	22	c Armstrong b Saunders	16
*Mr A. C. MacLaren b Trumble	1	(2) c Duff b Trumble	35
K. S. Ranjitsinhji lbw, b Trumble	2	(4) lbw, b Trumble	4
Hon. F. S. Jackson c Duff b Trumble	128	c Gregory b Saunders	7
L. C. Braund b Noble	65	st Kelly b Trumble	3
†A. A. Lilley b Noble	7	c Hill b Trumble	4
W. H. Lockwood run out	7	b Trumble	0
W. Rhodes c and b Trumble	5	not out	4
F. W. Tate not out	5	b Saunders	4
Extras (B 6, LB 2)	8	(B 5)	5
	262		**120**

ENGLAND	O.	M.	R.	W.	O.	M.	R.	W.
Rhodes	25	3	104	4	14.4	5	26	3
Jackson	11	0	58	0				
Tate	11	1	44	0	5	3	7	2
Braund	9	0	37	0	11	3	22	0
Lockwood	20.1	5	48	6	17	5	28	5
AUSTRALIA								
Trumble	43	16	75	4	25	9	53	6
Saunders	34	5	104	3	19.4	4	52	4
Noble	24	8	47	2	5	3	10	0
Trumper	6	4	6	0				
Armstrong	5	2	19	0				
Hopkins	2	0	3	0				

FALL OF WICKETS

Wkt.	Aus. 1st	Eng. 1st	Aus. 2nd	Eng. 2nd
1st	135	12	7	44
2nd	175	13	9	68
3rd	179	14	10	72
4th	183	30	64	92
5th	256	44	74	97
6th	256	185	76	107
7th	288	203	77	109
8th	292	214	79	109
9th	292	235	85	116
10th	299	262	86	120

Umpires: T. Mycroft and J. Moss

attempt at forcing the pace be considered the contributing factor? It could quite as easily have been dubbed "the match Clem Hill won for Australia", for his astounding catch to dismiss Lilley could equally be considered the reason for England's misfortune if we are looking for individual incidents. Or, why not credit Gregory's marvellous catching of Jackson, or Duff's dismissal of MacLaren as the turning-point in that last, fateful innings? Perhaps, too, it could possibly be the Australians' greater tenacity of purpose to win.

If reasons have to be sought for failure then the Selectors' choice, which must be found wanting, together with MacLaren's "petulant" manner of choosing Tate in place of Hirst as the wet pitch bowler, were prime causes.

CHAPTER 12

"To play the divil wid the bowlin'"

Feeling full of euphoria at the result of the fourth Test match, and having won the rubber, the Tourists could well have done with a complete rest. The nervous tension of the last few days had affected them and their Sunday "rest" was spent travelling back to London by train, for on Monday 28 July they were due to meet Essex at Leyton for a second time. A little respite, however, would be afforded to them before the final Test match at Kennington Oval as two of the four matches in their fixture list were to be of two days' duration only. Also on the eve of the last Test, on 9 August, there was the spectacle of the Coronation of King Edward VII to look forward to, at which the touring party were to have special seats.

The Essex county club were not experiencing a very successful season, but they had been buoyed up by their second win of the year having just beaten Derbyshire in an exciting game at Derby by 120 runs. The earlier fixture with the Australians in May had been quite spoiled by inclement weather, and the cricketing public of East London and metropolitan Essex were eagerly anticipating the return visit. Unfortunately, the county's ever cheerful veteran captain Harry Owen was not available, so on this occasion A. P. Lucas, the equally veteran deputy captain, was to lead them. Now playing for his third county after a long and honoured association with the game, Lucas had been a Test player against the Australians eighteen years previously, when most of his present opponents were small boys. However, some of the Australians were later to express their opinion that Mr Lucas was still amongst the top flight of English batsmen.

On their day Essex were a fine batting side, and against a for once rather wearied Australian attack they showed good mettle. Lucas and Fane set them off to a fine start, for although the pitch was damp it proved of little avail to Trumble and Saunders. It was dead enough for the Essex openers to watch the ball onto the bat. Fane batted in excellent vein, being in turn partnered by both of the Essex twins – Peter Perrin and Charlie McGahey. They all made runs but took their time in getting them. Lucas scored 26, Fane 81, Perrin 45 and McGahey 72. It was a pleasant sight to see "Charlie Mac" do so well against the Australian bowlers who caused him so much trouble on the recent Antipodean tour. Charles Kortright, who had been partnering McGahey and indulging in a big hit or two, fell to Ernest Jones in his second spell for 66. So far the batting had been soundness itself and a large total seemed most likely on the Leyton scoreboard, but "Jonah", the freshest looking bowler in the side, now proceeded to upend the innings in rather quick fashion. He spreadeagled Sewell's stumps with the last ball of an over of which Sewell, on his own admission, did not see one of them! Then he finished the County innings by doing likewise to "Sailor" Young, Tom Russell and Walter Mead. Even so, Essex could feel very pleased with themselves as their account closed with the creditable figure of 345.

By now it was the second day and the crowd got what they had come to see: a superlative innings from Victor Trumper. In the words of Guy Eden's poem:

> "And wid Essex, pore ould Essex, I'll remain a day or two,
> For I'm tould there's somethin' tasty in their bowlin'!"*

He did not remain a day or two – in the first innings he was at the crease for just ninety minutes, hitting all round the wicket to score 109 runs in dazzling vein. Whilst his team-mates Duff, Hill and Darling fell like leaves around him and could muster, with Gregory's help, but fifty runs between them, Victor at the other end was playing another beautiful and chanceless innings. The varied bowling talents of fast left-hander Young, the leg-"breaks" of McGahey, the medium slows – breaking both ways – of Walter Mead and Bill Reeves, were dispatched to every corner of the Leyton ground with a breathtaking variety of strokes faster than a run a minute. When he had made 109 (the scoreboard read 159 – 3) Vic was bowled by a ball from Mead that was considered unplayable. He received a tumultuous reception!

> "Oh! he's just a dandy batsman, he's a rajah, he's a toff
> Wid out any fancy feelin' for the 'on' or for the 'off'.
> He just takes his bat, and thin, wid one apologetic cough
> Sets to work to play the divil wid the bowlin'."†

*Guy Eden, "Victor Trumper", *Bush Ballads & Other Verses*, Sisley's Ltd, part verse iv.
†Ibid, verse vi.

But the Cornstalk innings, apart from Trumper, was a rather lack-lustre affair hardly living up to the great reputation they had made for themselves. Noble, however, played back-to-the-wall cricket, being 33 not out at the end, whilst Ernie Jones meted out the "long handle" treatment for a valuable 25 to help the Australians' total to a more respectable 232. Surprisingly to all present, Essex commenced their second venture 113 runs in hand.

For a second time the crack Essex bats produced the runs on the, by now, excellent Leyton pitch. Lucas reached his half century, looking everywise his old self, before Trumble bowled him. Perrin and McGahey, playing in their inimitable style – they were much alike in method – each passed the 50 mark, but the 184 runs which the county had added consumed all but three hours of the last day. So by the time the Tourists went to the wicket for their final innings, some 2 hours 50 minutes remained with 298 runs outstanding. That they got within 45 of them in that time was due in large measure to Trumper and Hill, despite a quiet start. Trumper played with more obvious care than usual, his initial fifty being scored at half the pace of his first innings, but once he felt certain that the result was no longer in doubt he attacked everything served up to him, hitting his second hundred of the match in brilliant style. Once again he delighted the Leytonians with the breathtaking spectacle of Trumper in full flight. The feat of two separate centuries in a match was thus performed for an Australian touring side for the first time.

> "Oh! it's all Killarney to him, if they shoot, or if they bump.
> By me sowl I've sat and watched him till me heart wid joy
> would thump,
> Just to see the saucy darlin' hook 'em off the middle stump
> Wid contimptous indiff'rence to the bowlin'!"*

When Trumper was LBW for 119 (Hill had made a valuable contribution of 59), the mighty Australians were in a safe position and the remaining bats continued to make runs quickly, so with four wickets in hand by the close they had nearly got them.

Ranji's Sussex were next on the list, the venue being, of course, their headquarters, the County Ground at Hove: a well marled pitch renowned for its scoring propensities and a veritable graveyard for bowlers' hopes, unless there happened to be a sea "fret" when the atmosphere could assist the spinner. The county of the "six martlets" was another fine run-getting side and, by the end of the season, was to come second to Yorkshire in the County Championship. Their bowling, however, though quite capable, was not always penetrative enough on their home ground to be decisive.

*Guy Eden, "Victor Trumper", *Bush Ballads & Other Verses*, Sisley's Ltd, verse vii.

AUSTRALIANS *v* ESSEX

At Leyton, 28, 29, 30 July.
Match drawn.

ESSEX

*Mr A. P. Lucas b Trumble	26		b Trumble	50
Mr F. L. Fane c Darling b Saunders	81		b Trumble	17
Mr P. Perrin c Kelly b Saunders	45		not out	58
Mr C. McGahey b Trumble	72		c Noble b Jones	59
Mr C. J. Kortright c Kelly b Jones	66		not out	0
Mr G. Tosetti b Trumble	15			
E. H. D. Sewell b Jones	0			
†T. M. Russell c Kelly b Jones	14			
H. Young b Jones	1			
W. Reeves not out	9			
W. Mead b Jones	4			
Extras (B 6, LB 5, NB 1)	12			
	345		**(3 wkts dec.)**	**184**

AUSTRALIANS

V. T. Trumper b Mead	109		lbw, b Reeves	119
R. A. Duff c Russell b Young	10		b Young	7
C. Hill b Reeves	15		c McGahey b Young	59
*J. Darling c Sewell b McGahey	19		b Mead	13
S. E. Gregory c Mead b McGahey	11		c Russell b Reeves	20
M. A. Noble not out	33			
A. J. Hopkins c Kortright b Tosetti	5		b Reeves	0
†J. J. Kelly b Tosetti	0		not out	8
H. Trumble run out	0		(6) not out	10
E. Jones c Russell b Mead	25			
J. Saunders b Young	0			
Extras (B 1, LB 4)	5		(B 16, LB 1)	17
	232		**(6 wkts)**	**253**

AUSTRALIANS	O.	M.	R.	W.	O.	M.	R.	W.
Trumble	49	15	97	3	31	10	81	2
Saunders	25	6	79	2	2	0	4	0
Noble	9	1	27	0	11	1	43	0
Trumper	13	4	43	0				
Jones	27.1	8	55	5	20	3	56	1
Hopkins	5	2	19	0				
Gregory	3	0	13	0				
ESSEX								
Young	13	0	64	2	18	1	66	2
McGahey	22	3	59	2	11	4	24	0
Mead	12	0	54	2	14	0	61	1
Reeves	5	0	35	1	8	0	62	3
Tosetti	5	1	15	2	6	1	23	0

FALL OF WICKETS

Wkt.	Essex 1st	Aus. 1st	Essex 2nd	Aus. 2nd
1st	58	29	30	15
2nd	136	82	107	116
3rd	177	134	178	158
4th	278	159	—	220
5th	310	175	—	237
6th	311	192	—	237
7th	321	192	—	—
8th	324	192	—	—
9th	337	228	—	—
10th	345	232	—	—

Umpires: W. A. J. West and A. A. White

In addition to Ranjitsinhji and Fry, three professional all-rounders – Joe Vine, Albert Relf and E. H. Killick – formed the nucleus of the regular eleven, together with Fred Tate, Cyril Bland and George Cox – the primary bowling attack – and stumper Harry Butt. Unfortunately, fast bowler Bland, suffering from strain, was unable to turn out, so Fred Tate's fast-medium bowling with

Albert Relf and George Cox would have to bear the brunt. A fine medium-paced stock right-hander was cheery Bert Relf, who delivered the ball edgewise on to the batsman with a sharp follow-through without checking his jerky run. From a quick rotary action he made the ball come smartly off the pitch, and with the least help from atmosphere or wind he could swerve the ball either way. At times a difficult bowler to play, for his length was impeccable, his sharp off-break was made by cutting the ball with the inside of his second finger. He also bowled one which went away from the bat, and a delivery that came straight through to effectively york the unwary. This was far from being the end of Relf's "bag of surprises", for there was also his notorious inswerver (from off to leg) bowled from the outside edge of the crease and, in doing this, he contrived, without bending the elbow, to get the right hand over the left side of his head. He was also a sound, strong and reliable bat.

The peculiarity of his flight was one reason why slow-medium-paced left-arm George Cox was so useful. He had a mannerism of rubbing the back of his hand across his mouth before starting his laboured jaunt up to the crease, which culminated in a pause prior to letting go of the ball. It went with his arm rather than swerving, and he cleverly disguised both a faster and slower delivery. In Joe Vine, the most capable all-rounder in the team, Sussex had a more than useful leg-break bowler whose pace was considerably faster than anyone else's. He had achieved the double the previous year of 1,190 runs and 113 wickets. But as opening batsman, the sheet-anchor, he had made his mark. Although he often had to hold up one end on "orders", he much preferred to have a go at the bowling and could effectively force the pace. Vine, too, as well as being the best professional bat in the side, was a brilliant outfield. A left-hander, who played in spectacles, Ted Killick was a good change bowler of leg-breaks and a sound and consistent batsman.

On the Australians' last visit Victor Trumper had thrashed the Sussex bowling to the tune of 300 not out, but although he commenced as if he might repeat the feat, he was out most unluckily for 21. Surprisingly, none of the other crack bats in the side could do much on the excellent Hove pitch and, however well Tate, Vine and Cox bowled, the Cornstalks seemed to be mesmerised by the cunning of Albert Relf. The Sussex side must have been delighted to find the telegraph reading 152 for 5. At this point Noble was joined by Armstrong. They played steadily and with circumspection; nevertheless, by the close of the first day they had added 200 runs together.

On Friday they continued their partnership in the same vein. Everyone on the field save Mr C. L. A. Smith and wicketkeeper

Butt turned his arm over. Charles Fry, who rarely bowled these days, yielded 42 runs in nine overs; Ranji and Bean were slightly less expensive. Noble hit them hard whenever he could but was otherwise restrained, and Armstrong batted with determination. They stayed in possession for nearly six hours. Finally, when Killick had Noble stumped for 284, the pair had added 428 runs together, the third highest partnership on record at that time in first-class cricket (and still the Australian record for the 6th wicket). Armstrong was undefeated for 172. It was quite a remarkable achievement as the batting was so free from fault. The Sussex side was glad to see the back of them when Darling applied the closure at 6 wickets for 580 runs.

With such a formidable total facing them the home county could do little, only Fry and Killick showing any real resistance. Ernie Jones and Trumble soon attended to the top of the order, then Saunders took care of the rest. Fred Tate, remaining not out at the end with 22 to his credit, must have had great personal satisfaction in playing Saunders' bowling so well. Facing the arrears of 395, Sussex were invited to follow on. Thus, with the last day well advanced and little prospect of a result, time was played out comfortably by Vine and Killick.

Journeying on to Cardiff, where the Tourists were to meet a combined Glamorgan and Wiltshire side on Monday 4 August, an enormous bank holiday crowd greeted them with much enthusiasm. For the two-day match the cream of these two second-class counties were joined by Silverlock, the Monmouthshire professional. The pitch was treacherous on the first day, and thus the Visitors soon dispensed with the Combined Counties for 121, the sternest oppositon coming from Mr W. H. Brain, the former Gloucester and Oxford University batsman, now representing Glamorgan.

On the Cornstalks' going in, being without the services of Trumper and Darling, they fared little better. Creber of Glamorgan and W. Overton from Wiltshire, both left-handers, bowled beautifully and had seven Australian wickets down for 48. However, Hopkins and Jones stopped the rot, both hitting the ball very hard, and when "Jonah"was bowled by Silverlock, wicketkeeper Carter played up well. These last three bats made the Tourists total a little more respectable – 148. Plainly they had underestimated their adversaries' strength.

With the Combined Counties batting again on the second day, the pitch having eased, they fought back admirably, Messrs Morgan, J. H. Brain and Medlicott all coping very well with the Tourists' bowling. It was Armstrong, however, who did most of the damage with his leg rollers to a leg-side field, but Medlicott coped so well as to be 50 not out when the innings closed at 178.

139

AUSTRALIANS *v* SUSSEX

At Hove, 31 July, 1, 2 August.
Match drawn.

AUSTRALIANS

V. T. Trumper b Relf	21
R. A. Duff lbw, b Relf	36
C. Hill c Smith b Relf	13
*J. Darling c Ranjitsinhji b Relf	0
M. A. Noble st Butt b Killick	284
A. J. Hopkins run out	32
W. W. Armstrong not out	172

Extras (B 12, LB 9, NB 1) 22

(5 wkts dec.) 580

†J. J. Kelly
H. Trumble
E. Jones
J. V. Saunders
} did not bat

SUSSEX

Mr C. B. Fry c Kelly b Jones	39	c Trumble b Saunders	11
J. Vine c and b Trumble	4	not out	50
E. H. Killick b Saunders	58	not out	60
A. E. Relf b Jones	0		
*K. S. Ranjitsinhji c Trumble b Jones	19		
Mr A. Collins lbw, b Trumble	5		
Mr C. L. A. Smith b Saunders	8		
G. Cox b Trumble	16		
†H. R. Butt c Hill b Saunders	2		
F. W. Tate not out	22		
G. Bean b Saunders	2		
Extras (B 4, LB 6)	10	(B 8, NB 1)	9

185

(1 wkt) 130

SUSSEX	O.	M.	R.	W.	O.	M.	R.	W.	FALL OF WICKETS			
										Aus.	Sx.	Sx.
Relf	54	15	142	4					Wkt.	1st	1st	2nd
Tate	41	9	136	0					1st	50	26	23
Vine	18	4	37	0					2nd	71	64	—
Cox	29	12	43	0					3rd	71	64	—
Bean	8	2	23	0					4th	90	104	—
Collins	15	3	52	0					5th	152	115	—
Killick	11.3	2	45	1					6th	—	134	—
Fry	9	0	42	0					7th	—	143	—
Ranjitsinhji ...	10	1	38	0					8th	—	145	—
AUSTRALIANS									9th	—	172	—
Jones	33	7	71	3	... 8	2	17	0	10th	—	185	—
Trumble	32	6	75	3	... 5	3	3	0				
Armstrong	13	7	7	0								
Saunders	12.1	5	22	4	... 10	0	41	1				
Noble					... 5	0	17	0				
Hopkins					... 5	1	24	0				
Duff					... 4	1	12	0				
Hill					... 2	0	7	0				

Umpires: F. Martin and W. Attewell

Time was short when the Australians went in to bat and they attempted to knock off the deficit, Gregory and Trumble in particular batting with alacrity. Extra time, however, was allowed to obtain a result, and the Visitors finished up victors with six wickets in hand, much to the spectators' satisfaction at two days of bright, attractive cricket.

AUSTRALIANS

v

GLAMORGAN and WILTSHIRE

At Cardiff, 4, 5 August.

Australians won by 6 wickets.

GLAMORGAN AND WILTSHIRE

Silverlock b Trumble	5	c and b Saunders	2
Mr H. E. Morgan c Noble b Trumble	1	c Jones b Armstrong	50
Mr J. H. Brain b Saunders	3	c Carter b Armstrong	34
Mr J. E. Stevens b Trumble	15	b Saunders	2
Mr W. S. Medlicott c Noble b Saunders	2	not out	50
Mr W. Smith c Gregory b Noble	25	b Armstrong	2
†Mr W. H. Brain not out	32	b Armstrong	8
Russell run out	10	c Gregory b Armstrong	5
Mr A. M. Miller b Noble	7	b Armstrong	1
W. Overton b Noble	6	c Trumble b Jones	15
H. Creber lbw, b Noble	2	lbw, b Armstrong	0
Extras (B 8, LB 3, NB 2)	13	(LB 7, NB 2)	9
	121		**178**

AUSTRALIANS

R. A. Duff c Smith b Creber	6		
J. J. Kelly c Silverlock b Creber	0	not out	42
C. Hill c Morgan b Creber	27	st W. Brain b Creber	32
S. E. Gregory c Morgan b Overton	0	b Russell	44
M. A. Noble lbw, b Overton	0		
*H. Trumble c Stevens b Creber	9	c Morgan b Russell	31
W. W. Armstrong c Stevens b Overton	3		
A. J. Hopkins not out	45		
E. Jones b Silverlock	39	c Creber b Miller	0
†H. Carter b Overton	16	not out	0
J. V. Saunders c Creber b Silverlock	0		
Extras (B 2, LB 1)	3	(B 5, LB 1)	6
	148	(4 wkts)	**155**

AUSTRALIANS	O.	M.	R.	W.	O.	M.	R.	W.
Saunders	14	7	20	2	22	5	56	2
Trumble	26	13	44	3	10	0	33	0
Noble	12	4	44	4	11	4	31	0
Armstrong					19.4	3	36	7
Jones					7	3	13	1
GLAMORGAN AND WILTSHIRE								
Creber	16	1	65	4	10	1	31	1
Overton	18	3	43	4	5	0	21	0
Smith	2	1	10	0	14	4	36	0
Silverlock	5	0	27	2	2	0	11	0
Russell					14	3	33	2
Miller					4.4	1	17	1

Umpires: R. Rogers and H. Coulson

A whole day free of cricket and a rest now came to the young men from the new Commonwealth before travelling to Southampton, where Hampshire were to be their hosts. One of the younger counties at the first-class game, Hampshire relied to a large extent upon a contingent of Army Officers whenever their service duties permitted. There were many good players amongst their ranks, but their appearances were somewhat irregular; this did not help form an evenly balanced side, and therefore the county were forced to rely heavily upon the services of a few hard-worked professionals. No longer were they skippered by Dr Russell Bencraft, now their Secretary, who did so much together with Mr Francis E. Lacey, the current Secretary of M C C since 1898, to make Hampshire first class. Owing to the recent war in South Africa few of the military men were able to assist: the arresting presence of Captain "Teddy" Wynyard was missing, Captain "Jungly" Greig was in India, and Captains Quinton, E. R. Bradford, and E. I. M. Barrett were in the Cape. So, from standing at seventh place in the Championship table in 1901 Hampshire were falling away badly.

Regardless of the county's misfortunes Mr C. Robson, enjoying his third year as captain, was ever serene in adversity. A good judge of the game and a clever tactician, he made a close study of opposing batsmen's weaknesses from his position behind the stumps and was forever scheming how to get them out. This jovial and kindly character, adept in his novel field placings, was also a useful bat. The lynch pin around which the eleven hung together was C. B. Llewellyn, the South African left-handed all-rounder. A wristy strokeplayer with a neat, crisp style, an excellent mid-off, but above all he was the type of bowler every county side desired to possess. Left-armed, of course, on the slow side of medium, he could turn the ball on the most favourable pitch to the bat, and if the pitch helped slightly his spin was vicious. Cleverly varying his pace, he turned the ball very sharply which, combined with consistent length, made him the devil to play. Having come to England with a representative South African side, Charles Llewellyn was considered good enough to be one of the chosen for England in the current Test series, and was to play for South Africa for many Test rubbers to come.

An additional attraction of this match was the reappearance of Major R. M. Poore in the Hampshire side, having just returned from the Boer War and still barely recovered from a broken arm. English cricket had not forgotten his whirlwind appearance in the 1899 season, when for two months he created sensation upon sensation by scoring 1,399 runs for the county in only 16 innings for the phenomenal average of 116.58. Among his seven centuries was a long score of 304 against Somerset, and his partnership with "Teddy" Wynyard of 411 for the 6th wicket became a record for first-class cricket at the time. Impressively tall, lean and leathery, using his commanding height and reach to smother length, Poore was a fast-pitch player who loved fast bowling, which he could cut sabre-like with military precision. His stance at the wicket was not unusual, but the secondary position he adopted appeared quite peculiar as he rose to his full height with the bat pointing to third man, whence he would off-drive, lunging forward with great power.

The county elected to bat, and Mr A. J. L. Hill opened with the consistent and capable professional A. W. Webb. "Brownie" Hill, a cheery character, like so many of the Hampshire amateurs, was an all-round sportsman excelling at rugby, hockey, tennis and rackets. A former Cambridge blue, one of the most stylish batsmen of the day and quite accomplished in all departments of the game, had he played regularly he would have risen to considerable eminence. They started well, but Saunders drew Hill forward and bowled him when he had made 15 excellent-looking runs. Major Poore displayed his cast-iron defence and Mr E. M. Sprot hit merrily, being the least troubled by the Cornstalk bowlers. Believing that attack was the best form of defence, Sprot, an aggressive bat with all the strokes, made top score of 33 before being caught behind by Carter from a Noble swerver. The middle order batting quite failed; Victor Barton, a professional who had purchased his discharge from the Army eleven years before and had served Hampshire well, was out for a duck. Robson, however, had a knock and together with Soar managed to get the Hampshire score past the 100 mark. All out for 130 runs – Trumble, Saunders and Noble experiencng little difficulty in claiming their wickets. Indeed, Monty Noble had taken 6 wickets for 33 runs in only twelve overs.

Now it was the Australians' turn. On a good pitch Llewellyn duped Duff and Trumper, then Hill and Gregory fell in quick succession to the hostile pace of lanky amateur fast bowler Hesketh Vernon Hesketh-Prichard, who managed to make the ball lift alarmingly at times. The Visitors were suddenly four down for 69 runs. Monty Noble went out to join his captain and found he was beaten time and again by Llewellyn's awkward deliveries. At the other end Darling, too, was in difficulties to the rising right-hand of Hesketh-Prichard (whose versatility extended to being an explorer, hunter and author of the famed "Don Q" detective stories). They consulted in mid-pitch – Darling would keep opposite the left-hander Llewellyn and Noble should handle Hesketh-Prichard. "The arrangement," Noble later recalled, "succeeding admirably. Darling pasted Llewellyn, and I hit the right-hander."* The Corn-stalk captain indulged in some quite remarkable hitting, and in the remaining 40 minutes of play that day they added 107 runs. Robson, behind the stumps, soon divined their intentions, "I know what you said to Darling," he commented to Monty Noble. Robson's guess was correct.

Continuing the following morning where they had left off, their partnership increased to 155 runs before Darling fell for 116. His big

*M. A. Noble, *The Game's the Thing*, Cassell & Co, p. 34.

hitting had been tremendous, carting Llewellyn five times for six, in an innings that lasted only 80 minutes. Noble batted on supremely, now partnered by Hopkins, and he too reached his hundred though he had, according to *Wisden*, "enjoyed some luck". Even so it was a skilful innings. The remaining batsmen fell easily to "Brownie" Hill's well-flighted and lively medium-fast bowling – they were all clean bowled.

Facing a deficit of 195 the Hampshire men obviously attempted to save the game, seeing that it was only to be a two-day match, and Major Poore dominated the innings. On going in first wicket down he carried out his bat for 62 runs. There was an interruption for

AUSTRALIANS *v* HAMPSHIRE

At Southampton, 7, 8 August.

Australians won by an innings and 79 runs.

HAMPSHIRE

Mr A. J. L. Hill b Saunders	15	c Hill b Saunders	5
A. W. Webb c Hopkins b Trumble	14	c and b Saunders	14
Major R. M. Poore c and b Noble	14	not out	62
Mr E. M. Sprot c Carter b Noble	33	run out	0
C. B. Llewellyn c Hopkins b Noble	2	c Hopkins b Trumble	4
V. A. Barton b Noble	0	b Trumble	6
Mr A. C. Johnston c Carter b Noble	5	b Trumble	0
Mr C. H. Bodington b Noble	0	lbw, b Trumble	1
*†Mr C. Robson b Trumble	17	b Trumble	12
T. Soar c Darling b Trumble	18	b Noble	2
Mr H. Hesketh-Prichard not out	5	lbw, b Trumble	0
Extras (B 4, LB 3)	7	(B 5, LB 5)	10
	130		116

AUSTRALIANS

V. T. Trumper c sub b Llewellyn	18	W. W. Armstrong b Hill	6
R. A. Duff c Sprot b Llewellyn	13	H. Trumble b Hill	2
C. Hill c Webb b Hesketh-Prichard	9	†H. Carter b Hill	0
*J. Darling c Sprot b Llewellyn	116	J. V. Saunders not out	9
S. E. Gregory c Hill b Hesketh-Prichard	9	Extras (B 6, LB 1, NB 1)	8
M. A. Noble st Robson b Llewellyn	113		
A. J. Hopkins b Hill	22		325

AUSTRALIANS	O.	M.	R.	W.	O.	M.	R.	W.		FALL OF WICKETS		
Trumble	23	3	53	3	28.4	10	52	6		*Hants.*	*Aus.*	*Hants.*
Saunders	10	1	37	1	24	9	33	2	*Wkt.*	*1st*	*1st*	*2nd*
Noble	12	4	33	6	4	0	21	1	1st	15	21	21
HAMPSHIRE									2nd	37	46	27
Llewellyn	22.1	2	129	4					3rd	66	48	32
Soar	8	1	34	0					4th	68	69	45
Barton	1	1	0	0					5th	68	224	60
Hesketh-									6th	78	266	62
Prichard	15	0	77	2					7th	78	293	68
Johnston	2	0	19	0					8th	93	295	98
Hill	12	1	43	4					9th	123	295	113
Bodington	1	0	15	0					10th	130	325	116

Umpires: A. Shaw and J. E. West

rain, but, far from helping the county to save the situation, it rendered assistance to Hughie Trumble. All, except Poore, fared ill with his mischievous deliveries, which earned him six wickets for 52 runs. So the Tourists won their remaining fixture before the last Test match by the healthy margin of an innings and 79 runs. They now had a complete rest from the toils of the cricket field with the pageantry and splendour of King Edward's Coronation the next day.

CHAPTER 13
Jessop's Match – The Fifth Test

It might appear, at a first glance, that there would be only academic interest in the fifth Test match at Kennington Oval. Australia had already won the rubber, and it could well be their intention to play for a draw. This, however, would have been against their avowed approach to cricket on the 1902 tour. But the cricketing public in general and English cricket in particular, although giving full credit to the Australians, were chagrined at the result of the rubber. They felt that England had been robbed of certain victory at Birmingham by rain and were convinced those same "elements" of misfortune had come to Australia's aid at Old Trafford. England by rights, they reasoned, should have been leading two games to one in the series. As English cricket pride was at stake, everybody hoped for a convincing win in this final encounter at The Oval.

Chastened by the spectre of Old Trafford before them, the Selection Committee, as the man in the street viewed it, saw reason at last by restoring Jessop and Hirst to favour in place of Ranji and the luckless Tate. Given a position for the first time in the series, although one of the original fourteen at Edgbaston, Tom Hayward replaced his Surrey colleague Abel.

After the excitement and tension of Manchester, nobody foresaw or was prepared for the remarkable struggle that ensued. In the event, the Oval Test developed into an even more exciting and tense contest, culminating in a last day so full of drama and suspense that many could not bear to watch and others were transfixed by the momentous struggle unfolding before their gaze. It was a long-drawn-out climax they were to remember for the rest of their lives, and it was one that cricket historians, by common consent, look back upon as one of the most dramatic Test matches of all time. But the result, a one-wicket victory for England, did so much to restore the confidence and self esteem of English cricket in the eyes of itself and its followers. They felt that justice had at last been done!

146

There had been much rain the previous day and Monday 11 August, though dry, seemed autumnal with a cold wind. The pitch, however, was rather slow but appeared to be in good condition. With the toss in his favour, Darling elected to bat first before the 12,000 brave souls attired in mackintoshes, scarves and overcoats – the customary dress for cricket in 1902! Their team was unchanged from Old Trafford. On an easy pitch Trumper and Duff commenced to go for the bowling off the opening attack of Lockwood and Rhodes, keeping pace with each other run for run. As usual Trumper's play was masterly. Hirst came on, proceeding to bowl as he had for Yorkshire at Headingley. Duff, however, pulled him right round to leg, a certain fourer. Dick Lilley, standing well back, leaped a yard or two to his left and, with outstretched hand, caught him with marvellous foresight. One down for forty-seven – first blood to Hirst and England.

Clem Hill took time to settle down and Trumper's run-rate dropped. Hill had most of the bowling until, with 11 to his name, Hirst's swerver was through him. Two down for sixty-three; the chilly crowd in overcoats applauding. With the English fielding very tight, Trumper opened his shoulders again, lifting the ball clear of the fielders' heads or finding the gaps. Lockwood, Rhodes, Hirst, Braund or Jackson: none seemed to trouble him. He played his strokes and was always looking for runs, but Jessop, cat-like, was cramping the off side so well that they were hard to come by in that direction. Attempting to do the same again to the ever dangerous Hirst, the great New South Welshman, essaying a pull drive to the on side, missed and was bowled. He had made 42 out of the 82 on the scoreboard. As the Australian captain Darling had fallen for a quiet 3 runs some 13 runs before, Australia had suddenly slumped to four down for 82. Noble and Gregory played cautiously until luncheon, slowly carrying the score to 107, but a few overs after the resumption, George Hirst – the bowler MacLaren had dropped at Manchester – on a still damp pitch clean bowled Syd Gregory. So the fifth wicket fell at 126 and all of them had been taken by George Herbert in a most convincing manner at a personal cost of 38 runs. By lunch the "Surrey Crowd" had nearly doubled – some 23,000 spectators now cheered their smiling Yorkshire hero. "We only need Noble's wicket now and the back of the Cornstalks' innings will be broken," was the general consensus of opinion.

By now Monty Noble had dug himself in and for all the bowling changes that were tried no one could shift him, not even Jessop. He compiled his runs carefully with the straightest of bats, taking no chances whatever, and Armstrong at the other end was even more painstaking. Hirst was still bowling in superlative style, making them play the ball, at times causing hurried strokes, even beating

147

them, but he could not break through their cast-iron defence. In this fashion their partnership added 48 careful runs until Jackson suddenly had both of them. Armstrong was bowled for 17 and Noble gave an easy return catch to end a sound and solid innings of 52, which had been invaluable to the Tourists at a time of crisis. It was not the kind of innings that Noble enjoyed playing but it was the necessity of the hour.

With seven gone for 175 Australia still had their backs to the wall. Hopkins and Hugh Trumble now came to the rescue, the former batting in good style and the latter enjoying a charmed life. When Trumble had made nine Dick Lilley dropped him, and the tall Victorian went on to be top scorer with an undefeated 64 runs after undergoing a remarkable series of lucky escapes. Nevertheless, Hughie Trumble was to earn his "tucker". Meanwhile, Hopkins fell for 40 to be eighth out at 256, then Kelly joined the fray and slowly totted up 39 runs before he was out to Braund only ten minutes before the drawing of stumps was due. However, in the same over and without the addition of a run, Saunders was neatly disposed of. Australia had managed to stay at the wickets all day and thus put themselves in a commanding position with 324 runs (though at one time it looked as if they would be lucky to get 200) and with two days left could hardly lose. They were criticised for the dilatoriness of their play, but, to be fair to them, Hirst's bowling caused them much difficulty and Jessop must have saved at least thirty runs alone on the off side. An amusing sidelight was Trumble's jesting at the ever alert Gloucester captain, "Come on, two, it's only Jessop," although he had no intention of attempting a run. He knew better!

England's luck, as seemed inevitable in 1902, was out once more. The real enemy fell in "buckets full" during the early hours of Tuesday morning. The rain was certainly enough to make a great difference to the pitch, and when MacLaren and Palairet came out to bat they were additionally handicapped by poor light, so much so that after some half-dozen overs they appealed against it and came in. This cost them forty valuable minutes' playing time. With the turf playing very awkwardly and giving considerable assistance to the bowlers, MacLaren, using his skill to the utmost, took fifty minutes to score ten runs; Palairet managed a little better. Exploiting the wet pitch to the full, Hugh Trumble, bowling his medium-paced off-breaks from round the wicket with four or five men on the leg side, was hoping for catches or leg before decisions. It was no surprise to the silent crowd when "Archie Mac", playing back as one came in to him, cocked it up to Armstrong at short leg. 31 for 1! Tyldesley came in and settled immediately to the pace of the wet surface and the pitch of the ball, but Palairet was soon bowled by the crafty Trumble. 36 for 2! Now accompanied by a near strokeless and uneasy Hayward, Johnny Tyldesley managed to keep pushing the score along, and the next twenty-six runs from the bat came from his alone. Australia's fielding was absolutely splendid in backing up the bowlers, Trumble at times making the ball lift awkwardly on the difficult turf, but Tyldesley hit anything he felt it safe to do so. After twenty minutes the scoreless Hayward was bowled by Trumble. 62 for 3, and the spectators grim and silent. Perhaps "Jacker" can stay with the admirable run-getting Tyldesley, they thought. Five more were posted on the scoreboard, two of them to Jackson, when Tyldesley faced Trumble and was clean bowled for 33 runs. Four wickets had now fallen, all taken by the devastating Trumble, when, without any further addition to the score, Saunders struck. Deceived by the pitch, Jackson was snapped up by Armstrong in the leg trap. Five wickets lost for only 67 runs – the Oval crowd were thunderstruck at the turn of events. It seemed the old, old story – England caught on a rain-damaged pitch with her premier batting failing once more.

The sun was struggling to break through the heavy clouds and a chilly wind had been blowing all morning. The slowly drying pitch, getting even more difficult as time wore on, would soon become disastrous for the batsmen. Jessop had joined Braund, Trumble and Saunders bowled on and on, and Jessopus decided to go for the bowling while runs were to be had at all. With bated breath the crowd watched him hammer Saunders, then turn his attention to the cunning Trumble's off-breaks, which were simply asking for it. His game was a calculated risk: he was hitting across the line of those off-breaks with his "cow shot", which depended so much on his eye to spot any variation in flight or pitch. In just eight minutes his score reached 13 when, chancing eye and bat across another one, he played too soon and was bowled. With six wickets down for 83 runs, it seemed certain now that England would have to follow on and their chances, with the luncheon interval almost upon them and the sun's warmth being felt, would be very slim indeed.

The pre-lunch session had furnished a morning of absorbing cricket, provided one could remain impartial, although only 94 runs had been scored. It had been a long, uphill struggle against capital bowling on a pitch that was becoming stickier than ever, backed up by alert and zestful fielding – it would be worse after lunch if the sun kept shining! "Cometh the hour, cometh the man", for whilst Braund defended as best he could getting behind the turning ball, George Hirst took upon himself the mantle of England's saviour. Setting out to attack Saunders and knock him off his length, he succeeded admirably with a succession of fierce pulls in removing him temporarily from the attack. In the next 45 minutes with free hitting he scored (with the aid of six fours and five threes) 43 runs out of the 54 added by the partnership, before falling to a hard caught and bowled off the ever steady Trumble. Seven were now out for 137 and still 38 runs were needed to avoid the follow-on. During this innings Len Braund had been beaten time and again by Trumble, balls shaving the stumps by the proverbial coat of varnish, but somehow he held on, continuing to do so when Lockwood joined him. Taking over the departed Hirst's role, Lockwood proceeded to have a go at the Australian bowling.

With some lusty hitting he reached 11, then, in going for another hard drive, Clem Hill at long-on badly missed him, so fluffing the chance of forcing the Englishmen to go in again. Nineteen runs were still needed for England to be safe. Lockwood and Braund battled on until the latter, after he had been at the wicket for an hour and a half with 22 hard-fought runs, hit a catch to Hill, who made no mistake this time. But the follow-on had now been saved and the English players were greatly relieved. Jessop, however, felt as thankful as if England had already won. The innings finally closed at 183, which happened to be considerably better than had seemed possible at lunch. Trumble and Saunders had bowled admirably, Hughie Trumble, in particular, earning his "tucker" for a second time. Always scheming how to get the Englishmen out, always dangerous and ever steady under punishment, he had the well deserved analysis of 8 wickets for 65 runs.

Commenting on the England innings and the weather conditions attendant on it, Gilbert Jessop remarks, "That overnight rain, though seemingly spoiling our prospects . . . was the one thing that made a definite issue of the match possible . . . if the wicket on the second morning had not been damaged by rain, it was highly probable that England would have occupied the wickets too long to have possessed much hope of dismissing Australia on the defensive in time to snatch a win."*

Comforted by so healthy a lead as 141, the Australians, when they entered the fray for the second time at 3.45, looked well set on the road to victory. The pitch was still soft and damp and, in the very first over, delivered by Rhodes, Duff was nearly caught. Hirst at mid-off tried to take the ball too close to his face — to his annoyance he dropped it. Now it was Lockwood's turn. Trumper was facing him, as always looking for runs. Playing a ball in the direction of cover point, he started to run. Duff shouted as he saw it going in Jessop's direction, refusing the call. By now in the middle of the pitch, Victor turned but slipped as· he tried to regain his crease. Jessop had acted with the speed of light in gathering the red missile and returning it to Lilley, who broke the wicket with Trumper still sitting on the ground yards from his crease. It was a turning-point for England in removing the great Trumper so

*G. L. Jessop, *A Cricketer's Log*, Hodder & Stoughton, p. 195.

cheaply; he had made 2 and the score was 6. This was the sort of thing that MacLaren always hoped for from Jessopus, and it had come off. He had run out Trumper for him! It was the Gloucester captain's reputation that had caused Duff's refusal and the resulting run out.

Reg Duff did not last much longer: with the scoreboard showing 9, Lockwood forced him to play on to his wicket. Darling joined a rather restrained Hill. It soon became obvious that the Australian captain was not going to force matters, he would have been foolish to do so after losing Trumper and Duff so cheaply, and, with the possibility of more rain, time was going to be just as important as run-getting. Lockwood and Rhodes bowled accurately and well, but the batsmen, though having difficulty in getting the ball away through the field, could probably have been more offensive in their methods if they had so wished. At 31 Bill Lockwood struck again, MacLaren holding a mishit from Joe Darling playing back. The Oval crowd found its voice.

With Noble settling himself in well MacLaren threw the ball to Braund. He knew of Monty Noble's dislike of the delivery pitched up on the leg stump that Braund disguised so well. With "Mary Ann" forced even more on the defensive, he was bowled off his pads by a ball he did not attempt to play. Four down for 71, with the ring becoming more excited at the England fight-back. Hill was steadiness itself, curbing his normal overwhelming desire to have a go at the bowling. He kept himself in check, realising that so much depended upon him remaining the sheet-anchor of the innings. Four more runs were added, Hirst having relieved Lockwood. Hill faced him and went to late cut the "away going" ball, getting right over it and playing it low down. Archie MacLaren pounced from first slip with rare premonition to take a marvellous one-handed catch only inches from the turf. Once more an incredulous Hill had to vacate the crease to delighted shouts from the massed spectators. Five down for seventy-five seemed unbelievable. But Hill had made 34 of them, taking an hour and thirty-five minutes to do so.

Armstrong now joined Gregory. He had his own methods of playing Braund's leg-breaks – he used his leg-guards. This brought forth ironic cheers from the concourse round the ring, but it was effective where time consumption was paramount. The runs had come very slowly, almost as an afterthought, but the bowling and fielding was very tight and nothing was being given away. Soon Braund had one through Syd Gregory's defence – 91 for 6 – and Lockwood, returning to the attack like a giant refreshed, was too fast for Hopkins, who was taken by Lilley standing well back. For the throng ranged around the Oval ground, it seemed incredible that the might of the Tourists had been humbled to seven dismissed for ninety-nine. Promoted in the batting order, Saunders joined the

151

solid and defensive Armstrong. Fifteen runs were slowly accumulated, mostly from Warwick Armstrong's broad bat. Saunders had made two when, facing Rhodes, he tried a big hit over the bowler's head, but Tyldesley, running full tilt from long-on, took a spectacular catch one-handed to reduce Australia to 114 for 8.

It was now time for drawing stumps, and Australia had consumed some two and three-quarter hours in getting those runs. Even in view of the conditions it was desperately slow going. Australia were 255 runs on with two wickets still in hand, and the prospects were very much in their favour. But perhaps England had an outside chance, if only they could remove the last two wickets cheaply and the weather remained fine. In the summer of 1902, it was a very big "if"!

The evening sky was clear, but Jessop relates how, on sitting down to dinner at The Great Central Hotel with some of his colleagues, they heard the familiar "pitter-patter". The heavens opened and the rain torrented down. Wednesday 13 August, however, dawned fine, though Kennington Oval was very wet, and it was nothing short of a miracle that play was possible before lunch. It says much for the absorbent properties of the Oval turf and the sterling work performed by Sam Apted and his groundstaff. But it was quite clear the pitch was totally unfavourable to the bat, suspicions of which were soon confirmed when the Australians resumed their second innings. The remaining two wickets did not last long, for Lockwood, somehow managing to keep his feet on the saturated turf, quickly removed Armstrong and Kelly for the paltry addition of 7 runs. All things considered, Bill Lockwood bowled superbly, having taken 5 wickets for 45 runs. With Australia all out for 121, this left England requiring 263 runs to win the match.

Few, if any, of the players on either side thought England would be lucky enough to reach three figures, let alone the formidable total required. Having to face Trumble, Saunders, Noble and Armstrong on a pitch that was turning quickly and on which the ball would get up abruptly to awkward heights, was hardly conducive to tranquil run-getting. Furthermore, it had been cut up badly by the previous day's play on it while still wet.

The Australians scented success from the opening ball of the innings. Trumble and Saunders bowled as men possessed and, on that pitch, the England batsmen were on the rack. MacLaren was the first to go with only 5 runs on the board; he played a defensive stroke to Saunders and stopped the ball – only to see it roll on to his wicket. Tyldesley entered, to be met immediately with a venomous turning one from the left-handed Victorian which crashed into his stumps. At 10, Saunders cleverly bowled Palairet in much the same way, but the ball this time after breaking the wicket beat Kelly, hitting him in the face. It took a few minutes for that worthy to be revived. Hardly ten minutes had elapsed and once more England had made a terrible start – 3 down for 10 runs. The far-famed "Surrey Crowd" felt a complete sense of hopelessness, and wondered if it would be all over by lunch. Their hopes, raised a little by the confident looking Jackson, were hardly buoyed up by an uneasy Hayward, who was very lucky to be dropped by Gregory at short leg off Trumble's bowling at 16. Slowly they lifted the total to 28 under a darkening sky when a shower drove them into the pavilion. Play was stopped for thirty-five minutes, and when Saunders resumed bowling he had Tom Hayward caught at the wicket from another vicious turner. Woe to England – 4 down for 31 and all of them taken by the triumphant Saunders at a cost of 9 runs.

Jackson had his eye in and was dealing with the difficult turning balls in his usual imperturbable manner, while Braund settled himself in carefully. It was a watching and waiting game: watching the popping red leather onto the bat and waiting for the short pitch or long-hop to punish. Not many came. It took a long while to add another seventeen runs, mostly from "Jacker's" straight bat. Now Trumble struck. Braund, playing back to the rising off-break, streakily put the ball behind him where Kelly somehow managed to clasp it to his body. The fifth wicket had fallen at 48. Half of the England side had gone, defeated by the treacherous pitch and the ability of two superb bowlers who were making the most of it. No wonder Darling saw no reason to change them. Few, if any, present thought the outstanding 215 runs could ever be obtained – the very idea was laughable!

It was now ten minutes past one, and there were still twenty minutes to go before lunch. The Hon. F. S. Jackson was playing admirably with 31 runs behind him. If only somebody could stay with him; it might well rain again and perhaps England could make a draw of it. The chilly and rather despondent spectators now saw Gilbert Jessop making his way out to the wicket, hoping against hope that he would bat with the care and mastery he had shown at Sheffield, although they would dearly love to see him knock the Tourists' bowling about. He started from the first ball he received, a healthy cracking single off Trumble. The next three balls from Saunders were dispatched with alacrity and some force for two, four and one respectively. Then a single through the on-side field off Trumble. He had scored nine from the initial five balls he had faced, all scoring strokes. The crowd noted how confident he looked. Now another over from Hughie Trumble, bowling round the wicket: two deliveries were played firmly back, then Jessop sprang down the pitch with a huge swing of the bat to loft Trumble high over his head right onto the pavilion awning – four runs! Cheers broke forth, nervous cheers; could he keep this up? But yes, the very next ball was walloped to the rails with a sure certainty of power and timing.

The spectators were in a frenzy of excitement as the very next ball he played deliberately into the on side for yet another single. Jessop was, for Jessop, being very careful. He was determined not to be greedily tempted into pulling the artful Hughie Trumble's off-breaks that were coming in to him, and although they were simply asking for it he contented himself with singles.

In the next over he faced Saunders, and the second ball was lustily driven for four to bring him up to 22. The fielders, who had been so smart and prophetic until Jessop came in, were just not certain where he was going to hit the ball, and so it was often through their defensive arc before they knew it. Putting all caution to the winds the Gloucester captain now sprang down the wicket with the apparent intention of hitting Saunders out of the ground, but he missed. The ball kept low and Kelly, most likely overawed by the sheer cheek of it, missed it too. A let-off, and the spectators sighed with relief; if only he would be more careful. "He'll throw his wicket away and we'll lose the match! That's for sure." But no – after another single from one of Trumble's off-breaks, he greeted his next ball from Saunders with a magnificent off-drive for four high over Armstrong at cover point. Now on 27, Jessopus hit Saunders again very hard and Trumper, dashing in full pelt, just got his hand to it as it swerved away from him at long-off. A palpable chance, but few fielders other than Trumper would have even got near it. With luncheon looming, Jessop took another single from Trumble.

In those twenty minutes, 39 runs had been put on – 29 from Jessopus, 8 from Jackson and two extras. The score had risen to 87 for 5 and both batsmen had played superbly, but the talk amongst the lunchtime crowds was of the "Croucher". Could he possibly keep up this terrific hitting, especially on such a pitch so favourable to the bowlers? If he could, with "Jacker" to stay with him and still Hirst, Lockwood, Lilley and Rhodes to come, it might barely be an outside possibility that they could get those 176 runs to win.

The Australians were returning to the field of play quite certain they would soon account for Jessop – he would probably get himself out – then they would have time and runs enough to account for the rest. A contingent of New South Wales Lancers, over for the Coronation and sitting just in front of the press box, "cooee-ing" the England players, were fairly vociferous in their opinions. "All over by tea," they said, and their views of the "Croucher" were far from flattering. But before the large crowd, which had swollen to some 18,000 souls (news had travelled quickly that Jessop was on the kill) the England pair came out from the pavilion gate: Jackson – tall, erect, with upturned moustache and wearing a scarf around his throat with all the nonchalance of a cavalry officer, then Gilbert Jessop – a well-built, compact figure with the light of battle in those blue-grey eyes darting hither and yon beneath the large Gloucestershire cap, jauntily swinging his bat from the thick wrist of a sinewy, muscular forearm.

The warmth of the sun was making itself felt as each batsman opened his after-luncheon account with a single. The pitch, apparently a trifle easier now, was still damp and worn enough for the ball to turn and lift. Another run to Jessop, then, in the next over, he late-cut Trumble for four so swiftly along the turf that the slips could only stand and stare. Hugh's next delivery yielded a single to the on side, Jessop stifling his greed once more, then four byes and the hundred was up on the telegraph in just 80 minutes from the commencement of England's innings. All things considered, it was good going after the appalling start. Now Trumble, although suffering at the Gloucester captain's hands, was bowling as craftily as ever and, pitching them shorter and shorter, was making Jackson play and miss. A single to Jessop (the field were well spread out to him now) then Trumble beat "Jacker" all ends up.

Although still treating Trumble with a certain amount of respect, Jessopus had little for Saunders. The Victorian's suspect action had no terrors for him: a drive past long off yielded three runs, it would have been four had the outfield not been so wet, then a single. Jackson was faltering, and the crowd died a thousand deaths as he snicked one behind. Kelly got a hand to it but it fell just out of Trumble's reach in the slips. In Hugh Trumble's next over Jessopus raised the crowd's blood-pressure, first with a three then, after a single from "Jacker", a most ferocious cut through the slips to the distant corner of the Vauxhall end. Frenzied with delight at Jessop's fireworks the spectators cheered themselves hoarse as five runs were rushed at break-neck speed. With a single off the next ball he received Jessopus reached his fifty, made out of 70 added since he came in – it had taken just 43 minutes! Playing with a perfection of judgement and timing he was in absolute command of the bowling, which, by now, was showing signs of wilting under the onslaught of his brilliant attack:

> "At one end stocky Jessop frowned,
> The human catapult,
> Who wrecks the roofs of distant towns
> When set in his assault."*

Acknowledging the cheers from the crowd, which had increased to 22,000, he cut Saunders off the middle stump, beautifully square, from the next ball delivered to him. Again the field of Cornstalks did not see it leave the bat. The following two balls he played

*Verse from poem by Ralph D. Paine (1897).

quietly. Trumble was bowling to a sorely tried Jackson again. He was beaten by a beauty and immediately missed by Armstrong in the slips; it was an over that must have seemed a nightmare for the Yorkshire amateur. If Saunders had already been mauled by the "Human Catapult", he was now slashed to ribbons – the next over yielded 17 runs! With his hands rapidly clasping and unclasping the bat handle in his crouching position as Saunders ran slantwise in, Jessop was down on his left knee sweeping the ball to the square leg boundary through a paralysed field. Hardly had the cheering died as Saunders ran in again. Jessopus leapt out of his crease and pulled him fiercely round to leg for a second four. By now completely dominated, Saunders bowled a full toss which the Gloucester captain gloriously mowed out of sight over the ring at square leg. His fourth ball was a half volley – majestically Jessopus pulled it to the square leg boundary again. The fielders were in a turmoil at this onslaught. They just did not know where to stand in a desperate attempt to intercept those devastating field-piercing hits. Saunders' fifth ball was driven hard to the off and yielded a single. Four fourers and a single from successive deliveries: no wonder there was a tumult of cheers and applause. "This was Jessop on the kill, all right," laughed the excited spectators. Saunders' analysis now evoked a sorry sight: 4–75!

The "Human Catapult" had pillaged 71 runs. He took another run from Trumble and the telegraph read 145 when Darling, taking pity on Saunders, replaced him with Armstrong at the Vauxhall end. Immediately, Armstrong requested five men on the leg-side boundary. For his first over the awkward leg-rollers, bowled outside the leg stump, staunched the flow of runs, but Jessop took a single from the last ball. Then with a two off Trumble he reached 75, and the partnership was worth 100 exactly. His stay at the crease so far was only 57 minutes. Armstrong was bowling to him again, but Jessopus had his answer to the packed leg field. Stepping back he cut him to the empty off side for four runs. Three balls later, with a hefty smack he placed Armstrong through his own leg boundary ring for yet another fourer – how the crowds yelled to relieve their tense nerves.

The partnership had put on 109 runs, and the telegraph read 157 for 6 with Jackson 49 and Jessop 83. They had been together for 67 minutes in this sensational fight-back, and while Jessopus was decimating the Tourists' attack and treating it as if it were "village green stuff", "Jacker", who had been so steady in the morning, was ill at ease. Morally, Hugh Trumble had defeated him many times before he put one back straight into the bowler's capacious hands. The time was two minutes past three. The broad, smiling figure of George Hirst, ever a favourite with the crowd, survived a confident LBW appeal from Trumble immediately on arrival at the wicket.

Both Fry and E. M. Dowson, who were sitting on the pavilion balcony pretty well behind the bowler's arm, were uncomfortable about it, but Trumble picked up the ball without any apparent discontent at the umpire's decision. Jessop was as horrified as the spectators when the ball struck George on his pad.

But George Hirst did not turn a hair. He lustily pulled Armstrong for two fours, then Jessop took a single. Trumble was still bowling his crafty medium-paced off-breaks round the wicket from the pavilion end, but Jessop proceeded to mete out the same treatment to him that he had previously given to Saunders. A straight drive into the pavilion balcony – for which he was only accredited with four runs – a hit for two, a second two and then another cracking hit, driven straight, to the top of the pavilion again – to be "fielded" by the Worcester captain Harry Foster! Pandemonium reigned around the ring at such hurricane hitting. Twelve runs had come off that over and Jessop's score was 96. From the very next ball, off Armstrong, he reached his century with a beautiful late cut. It was now ten minutes past three – it had taken him just 75 minutes. The applause that greeted Jessop had to be heard to be believed. Hats were thrown in the air; scarves, umbrellas and walking-sticks were waved; and spectators cheered in a tumult of excitement. Unfortunately, this must have upset Jessop's concentration, for, after another sweep to the square leg boundary, he tried to sweep again off the last ball of Armstrong's over only to give Noble an easy catch at short leg. Having scored 104 out of the 139 runs added whilst he was at the wicket in 77 minutes, Jessop had performed the fastest century in Anglo-Australian Test cricket, a record which still endures.

As he returned to the pavilion he was given another remarkable ovation from the ring. The Australian players, too, applauded him in a most warm and hearty fashion in genuine admiration of the kind of innings they would witness but once in a lifetime. But for Jessopus, and the kind of innings that he could play, this effort he referred to as being "restrained". It must be recalled that it was performed on very much a bowler's pitch and at a very critical stage of a Test match. George Hirst, who watched the closing stages of that innings at close hand, says, "It was a great treat to me watching their bowlers' faces change with wonder and consternation in their efforts to try and block his shots by changing the field."[*] Dick Lilley, viewing from the pavilion, said, "The odds against him were practically unlimited. Although he scored at such a tremendous pace, it was the result of magnificent batting . . . His timing and placing were simply perfect, and he hit the bowling mercilessly to all parts of the field."[†] Charles Fry comments, "Jessop let

[*]C. J. Britton, *G. L. Jessop*, Cornish Brothers Ltd, p. 125.
[†]A. A. Lilley, *Twenty-Four Years of Cricket*, Mills & Boon, p. 126 (abridged).

himself loose like a catapult at the bowling and scattered it to smithereens. If ever an innings ought to have been filmed, that was the one."*

After seeing this exciting innings which had so transformed the game, the large crowd realised, as Joe Darling and his team must have done, that England at 187 for 7 wickets could now possibly win. It was still an outside chance – 76 runs were still needed. The Australians would do their level best to deny them. Their fieldsmen moved back to closer positions to frustrate the remaining batsmen, and their bowlers bowled with hope renewed. Lockwood was now partnering Hirst, and Hirst had taken on Jessop's mantle, pulling Saunders to the leg boundary and off-driving him for another four to post 200 on the scoreboard. Again the applause from inside the crowded Oval was tremendous as the batsmen bent to their task once more. Hirst kept the telegraph ticking over when, at 214, Lockwood put his leg in front to Trumble. Forty-nine runs still to get and only two wickets to fall. Lilley came in and scored two. Bustling for runs as he was wont to do, he very nearly played Saunders on to his wicket at 219, and at 222 Trumble, bowling round the wicket almost from the very edge of the crease to make his off-break as awkward as possible, nearly caught and bowled him. The fielders strained every nerve and muscle to save runs. Noble threw himself full length in a desperate attempt, and Darling's stopping was little short of miraculous, but somehow Lilley and Hirst punctured the tight, constrictive ring.

To shouts of "Play up England!" Lilley hit a fourer and Hirst, with complete equanimity, raised the 230 on the board with a solid looking square cut for four off Saunders. Three singles were added, then another four from Hirst. Overwrought members of the crowd could scarcely bear to watch for fear of seeing a wicket fall – some, unable to endure the extreme tension in the electric atmosphere, fainted. One spectator was reported to have gnawed the handle of his umbrella, and another kept wrapping up his gloves methodically in his scorecard! Lilley, still bustling for runs and wanting to get it over and done with, drove Trumble for four to pass the 240. More cheers, hats, umbrellas, and arms waved, then a tight-lipped silence as the grim and hard-drawn-faced Australians settled themselves in the field once more. They were paying in full measure for their lost chances now.

Stern, phlegmatic even, in defence, George Hirst was taking no chances, scoring only when he was certain it was safe to do so. The strain between each ball, with Hirst unconcernedly patting the turf with his bat, was becoming unbearable for the suffering crowd. England had reached 248 – fifteen runs to win – when Dick Lilley,

*C. B. Fry, *Life Worth Living*, Eyre & Spottiswoode, p. 235.

over-eager to punish a half volley from Trumble, clouted it hard in the direction of deep mid-off. But instead of it trimming the turf as he had intended, the ball lifted sufficiently for Joe Darling to throw himself at it to take a splendid catch. Thus ended an invaluable innings. Lilley had helped Hirst to add 34 priceless runs. But the fear of another Old Trafford finish was now uppermost in the spectators' minds. The prospect of being so near yet so far from victory, and the thought that the slender thread upon which it depended could be sundered by just one delivery: the ideas made strong men weak. Even more could not bear to watch; some, in helpless agony, left the ground.

England's last man and sole remaining hope, Wilfred Rhodes, was a man of proven ability in such a tense situation. Bred in a nursery of stern cricket, his Yorkshire background had stood him in good stead in many a tight corner of a Roses match. He was about to join at the wicket his friend, county colleague and fellow-Kirkheatonian. There is little doubt that both of them knew they would stay there until victory was secure; they had a job to do and they would see it through. "Fifteen runs to get and two Yorkshiremen to do it!"

In an atmosphere of indescribable tension Rhodes faced the last ball of Trumble's over; he played it back coolly. Noble was bowling from the Vauxhall end and Hirst played a single off the first ball to reach his 50, which had come in the surprisingly quick time of 65 minutes. An hysterical outburst of cheering greeted this, whilst the Australians grimly reset themselves for Rhodes. Noble's handsome features bore an enigmatic look as he walked back to his mark, planning and scheming Rhodes' downfall. It nearly worked—Rhodes got an edge, but the ball went through the slips for four runs. Ten to win, calculated the spectators, as white-faced and worried they settled again – not even daring to breathe in case they put the batsmen off. Before Noble's over ended Rhodes again played uppishly through the slips, Armstrong got a hand to it, but he was off balance and the ball fell from his grasp. Repeated incidents of this kind were enough to cause heart-attacks in the most placid of men round the ring.

The suffering spectators watched George Hirst, with time and in an anxiety consuming manner, go through the motions of drawing his hands first up one padded leg then the other before settling himself to receive each ball. From Trumble's next over, he placed the first delivery neatly to leg and they ran a single. Rhodes had the rest of the over to deal with, nearly giving Trumble's grasping hands a return catch from one delivery. Noble again, and Hirst took one run from the first ball, Rhodes once more playing out the rest of the over. It was ten minutes past four; the sun had gone, the sky had completely clouded over. Eight runs to get as Trumble commenced

159

his thirty-third over of the innings. A single from Hirst, a single to the off by Rhodes, then another single by Hirst, but a hectic overthrow enabled them to run a second. Amid cheers the throw-in hit Hirst smartly on the shoulder and he laughed good-humouredly. The faces of the Australians showed desperation. From the last delivery Hirst deliberately played another firm single to keep the bowling; it started to drizzle.

Two to tie and three to win! Would the rain keep off? The nervous exhaustion of the crowd was almost complete as the anxious minutes, seeming like hours, passed, as Noble bowled to Hirst amid the crowding field of straining, tight-lipped Australians. Calmly dealing with each of the first five deliveries, the solid, reassuring figure of George Hirst was seen playing the last ball through the gap. Another single – one to tie; he kept the bowling. Desperately the field crept closer amid a deathly silence. This was Australia's last chance as Trumble ran up to the wicket – but Hirst came forward and pushed the ball sturdily between the bowler and mid-off. Rhodes, backing up his county comrade well, had made the crease at the Vauxhall end. A tie! "We can't lose now!" Pandemonium reigned: howls, cheers and yells! Quite beside himself, a parson dashed howling onto the pitch. Hirst smiled, Rhodes permitted himself a grin, even Noble was able to laugh, but Clem Hill stood at long-on, eyes downcast with despair. Under a darkening sky the game continued. Rhodes, not to be tempted, played the next three balls with care and determination. Trumble paused before his fifth ball, rubbed it in the sawdust pile again and bowled. Coming forward, Rhodes crisply drove it between Trumble and Duff at mid-on. He ran, and went on running for the shelter of the pavilion.

England had won at last. The vast concourse of spectators erupted onto the pitch and surged round the scurrying players as they too ran pavilionwards. George Hirst, caught up in the mêlée, was carried, like the hero he was, for the last few yards. In a pressing throng they gathered in front of the Oval pavilion, and shouted and cheered for the players. The pent-up emotions of the followers of English cricket were loosened from the straining bonds of nerve-wrack of the past few hours. They simply laughed, waved, cheered and yelled in the drizzling rain. They shouted for Jessop; they called for Hirst; they "hurrahed" for every one, until the ever present enemy – rain – drove them home. They were happy; English cricket had been completely vindicated.

The Australians took their defeat gallantly, congratulating the England players, and Gilbert Jessop most warmly of all. As Hugh Trumble said, "The only man living who could beat us, beat us." Jessopus. Gerald Brodribb summed it up admirably in his biography of Jessop. "There is no doubt," he commented, "that Wednesday, August 13th, 1902, must count as one of the greatest days in the

ENGLAND *v* AUSTRALIA

(5th TEST)

At Kennington Oval, 11, 12, 13 August.
England won by 1 wicket.

AUSTRALIA

V. T. Trumper b Hirst	42	run out	2
R. A. Duff c Lilley b Hirst	23	b Lockwood	6
C. Hill b Hirst	11	c MacLaren b Hirst	34
*J. Darling c Lilley b Hirst	3	c MacLaren b Lockwood ...	15
M. A. Noble c and b Jackson	52	b Braund	13
S. E. Gregory b Hirst	23	b Braund	9
W. W. Armstrong b Jackson	17	b Lockwood	21
A. J. Hopkins c MacLaren b Lockwood	40	c Lilley b Lockwood	3
H. Trumble not out	64	(10) not out	7
†J. J. Kelly c Rhodes b Braund	39	(11) lbw, b Lockwood	0
J. V. Saunders lbw, b Braund	0	(9) c Tyldesley b Rhodes	2
Extras (B 5, LB 3, NB 2)	10	(B 7, LB 2)	9
	324		**121**

ENGLAND

*Mr A. C. MacLaren c Armstrong b Trumble ...	10	b Saunders	2
Mr L. C. H. Palairet b Trumble	20	b Saunders	6
J. T. Tyldesley b Trumble	33	b Saunders	0
T. Hayward b Trumble	0	c Kelly b Saunders	7
Hon. F. S. Jackson c Armstrong b Saunders	2	c and b Trumble	49
L. C. Braund c Hill b Trumble	22	c Kelly b Trumble	2
Mr G. L. Jessop b Trumble	13	c Noble b Armstrong	104
G. H. Hirst c and b Trumble	43	not out	58
W. H. Lockwood c Noble b Saunders	25	lbw, b Trumble	2
†A. A. Lilley c Trumper b Trumble	0	c Darling b Trumble	16
W. Rhodes not out	0	not out	6
Extras (B 13, LB 2)	15	(B 5, LB 6)	11
	183	(9 wkts)	**263**

ENGLAND	O.	M.	R.	W.	O.	M.	R.	W.
Lockwood	24	2	85	1	20	6	45	5
Rhodes	28	9	46	0	22	7	38	1
Hirst	29	5	77	5	5	1	7	1
Braund	16.5	5	29	2	9	1	15	2
Jackson	20	4	66	2	4	3	7	0
Jessop	6	2	11	0				
AUSTRALIA								
Trumble	31	13	65	8	33.5	4	108	4
Saunders	23	7	79	2	24	3	105	4
Noble	7	3	24	0	5	0	11	0
Armstrong					4	0	28	1

FALL OF WICKETS

Wkt.	Aus. 1st	Eng. 1st	Aus. 2nd	Eng. 2nd
1st	47	31	6	5
2nd	63	36	9	5
3rd	69	62	31	10
4th	82	67	71	31
5th	126	67	75	48
6th	174	83	91	157
7th	175	137	99	187
8th	256	179	114	214
9th	324	183	115	248
10th	324	183	121	—

Umpires: C. E. Richardson and A. White

history of cricket. So England beat the Australians, and, for the first time in the series, also beat the rain."*(See p. 162.)

> "With Trumble trounced into the pavilion
> (Poor Saunders had suffered the same)
> The crowd roared hoarse-voiced like a million
> At the 'Croucher's' hurricane game.

"Fifteen to win as Rhodes strode to the wicket
Said George Hirst 'come do as thy're bid,
'Let's get them in singles, safe cricket,'
And get them they certainly did.

"It was Rhodes' single for victory – a neat'un,
To restore England's lost health, life and fame,
Now the Cornstalks knew they were beaten,
Just in time, for down came the rain!"

*G. Brodribb, *The Croucher*, London Magazines Editions, p. 19.

CHAPTER 14

Darling's Darlings – Five Wins in a Row

The Australians were not too disappointed at the loss of the fifth Test match – they already had the satisfaction of having won the rubber. Joe Darling was astute enough to realise that all the luck of the elements had been on their side, and that had the summer been drier, the boot might have been on the other foot!

After the excitement and nervous tension of the cliffhanger they had been engaged in during the past three days, some rest and relief from the continual round of cricket would have been welcome. Their fixture card, however, did not allow for this for on the morrow, Thursday 14 August, the Tourists were due to appear at Lord's to try conclusions with a team entitled "M C C and Ground". In the event, their opponents were none too strong even though it was captained by A. P. Lucas and sported the names of Ranji, "Sailor" Young, Walter Mead and Harry Carpenter of Essex.

Perhaps it was not surprising that the game was something of an anti-climax, but even so there was some good cricket. After the rain of the previous evening Lucas won a toss he would have preferred to lose as he could not chance putting the Tourists in to bat. Mr W. Findlay, the Oxford vice-captain and eventual successor to Sir Francis Lacey as Secretary of MCC, had the pleasure of opening their innings with Carpenter, and both fell immediately to Bill Howell, making a welcome return to the attack. The Middlesex amateur and former Etonian Mr H. B. Chinnery played a sound innings of 37 assisting first Thompson, the Northants all-rounder, and Ranjitsinhji. The latter had regained his form in grand style with 60 runs before he "brought his innings to an inglorious conclusion",* being caught by Duff from one of Armstrong's leg-rollers. On the damp pitch M C C did reasonably well to score as many as 212. Howell's six wickets were taken at an average of 17.50 runs apiece in forty overs.

*Wisden, 1903, p. 285.

Trumper and Duff started in their usual brilliant fashion, but both were quickly out the following morning; then, with Darling clean bowled by "Sailor" Young, the Cornstalks were suddenly 3 down for 102. Hill, playing carefully but always looking for runs, was joined by Noble. Before long they had the upper hand of the bowling, Monty Noble indeed batting in his most attractive manner. Untroubled by the bowling changes, he soon had 70 runs to his account, and, when looking well set for his century, he fell to the fast medium pace of Thompson. Hill, too, had hit splendidly all round the wicket but seemed to be troubled sorely between 60 and 70. Fortunately for him, he recovered his batting composure and, now partnered by Syd Gregory, scoring in ebullient mood, Clem reached 136, his highest score and his fourth hundred of the tour. The Cornstalks were 349 for 5 and Gregory performed in his brightest vein, producing some of the best cricket he had so far played this season. He, too, seemed certain to reach the three figure score that had so far been eluding him; alas, Mead caused him to put a leg in front for 86. The innings closed at 427, M C C having tried the abilities of eight men with the leather.

Chasing 215 runs to make the Australians bat again, the laconic Carpenter batted stubbornly and with great patience, whilst his M C C colleagues came and went. It was only when Mr W. Smith (one of the Smiths of Witney and of London County fame) joined him that stout resistance was apparent at both ends. Armstrong had been kidding them out; but Mr Ernest Smith of Yorkshire played a brilliant game towards the closing stages, hitting out well for 48 runs. Carpenter (66), W. Smith (21) and E. Smith together accounted for 135 of M C C's 181 total. Warwick Armstrong's bowling had been very effective – 6 for 46 and 9 wickets in the match: a considerable contribution to the Tourists' innings and 34-run triumph.

Having so recently suffered such a drubbing at the hands of the "Croucher", one may well imagine the Visitors' mixed feelings at the prospect of seeing him again so soon. They met Gloucestershire at Cheltenham on Monday 18 August, where the county had in the previous match succumbed rather badly to Yorkshire on a rain-soaked pitch. As usual, the Cestrians were hard put to it to raise a side but managed to secure the services of William Woof, in his day a fine slow-left-hand bowler, who had last turned out for them eight years before. As it was raining, most of the dismal day was spent in the pavilion. Winning a toss of doubtful value Darling decided to bat, only about twenty minutes' play being possible in the late afternoon. During this short period the Australians scored 21 runs for the loss of Duff, giving Woof, the Cheltenham School coach, his first wicket in first-class cricket for many a long day.

AUSTRALIANS *v* MCC and GROUND

At Lord's 14, 15, 16 August.
Australians won by an innings and 34 runs.

MCC AND GROUND

†Mr W. Findlay b Howell	7	c Trumble b Howell	4
H. Carpenter b Howell	1	b Armstrong	66
Mr H. B. Chinnery c Trumble b Howell	37	lbw, b Armstrong	2
G. J. Thompson c Trumble b Howell	23	lbw, b Armstrong	0
K. S. Ranjitsinhji c Duff b Armstrong	60	c Duff b Trumble	10
*Mr A. P. Lucas c Duff b Armstrong	27	c Kelly b Trumble	11
Mr E. Smith c Hill b Armstrong	3	b Trumble	48
Mr W. Smith c and b Noble	20	st Kelly b Armstrong	21
Mr H. J. Stevenson b Howell	12	c Noble b Armstrong	3
H. Young c Hill b Howell	14	b Armstrong	0
W. Mead not out	0	not out	4
Extras (B 3, LB 5)	8	(B 6, NB 3, LB 3)	12
	212		**181**

AUSTRALIANS

V. T. Trumper c E. Smith b Mead	29	A. J. Hopkins lbw, b Thompson	27
R. Duff c Young b Stevenson	36	H. Trumble b Thompson	7
C. Hill b Carpenter	136	†J. J. Kelly not out	3
*J. Darling b Young	3	W. P. Howell c Young b Mead	1
M. A. Noble c W. Smith b Thompson	70	Extras (B 11, LB 3, NB 3)	17
S. E. Gregory lbw, b Mead	86		
W. Armstrong run out	12		**427**

AUSTRALIANS	O.	M.	R.	W.	O.	M.	R.	W.
Trumble	15	6	31	0	17.3	4	51	3
Howell	40	11	105	6	19	8	41	1
Armstrong	27	10	53	3	21	4	44	6
Noble	3.4	0	15	1	15	6	33	0
MCC								
Mead	32.2	10	90	3				
Young	28	4	80	1				
Thompson	11	1	43	3				
E. Smith	15	1	57	0				
Stevenson	17	2	78	1				
Ranjitsinhji	5	1	24	0				
W. Smith	5	0	13	0				
Carpenter	5	0	25	1				

Umpires: J. Phillips and J. Moss

Tuesday saw Trumper toying with the bowling, Hill playing second fiddle to his brilliant strokemaking. Attacking Woof and Jessop's medium fastish off-breaks, Trumper quickly reached his 50 only to lose his partner Hill at 84. Seeing that Darling was in excellent batting trim Victor commenced to experiment, bringing off many daring and novel strokes that must have delighted Jessop. Scorning the probability of losing his wicket, he leapt into the attack. Thus he and Darling added 66 runs in less than half an hour, but with the risks he was taking it was not surprising that he gave three possibilities to the field. Then Jessop had the success of Darling's wicket, caught by Bateman Champain at long-on, and had Noble caught in the same way shortly after. Owing to the fall of these two wickets and Gregory's (caught behind off Jessopus), Trumper, for the sake of his side, reverted to his more immaculate and less dangerous strokeplay. Quickly reaching his ninth hundred of the tour, he continued with faultless cricket until he, too, holed out to Bateman Champain at long-on from an admiring Jessop. Armstrong, meanwhile, had played himself in and was scoring rapidly, but had the misfortune eventually to run out of partners when the Australian score reached 312 runs. Jessop had bowled steadily and splendidly under pressure with 7 wickets to his credit for 91, and the Cestrians' fielding had been first-rate.

The County started their account fairly well – Sewell had a confident opening knock of 33 – but once Armstrong and Hopkins came on the Cestrians slumped as badly as they had to Yorkshire. Even Jessop was out for 13. The latter part of the innings could be described as a procession. All out for 152 the western shire were invited to follow on. Armstrong, with 4 for 35, and Hopkins, 4 for 11, were the angels of destruction.

During the County's second venture the Cornstalks thought that the "Croucher" was going to flay them again. Vigorously he went onto the attack, so severely punishing the two bowlers that a change appeared imminent. With 43 behind him and completely in command of the situation, the Gloster captain was, alas, run out. Nobody had stayed at the other end; wickets had tumbled – six had fallen for 69 runs. Troup and Board now became associated and restored the somewhat ailing Cestrian total to a certain respectability. At the end, when all had fallen again to the subterfuge of Armstrong and Hopkins, Mr Troup remained stolidly unbeaten for 45 runs. Closing finally at 150 runs, they could not quite force the Tourists to bat again. Armstrong and Hopkins were well satisfied, the former having 8 wickets in the match for 109 runs and the latter 9 wickets for 76. Once more the Australians had won without having to go in a second time.

It had not been possible to arrange for the Tourists to visit Kent during Canterbury Cricket Week, for it would have been just prior to the fifth Test match; therefore, they were due to play the "county of the prancing horse" at the St Lawrence Ground, Canterbury, twelve days later. Their previous visit in 1899 had occasioned them a surprise defeat, due in some measure to C. J. Burnup, just down from Cambridge. "Pinky" Burnup had taken 8 of their wickets for 51 runs with his swing bowling, then rather new to them. The same young gentleman had figured prominently against them, too, in 1896 when he made a fine century off their attack at the time that Jones was at his peak.

Predominantly a county of amateurs with a leavening of class professionals, Kent, in the team due to meet the Cornstalks, could

AUSTRALIANS
v
GLOUCESTERSHIRE

At Cheltenham, 18, 19, 20 August.

Australians won by an innings and 10 runs.

AUSTRALIANS

V. T. Trumper c Champain b Jessop ..	125
R. A. Duff c and b Woof	2
C. Hill c Sewell b Woof	34
*J. Darling c Champain b Jessop	39
M. A. Noble c Champain b Jessop	10
S. E. Gregory c Board b Jessop	0
W. W. Armstrong not out	56
A. J. Hopkins b Jessop	19
E. Jones c Brownlee b Jessop	14
†H. Carter b Woof	1
W. P. Howell c Wrathall b Jessop	6
Extras (B 4, NB 2)	6
	312

GLOUCESTERSHIRE

Mr C. O. H. Sewell c Armstrong b Howell	33	c Carter b Hopkins	13
H. Wrathall run out	18	b Armstrong	0
T. Langdon c Hill b Armstrong	28	b Hopkins	1
Mr F. H. B. Champain b Hopkins	27	b Hopkins	1
*Mr G. L. Jessop b Armstrong	13	run out	43
Mr R. W. Rice b Hopkins	7	c and b Armstrong	4
Mr W. Troup c Hill b Armstrong	1	not out	45
†J. H. Board b Armstrong	8	c Carter b Armstrong	29
Mr L. D. Brownlee b Hopkins	6	b Hopkins	3
W. A. Woof c Darling b Hopkins	3	c Noble b Hopkins	0
E. Spry not out	2	b Armstrong	0
Extras (B 2, LB 4)	6	(B 7, LB 4)	11
	152		150

GLOS.	O.	M.	R.	W.	O.	M.	R.	W.
Woof	30	1	135	3				
Jessop	29.5	3	91	7				
Spry	13	0	80	0				
AUSTRALIANS								
Howell	16	2	54	1				
Noble	10	3	46	0				
Armstrong	16	4	35	4	24.3	6	74	4
Hopkins	9.4	4	11	4	24	8	65	5

Umpires: W. Richards and C. E. Richardson

boast in addition to Jack Mason, the current captain, the former skipper Frank Marchant and two future holders of that office, C. J. Burnup and Cloudesley Marsham. The young amateurs were either all-round cricketers or all-round sportsmen: Sam Day, still at Cambridge, was a Corinthian, as was Burnup, and Dick Blaker, also still a Cantab, was a soccer blue. They were a very strong side in all departments of the game with their all-rounder captain Mason, who had represented England in Australia in 1897–8, Mr Walter Morris Bradley, a straightforward, aggressive fast bowler, who had played in two Tests in 1899, and a supremely accurate young left-arm-slow bowler in Colin Blythe, already hailed by knowing players as the equal of Wilfred Rhodes. Blythe, known to all as "Charlie", had recently toured the Antipodes under MacLaren. Their wicketkeeper Fred Huish was one of the outstanding stumpers of the day and was considered worthy of international honours.

Mason and Alec Hearne bowled well. The former, a stock fast-medium, had Trumper LBW for 15, and Hearne, who could move the ball from leg and at good medium pace, had Clem Hill in two minds and bowled him. Then Darling, playing a hitting game, was beautifully caught off the same bowler by Burnup in the deep. Reg Duff was out in a most unusual fashion, for Huish, in attempting to run out Noble, kicked the ball at the wicket; it missed the batsman's stumps only to break the wicket at the other end with Duff still out of his ground. Blythe was now hypnotising the batsmen, and only Noble seemed to be able to counter him. Attacking them on a perfect pitch, this most artistic of bowlers continually altered his pitch and pace and varied the left-hander's natural break with the one that came with his arm. This master of flight and spin, quite unafraid of being hit, soon finished off the Cornstalks' innings. To everyone's surprise, in two and a quarter hours the mighty Australians had been removed for 154 runs.

On Kent going in, Burnup and Mason, their two heaviest scorers, were both sent back quickly and it was left to Sam Day, the eldest of three cricketing brothers, and the young professional James Seymour to repair the damage. Making a short stand in terms of runs, for they were very hard to score off Trumble and Saunders, they looked more comfortable in the middle than the rest of their colleagues. Day, a fine player on all kinds of pitches, was unfortunate to be out LBW to Trumble when he had made 20. But this wicket started a landslide, for Trumble bowled so beautifully and was so irresistible that in his next seven overs and five balls he carried the rest of the county bats for just 11 runs. Seymour, a polished player with a wide range of strokes, played back to him and kept his wicket up for 26 runs out of the Kent total of 77.

The Australians, somehow, could not get going in their second innings either. Blythe, Mason and Hearne they found difficult to score from, except for Victor Trumper. He played Blythe superlatively and hammered the other bowlers, and when Bradley came on Vic drove him. Then, when the fast bowler pitched short he pulled him mercilessly. As wickets were falling at the other end, Trumper took no risks until he was unluckily run out for 69. It was Hearne who was proving most troublesome, but Hopkins played a defensive game to allow Trumble to hit Hearne and Blythe at the other end, and Trumble made a gallant 30 before he fell. Kent's bowling was accurate and her fielding tight, Burnup making some excellent stops in the outfield and taking a fine catch to dispose of Darling. Although he took only two wickets, it was "Charlie" Blythe who puzzled the Tourists most. After dancing up to the wicket with his left arm tucked under his armpit and letting the ball go with plenty of air from a long final stride, they found his flight so difficult to gauge. Even when he was hit, it did not seem to worry him; he still kept his length.

The Australians had made 209 so Kent faced a total of 287 runs to win with plenty of time to obtain them. Perhaps with a little luck they might repeat their success of three years before. Burnup and Marsham got off to a good start and by the close on Friday night they had made 135 for the loss of four wickets, with "Pinky" Burnup having made 43. His stance at the wicket was somewhat reminiscent of Jessop's – he held the bat handle low down and he crouched.

With the weather living up to its usual form for 1902, it rained heavily in the night. This was most unfortunate for the county as they had to face Trumble and Saunders on a rain-affected pitch on Saturday morning. Their remaining batsmen could do nothing in the prevailing conditions against the Cornstalk spinners. In little more than an hour and a quarter's play Kent had tumbled to defeat by a margin of 89 runs.

Surprisingly, the Tourists had not previously met Middlesex this season, but at Lord's on Monday 25 August the omission was about to be repaired. The metropolitan county always in its history had had a wonderful selection of class amateurs, but rarely were sufficient available, except in August, to be able to deploy this strength of amateur talent in the field. Fortunately, a late meeting with the Australians meant that Middlesex could be represented by a strong eleven, only two of whom were professionals. These were, of course, the ever faithful bowlers Jack Hearne and Albert Trott. The county were in the throes of a poor season: dramatically, they had dropped from second place in the Championship Table in 1901 to a lowly position this year.

There had been much more rain about over the weekend, so with a cool wind and a pale, drawn sun, the toss was again one which it may have been of advantage to have lost. It was a pitch made for Trumble, who commenced the bowling assisted by Armstrong in place of Saunders, who was being rested. Quickly changing to round the wicket as he was turning so prodigiously, he had James Douglas, who liked soft pitches, leg before for 2 runs. George Beldam, the famous cricket photographer and a very gifted batsman, joined Pelham Warner. Runs were hard to obtain in the prevailing conditions, and they both defended with the greatest caution, scoring from the occasional loose ball. Beldam's defence was impressive. He had made a faultless 155 not out against Surrey only a month previously, which had been highly praised, but he was the first of the pair to fall, for 32, inevitably to Trumble bowling his

AUSTRALIANS *v* KENT

At Canterbury, 21, 22, 23 August.
Australians won by 89 runs.

AUSTRALIANS

V. T. Trumper lbw, b Mason	15	(3) run out	69
R. A. Duff run out	36	(1) b Blythe	6
C. Hill b Hearne	8	(4) run out	7
*J. Darling c Burnup b Hearne	6	(5) c Burnup b Mason	10
M. A. Noble run out	43	(6) b Blythe	28
S. E. Gregory lbw, b Blythe	0	(7) lbw, b Mason	16
W. W. Armstrong c Bradley b Blythe	1	(2) st Huish b Hearne	6
A. J. Hopkins c Seymour b Blythe	24	not out	18
H. Trumble st Huish b Blythe	8	c Blythe b Hearne	30
†H. Carter not out	6	c Mason b Hearne	9
J. V. Saunders b Hearne	2	run out	0
Extras (B 1, LB 2, W 1, NB 1)	5	(B 8, LB 2)	10
	154		**209**

KENT

Mr C. J. Burnup b Trumble	6	c and b Trumble	43
*Mr J. R. Mason b Saunders	7	(5) c Armstrong b Trumble	24
Mr S. H. Day lbw, b Trumble	20	lbw, b Noble	14
J. Seymour not out	26	(7) b Saunders	2
Mr C. H. B. Marsham b Trumble	2	(2) b Trumble	14
A. Hearne b Trumble	0	(4) b Noble	26
Mr F. Marchant b Trumble	8	(6) c Noble b Saunders	15
Mr R. N. R. Blaker b Trumble	0	c Noble b Saunders	18
†F. H. Huish lbw, b Trumble	3	c Trumble b Saunders	11
C. Blythe run out	1	not out	7
Mr W. M. Bradley c Hill b Trumble	0	c Trumper b Saunders	10
Extras (B 4)	4	(B 11, NB 2)	13
	77		**197**

KENT	O.	M.	R.	W.	O.	M.	R.	W.
Mason	10	1	31	1	(3) 15	2	48	2
Blythe	17	4	50	4	(1) 23.2	8	71	2
Hearne	11	1	39	3	(2) 19	6	50	3
Bradley	6	0	29	0	... 7	3	23	0
Burnup					... 1	0	7	0
AUSTRALIANS								
Trumble	19.5	10	30	8	...36	7	92	3
Saunders	18	6	43	1	...17.2	5	43	5
Armstrong	1	1	0	0	...6	1	14	0
Noble					...12	2	35	2

FALL OF WICKETS

	Aus.	Kent	Aus.	Kent
Wkt.	1st	1st	2nd	2nd
1st	37	6	8	31
2nd	52	30	42	62
3rd	60	50	61	79
4th	112	56	99	114
5th	112	56	105	138
6th	112	64	147	144
7th	117	64	151	158
8th	140	76	197	174
9th	147	77	209	183
10th	154	77	209	197

Umpires: W. A. J. West and H. Shaw

hardest for leg in front decisions. Very quickly the tall Victorian bowled the elder Douglas brother, R. N., who was too late making his stroke. C. M. Wells, on his day a most capable bat, was quickly snapped up by Trumper in Armstrong's leg trap.

Whilst all these wickets were falling Warner, in his Harlequin cap, had been surely placing the ball, deliberately and carefully. Now he, too, succumbed to Hugh Trumble's artfulness. A fine innings of 58 was handsomely applauded by the large body of spectators. Neither Trott nor Bosanquet tarried long, Trumble again being responsible, but the Middlesex captain Gregor MacGregor was determined to stay. He was now partnered by the Old Pauline and future South African Test player Reggie Schwarz: the pair attempted to put a certain amount of respectability on the face of the Lord's scoreboard. Both batted well and managed to hit the now tiring Trumble; nevertheless, he succeeded in an LBW decision which removed MacGregor for 20 runs. With assistance from R. W. Nicholls, who chanced his arm for a well-hit 23, the Middlesex innings was brought to a close after four hours for 204. Trumble's excellent analysis was 8 wickets for 101 runs from 52 overs and 3 balls.

To the surprise of all present Kelly and Hopkins came out to open for the Australians, but the gambit was unsuccessful as Jim Kelly did not trouble the scorers. Bosanquet, who was at this period experimenting in private with his googly (an off-break delivered with a leg-break action) generally bowled slow leg-breaks, though occasionally he reverted to the fast-medium style of his Oxford days. It was the slow leg-break that deceived Kelly. Now, to the crowd's delight, entered Trumper, who quickly induced MacGregor to take Bosanquet off and replace him with Albert Trott. It made little difference to the scoring, for Trumper punished both Trott and Beldam's round-the-wicket medium pacers. George Beldam, who was really beginning to develop his bowling this season, came off the pitch "fizzing" with spin and could make the ball go with his arm. He claimed Hopkins' wicket for 17 runs, then Wells and Hearne took over the attack.

The success which had been denied the other bowlers came immediately to stalwart Jack Hearne: Duff was removed for 5, Hill for 23, then the lordly, strokemaking Trumper was caught by Trott in the slips for 69. Noble took root, but Joe Darling was magically stumped by MacGregor off one of C. M. Wells' subtle slow leg-breaks. The Cornstalks were now six wickets down for 144. Armstrong joined Noble, and together they made runs in capital form until Monty Noble was clean bowled by Albert Trott for 40. Then there was another fine MacGregor stumping off Wells (the slower ball, delivered from the palm of his hand) to remove the run-hunting Armstrong, who had made 39. MacGregor, the former England wicketkeeper, was having a grand day, for he now caught Syd Gregory, this time from a Beldam "spinner". The Tourists finally closed their first account for 232 runs.

Highly satisfied in having removed Darling's darlings so cheaply, Middlesex returned to the wickets only 28 runs behind. But before the arrears were overcome the reliable opening bat James Douglas was back in the pavilion. So George Beldam came out to join

"Plum" Warner. Playing a very fine innings, he showed with the use of much excellent strokeplay how the Tourists' bowling could be treated by a careful and determined bat. Countering many good balls from Trumble and Howell he saw the demise of his county colleagues Warner, R. N. Douglas, Wells and Trott. Trott had injured his knee but, even so, managed to score 21 before playing Hopkins into Syd Gregory's hands at cover, in somewhat similar fashion to Wells. Looking everywise as handsome in his methods as he appeared later in his own book, *Great Batsmen – Their Methods at a Glance*, Beldam seemed worth a century. Alas, Bill Howell bowled him for 75. Bernard Bosanquet was playing under great difficulties (he had sprained his shoulder when fielding), but batting pluckily together with MacGregor they both made runs. Theirs was the virtual end of the county innings, so setting the opposition 176 to win.

This time Trumper and Duff came out first and set about the Middlesex bowling as if they meant to get the runs quickly, but three wickets were lost for 49. It was Noble and Armstrong who rode the difficulties of Wells, and, regardless of MacGregor's bowling changes, hammered 95 runs in seventy-five minutes – Warwick Armstrong, who was out first, being particularly aggressive. With 32 runs needed Hopkins, in his most lively style, helped Noble to polish them off. Due in large measure to Trumble's 12 for 149, seven of them LBW, the Australians were triumphant by six wickets.

The last county side that the Tourists played was Lancashire in a return encounter on the Aigburth Ground at Liverpool, commencing on Thursday 28 August. Their earlier game against the County Palatine had been entirely ruined by rain after the first day and those same "elements of misfortune" were to have their effect upon the current fixture. The Lancashire side that entered the field was far weaker than the previous one that had entertained the Australians, and that they were to run this powerful touring team so close to defeat reflected great credit upon them. Being without Barnes, E. E. Steel, Willis Cuttell, Webb and Sharp reduced the penetration of their attack, and having no regular wicketkeeper handicapped them considerably, though Lees Radcliffe of Rochdale, who officiated behind the stumps, served them creditably.

To help relieve MacLaren's extremity Joe Darling courteously agreed to Alexander Kermode, the N S W fast bowler, who had just taken up residence and would not be qualified until 1904, being included in the county side. Of the stalwarts who met the Australians early in June, besides MacLaren himself, there remained only Tyldesley, Albert Ward and James Hallows. More in hope than expectation a young twenty-year-old, G. Littlewood, a slow left-hand bowler on the Old Trafford groundstaff, was played on the

AUSTRALIANS *v* MIDDLESEX

At Lord's, 25, 26, 27 August.

Australians won by 6 wickets.

MIDDLESEX

Mr P. F. Warner lbw, b Trumble	58	lbw, b Trumble	25
Mr J. Douglas lbw, b Trumble	2	b Trumble	6
Mr G. W. Beldam lbw, b Trumble	32	b Howell	75
Mr R. N. Douglas lbw, b Trumble	3	lbw, b Trumble	8
Mr C. M. Wells c Trumper b Armstrong	10	c Gregory b Hopkins	2
A. E. Trott c Hopkins b Trumble	6	c Gregory b Hopkins	21
Mr B. J. T. Bosanquet b Trumble	3	lbw, b Trumble	25
*†Mr G. MacGregor lbw, b Trumble	20	b Howell	20
Mr R. O. Schwarz c Trumble b Howell	32	c Hopkins b Noble	3
Mr R. W. Nicholls c Armstrong b Trumble	23	not out	4
J. T. Hearne not out	0	c Darling b Noble	3
Extras (B 4, LB 9, W 1, NB 1)	15	(B 4, LB 5, W 1, NB 1)	11
	204		203

AUSTRALIANS

†J. J. Kelly lbw, b Bosanquet	0		
A. J. Hopkins c Hearne b Beldam	17	(6) not out	19
V. T. Trumper c Trott b Hearne	69	(1) b Wells	23
R. Duff b Hearne	5	(2) c MacGregor b Wells	22
C. Hill c Bosanquet b Hearne	23	(3) b Beldam	1
M. A. Noble b Trott	40	(4) not out	59
*J. Darling st MacGregor b Wells	6		
W. Armstrong st MacGregor b Wells	39	(5) b Wells	47
S. E. Gregory c MacGregor b Beldam	15		
H. Trumble b Wells	4		
W. P. Howell not out	12		
Extras (B 1, LB 1)	2	(B 4, LB 1)	5
	232	(4 wkts)	176

AUSTRALIANS	O.	M.	R.	W.	O.	M.	R.	W.
Trumble	52.3	20	101	8	33	13	48	4
Armstrong	34	11	59	1	18	1	46	0
Noble	14	3	24	0	14.4	4	29	2
Howell	4	2	5	0	12	4	19	2
Hopkins					14	1	50	2
MIDDLESEX								
Bosanquet	4	0	16	1				
Beldam	15	5	33	2	16	4	38	1
Trott	11	1	45	1	5	0	24	0
Wells	11.4	0	61	3	14	2	49	3
Hearne	25	3	75	3	12	4	38	0
Warner					4	1	16	0
Schwarz					3.2	1	6	0

Umpires: A. Shaw and J. Carlin

strength of his 9 Leicestershire wickets in the previous match. To MacLaren's surprise and delight the novice came off, capturing the first three wickets – Trumper, Duff and Noble – for a handful of runs. Littlewood, bowling in harness with the burly Kermode, surprised and humbled the mighty Cornstalks, who were tumbled out for 138 runs; only Hill with 28 and Gregory's undefeated 32 preventing a débâcle. Both bowlers captured 5 wickets apiece in the equally shared 36 overs.

Hardly believing in their good fortune the Lancastrians commenced to bat with a will, replying with 61 for 2 wickets at the close, the left-handed amateur opener Garnett playing very steadily for 32. Their favourable position, however, was completely nullified by overnight rain and early morning sunshine. Saunders and

AUSTRALIANS *v* LANCASHIRE

At Liverpool, 28, 29, 30 August.

Australians won by 18 runs.

AUSTRALIANS

V. T. Trumper c Stanning b Littlewood	4	b Kermode	6
R. A. Duff c and b Littlewood	13	b Littlewood	22
C. Hill b Kermode	28	c and b Kermode	24
M. A. Noble lbw, b Littlewood	0	b Littlewood	14
*J. Darling b Kermode	10	c Garnett b Littlewood	10
W. W. Armstrong b Littlewood	14	c Hollins b I'Anson	5
A. J. Hopkins b Kermode	0	c Ward b Littlewood	1
S. E. Gregory not out	32	c Radcliffe b Littlewood	12
H. Trumble c Kermode b Littlewood	5	b Littlewood	0
†J. J. Kelly b Kermode	16	b Littlewood	5
J. V. Saunders b Kermode	4	not out	0
Extras (B 10, LB 2)	12	(B 5, LB 1)	6
	138		**105**

LANCASHIRE

Mr H. G. Garnett b Trumble	32	c Hopkins b Trumble	28
A. Ward c Hill b Armstrong	17	lbw, b Trumble	2
J. T. Tyldesley c Armstrong b Trumble	21	c Kelly b Saunders	4
G. Littlewood c Hopkins b Saunders	2	c Trumper b Trumble	6
*Mr A. C. MacLaren b Saunders	0	c Gregory b Saunders	3
J. Hallows not out	32	c Trumper b Noble	14
Mr J. Stanning b Trumble	0	c Hopkins b Trumble	14
J. I'Anson st Kelly b Saunders	0	c Kelly b Saunders	0
Mr F. H. Hollins b Saunders	9	c Noble b Saunders	27
A. Kermode c Darling b Saunders	2	c Darling b Trumble	0
†L. Radcliffe c Trumper b Saunders	3	not out	6
Extras (B1, LB 1)	2	(LB 1)	1
	120		**105**

LANCASHIRE	O.	M.	R.	W.	O.	M.	R.	W.
Littlewood	18	6	49	5	15.5	3	49	7
Kermode	18	2	68	5	13	3	43	2
I'Anson	1	0	3	0	3	1	7	1
Hallows	1	0	6	0				
AUSTRALIANS								
Trumble	29	9	53	3	20.4	5	44	5
Saunders	20.4	7	52	6	15	1	37	4
Armstrong	8	4	13	1				
Hopkins					2	0	8	0
Noble					3	0	15	1

FALL OF WICKETS

Wkt.	Aus. 1st	Lancs. 1st	Aus. 2nd	Lancs. 2nd
1st	10	47	13	2
2nd	27	55	21	7
3rd	27	61	46	41
4th	54	61	64	47
5th	77	89	91	52
6th	77	89	94	93
7th	81	90	100	93
8th	91	102	100	93
9th	134	116	105	94
10th	138	120	105	105

Umpires: T. Mycroft and F. Martin

Trumble, bowling under conditions most advantageous to them, scattered the remaining 8 wickets for the addition of 59 runs. The graceful left-handed all-rounder James Hallows, being the only Red Rose capable of judging the pace of the pitch, was still in possession with 32 runs to his name at the innings' conclusion.

With eighteen runs in hand and the pitch still very difficult, Darling's orders to force the game were hardly successful. Littlewood had a field day, though it was Kermode who removed the biggest guns of Trumper and Hill. When all-rounder I'Anson had Armstrong caught, the score was 5 wickets for 91 runs, but Littlewood, taking advantage of the pitch, captured the remaining 5 for the paltry addition of 14 runs. His analysis of 7 for 49 in the innings and 12 for 98 in the match against such opposition was astonishing.

With 124 required for victory Archie MacLaren and Johnny Tyldesley commenced the last innings, but magnificent bowling by Saunders backed by superlatively keen fielding saw both the opening pair out for 7 runs. Garnett again played up well for 28 and, by the time of drawing stumps, only 49 were still wanted with 5 wickets in hand. Determined not to lose, if at all humanly possible, Trumble and Saunders bowled as men possessed on Saturday morning backed by a mustard-keen field. Lancastrian hopes were heightened by a last-ditch stand by Messrs Stanning and Hollins, the former having represented the county in only one match this season and the latter in but two. Hollins' doughty knock of 27 was a good one and nearly won the game, but Saunders was not to be denied. Six runs later, all scored by wicketkeeper Radcliffe, Kermode fell to Trumble and the Cornstalks' bacon had been saved by just 18 runs. It had been a close run thing, the match might so easily have been lost, but Darling's darlings had saved their reputation.

CHAPTER 15
Festival Cricket

Their county programme now complete, the Australians still had five more fixtures in hand before concluding their tour. These were all against representative sides and were, by nature, end of season festival matches. A little more lighthearted, perhaps, but still cricket matches to be played hard and won.

Travelling to Harrogate on their way to the Scarborough Festival, where a Gentlemen and Players game was currently in progress, the Tourists met a team entitled "Eleven Players of England", a kind of "Players" Second Eleven. All well known and highly regarded professionals: Vine, Relf, Killick and Tate of Sussex, Quaife and Devey of Warwickshire, Arnold and Gaukrodger of Worcestershire, Washington, the young Yorkshire left-hander, Llewellyn, the Hampshire South African, and Albert Trott of Middlesex.

The commencement was delayed by the effects of weekend rain and the September morning dew, therefore the "Professors" by winning the toss were somewhat at a disadvantage in electing to bat. Quickly disposing of Joe Vine and Irving Washington, Saunders was continuing in the prolific wicket-taking vein of recent weeks, but the slippery turf handicapped Ernie Jones. Jack Devey played circumspectly until he was run out for 35, though the diminutive Willie Quaife batted in beautiful style sharing a 72-run stand, made in 90 minutes, with bespectacled Ted Killick. They raised the total to 165 before Quaife was caught off "Jonah" for 58, this being the only occasion the bat dominated. With Killick surprised by Hopkins for 47, the Players succumbed quietly for 184 runs.

Having rested Noble, Gregory and Kelly, the Cornstalks' batting might have been thought to be below strength, but Trumper and Duff got them off to a good start of 59 without being separated at the close. Tuesday morning saw Trumper carrying on where he had left off the night before. Giving a most polished and lustrous display of the batsman's art, he delighted the five thousand spectators as he

176

quickly raced to his tenth hundred of the tour. Duff and Hill had not lasted long and so, with Darling's help, 89 runs were pillaged in a mere forty minutes. Two-thirds of them were scored from Trumper's flashing blade before he was stumped when the 200 had been hoisted. Victor had made 127 of them in one hundred and five minutes. With 67 to Darling, 58 from Hopkins, 19 to Trumble and 22 by "Sep" Carter, cudgelled from, by now, weary bowlers, the Tourists' account closed at 359 runs. Ted Arnold and Fred Tate were the most successful bowlers with 3 wickets each.

With the light failing rapidly the "Professors" lost two quick wickets – Devey deceived in the gloom by Ernie Jones' pace and Washington caught at mid-off from Saunders – each for a duck. They came in hoping to do better on the morrow, but the gloomy light of evening presaged the "watering pot" to effectively dampen the Players' hopes of making the opposition bat again. It was Howell who struck first next morning by getting both Quaife's and Arnold's wickets, then, with Vine and Relf disposed of, the remainder could do little to hold out in a strong wind against such formidable odds. Saunders (5–44) and Howell (3–42) proved too much for them and they left the field with the Australians victors by an innings and 47 runs and plenty of time to get to Scarborough.

A large crowd greeted the Tourists next day for their fixture with Mr C. I. Thornton's XI, a powerful side containing no less than seven Yorkshiremen. "Buns" Thornton had hoped to make it even stronger with MacLaren and Braund, but at the last minute they were not available. Winning the toss on a bright morning after the previous day's gale, during which the Players' match had been concluded without "bails", the Hon. F. S. Jackson found himself playing a captain's innings after his early batting had failed. Jack Saunders had quickly accounted for Tunnicliffe, Tyldesley and T. L. Taylor; then Trumble, after his rest from bowling in the last game, dislodged opener A. O. Jones, R. E. Foster, and George Hirst. With Thornton's XI having lost six wickets for 79 runs Jackson's back-to-the-wall innings was a superb effort. Assisted initially by George Thompson of Northants and latterly by a debonair "Schof" Haigh, "Jacker's" 72 runs helped lift the Thornton XI score to 198, far more than at one time seemed possible. Trumble and Saunders shared the wicket equally, but Noble and Armstrong had bowled well without success attending their efforts.

Fresh from his wondrous batting at Harrogate, Trumper set about the combined left-handed talents of Hirst and Rhodes. But the guileful Wilfred proved too much for Duff and Armstrong, the latter having gone in first wicket down as Hill was feeling unwell. It was left to Hugh Trumble as night-watchman to assist Trumper in the closing overs. Enjoying his promotion in the batting order, the giant

177

AUSTRALIANS
v
XI PLAYERS OF ENGLAND

At Harrogate, 1, 2, 3 September.

Australians won by an innings and 47 runs.

ELEVEN PLAYERS OF ENGLAND

J. Vine c Darling b Saunders	5	c Armstrong b Hopkins	34
J. Devey run out	35	b Jones	0
I. Washington c Armstrong b Saunders	7	c Jones b Saunders	0
W. G. Quaife c Saunders b Jones	58	c Hill b Howell	18
E. Arnold b Saunders	14	b Howell	0
A. E. Relf b Saunders	0	b Saunders	32
E. H. Killick c Jones b Hopkins	47	c Howell b Saunders	1
C. B. Llewellyn lbw, b Hopkins	2	c Jones b Howell	17
A. E. Trott b Hopkins	1	c Armstrong b Saunders	6
†G. Gaukrodger not out	1	b Saunders	10
F. W. Tate b Jones	7	not out	0
Extras (B 5, LB 2)	7	(B 8, LB 1, NB 1)	10
	184		**128**

AUSTRALIANS

V. T. Trumper st Gaukrodger b Vine	127	E. Jones c Arnold b Trott	0
R. A. Duff lbw, b Tate	21	†H. Carter c Trott b Tate	22
C. Hill st Gaukrodger b Arnold	15	W. P. Howell c Killick b Trott	4
*J. Darling b Arnold	67	J. V. Saunders not out	8
W. W. Armstrong b Llewellyn	0	Extras (B 12, LB 4, W 2)	18
A. J. Hopkins b Tate	58		
H. Trumble c Vine b Arnold	19		**359**

AUSTRALIANS	O.	M.	R.	W.	O.	M.	R.	W.
Jones	16.4	5	46	2	9	4	11	1
Saunders	23	8	44	4	17	4	44	5
Howell	15	5	45	0	16.2	4	42	3
Armstrong	12	4	21	0				
Hopkins	11	4	21	3	9	3	21	1
PLAYERS								
Llewellyn	14	1	80	1				
Tate	19.3	5	87	3				
Arnold	23	5	79	3				
Vine	7	1	44	1				
Trott	17	1	51	2				

Umpires: T. Mycroft and G. Porter

Victorian made 38 runs before Rhodes bowled him. But it was Trumper whom the large crowd delighted in until he too fell victim to Yorkshire's slow left-hander, leg before wicket for 62 runs. Then Noble put the Australians in sight of the Thornton XI score and Hopkins, playing delightfully free cricket and carrying his bat for 49 through the remainder of the innings, raised the Cornstalk total to 247.

By the end of Friday, the second day, Thornton's men were in some disarray – just 38 runs on with six wickets down. Only John

Tyldesley of the recognised bats remained between the Tourists and victory, but Tyldesley could not be disposed of. He stayed to make a gallant 88, then Haigh and Rhodes put a better complexion on things by hoisting the 200 on the telegraph. Jackson now did some mental calculations: as it was now nearly three-thirty and it had been agreed to draw stumps at 5 o'clock, the opposition needed 154 to win so he would declare and make a match of it.

Surprisingly, Gregory came out as opener, got off the mark quickly, but was yorked by Haigh at 19. Trumper and Armstrong then, determined to polish off the outstanding runs, put bat to ball in such electrifying fashion that 82 were added in the next forty minutes. Continuing in this fashion, if time had been played out in full the Australians would have easily obtained them, for at the five o'clock finish they wanted only 34 to win with six wickets in hand. Certainly a moral victory to them if not an actual one.

Travelling from one festival at Scarborough to another being held at Hastings, the Tourists found themselves faced by a formidable foe in the shape of Dr Grace and the "South of England". They always enjoyed visiting Hastings, a town and ground which had fond memories for them, and they delighted in the company, off and on the field, of W. G. himself. Victor Trumper always felt it was an honour and a privilege to meet him, so did Monty Noble; those touring for the first time may have been a little overawed, but the kindly Doctor would soon put them at their ease.

The South of England side was tremendously strong in batting. "Pinky" Burnup, having enjoyed a wonderful season, had just scored a beautiful 107 on a rain-damaged pitch here at Hastings in the previous match of the festival. (Perhaps the Cornstalks were pleased that the other century-maker in that game, Gilbert Jessop – 109 runs in under eighty minutes – was not playing!) As well as Bobby Abel, one of the heaviest scorers of the season, the team included Tom Hayward, Len Braund, Jack Mason, Sam Day, Ted Dillon, Joe Vine, wicketkeeper Jack Board and George Gill.

With Darling resting himself, Howell and Kelly, the Australians did not score as many runs as they should have done. Braund and Gill bowled so finely as to take the wickets of all the accredited bats in the side and Burnup, with his swing bowling, accounted for the tail. Noble, batting in his most determined manner for 63, Hopkins, playing his most resplendent style for 74, and Hugh Trumble, not out 27, were the only ones to do anything of note. But 249 runs by mid-afternoon was to be quite inadequate.

The South scored heavily, and everybody made runs. For once Trumble and Saunders could not lure opponents to their fate, and even Ernie Jones was comparatively innocuous. Burnup and Abel hoisted the hundred before they were parted, then Tom Hayward scored 106, Braund, Mason and Day made thirties and forties and

AUSTRALIANS
v
C. I. THORNTON'S XI

At Scarborough, 4, 5, 6 September.

Match drawn.

MR C. I. THORNTON'S XI

Mr A. O. Jones c Darling b Trumble	31	b Saunders	1
J. Tunnicliffe b Saunders	9	c Trumble b Saunders	4
J. T. Tyldesley b Saunders	0	b Noble	88
Mr T. L. Taylor c Noble b Saunders	3	st Kelly b Saunders	0
*Hon. F. S. Jackson c Hill b Trumble	72	b Trumble	11
Mr R. E. Foster b Trumble	5	b Saunders	6
G. H. Hirst lbw, b Trumble	14	c Darling b Armstrong	5
G. J. Thompson c Darling b Saunders	18	c Trumper b Noble	12
S. Haigh b Saunders	28	not out	30
W. Rhodes c Duff b Trumble	0	not out	25
†D. Hunter not out	4	lbw, b Saunders	11
Extras (B 10, LB 3, NB 1)	14	(B 1, LB 8)	9
	198	**(9 wkts dec.)**	**202**

AUSTRALIANS

V. T. Trumper lbw, b Rhodes	62	lbw, b Thompson	55
R. A. Duff lbw, b Rhodes	1		
W. W. Armstrong b Rhodes	6	c Hunter b Thompson	37
H. Trumble b Rhodes	38		
C. Hill lbw, b Thompson	5		
*J. Darling c Jones b Haigh	20	not out	9
M. A. Noble c Hunter b Thompson	39		
S. E. Gregory c Hunter b Haigh	10	b Haigh	12
A. J. Hopkins not out	49	b Jackson	1
†J. J. Kelly run out	4		
J. V. Saunders c Hunter b Thompson	0		
Extras (B 12, W 1)	13	(B 4, LB 2)	6
	247	**(4 wkts)**	**120**

AUSTRALIANS	O.	M.	R.	W.	O.	M.	R.	W.
Noble	15	1	39	0	10	2	22	2
Trumble	39	17	62	5	37	20	55	1
Saunders	25.4	6	74	5	39	10	95	5
Armstrong	11	5	9	0	12	2	21	1
MR C. I. THORNTON'S XI								
Hirst	8	0	40	0				
Rhodes	36	6	95	4	7	1	34	0
Haigh	19	3	65	2	8	1	28	1
Thompson	15.3	4	32	3	5.5	0	36	2
Jackson	4	3	2	0	4	0	16	1

Umpires: A. Pike and Whitehead

W. G., with 17 not out and the South total past 400, declared. It had been left to Noble and Armstrong to be successful with the ball.

Facing a deficit of 154, Trumper and Duff went for the runs until the latter, trying to force a medium-paced off-break from Tom Hayward, was LBW for 36. The festive crowd was being enthralled by Trumper, who was doing exactly what he liked with all the bowlers. As the luncheon interval approached his scoring-rate increased; he reached his eleventh century of the season amid excited acclaim. But the arrears had only just been accounted for, so Trumper had no intentions of throwing his wicket away. Two wickets for 165 at lunch – eleven runs ahead, it seemed as if a draw was in prospect.

Soon after the restart, however, a change came over the game. Vine started another spell of bowling with his fast leg-breaks, and Noble was clean bowled and Gregory caught and bowled. Then, ill luck to the Australians: Mason took a splendid catch in the deep to dismiss Trumper, their main hope. *Wisden* laconically comments, "Trumper's 120 was one of his finest displays."*

In the next hour and a half Vine took complete command. The rest of the Cornstalks were bewitched by those leg-breaks sent down at such a ripping pace, only Trumble (29) and Armstrong (10) reaching double figures. The Australians looked as if they were slipping to defeat, and the eminent Doctor chuckled through his beard. Joe Vine earned his undying gratitude with 7 wickets for 31 runs.

With little more than an hour's play left the South needed 95, and they were determined to get them. They hit out at everything possible on the Doctor's orders, but three were caught in the country, Trumper being responsible for the downfall of Mason and Braund. Right up to the last over it was touch and go, but time saved the Australians. The South were just eight runs short of victory with 5 wickets still in hand. Doctor Grace's merry men had given them a bit of a fright!

On the same day, 11 September, that Yorkshire, the Champion County, were due to meet "The Rest of England" at Lord's, the Australians were sitting in the dressing-room watching the rain at Bournemouth. It had set in about 6 a.m. and continued unabated; at noon, play was abandoned for the day. Hopefully, they were due to meet another team styled "South of England" at the attractive municipally-owned Dean Park. The only similarities with the side of the same name they had just met were Joe Vine, George Gill and Jack Board. Otherwise, under "Sam" Woods' leadership, it consisted of Charles Fry, Hampshire's E. M. Sprot, Hayes and Brockwell of Surrey, C. J. B. Wood of Leicestershire, Ted Arnold of Worcester and Fred Tate of Sussex.

Friday was a much better day and a fair crowd of spectators made its way to the cricket ground, sampling the novelty of a new mode of transport in Bournemouth – the municipal electric tram cars – for these vehicles had only been running six weeks. The pitch was a treacherous one, indeed it remained so throughout, and the ball was

* *Wisden* 1903, p. 292.

AUSTRALIANS
v
SOUTH OF ENGLAND
At Hastings, 8, 9, 10 September.
Match drawn.

AUSTRALIANS

V. T. Trumper b Gill	16	c Mason b Gill	120
R. A. Duff c Board b Gill	20	lbw, b Hayward	36
C. Hill b Braund	14	b Gill	17
M. A. Noble b Braund	63	b Vine	4
S. E. Gregory lbw, b Braund	1	c and b Vine	5
W. W. Armstrong b Braund	18	b Vine	10
A. J. Hopkins c Board b Burnup	74	b Vine	4
*H. Trumble not out	27	b Vine	29
†H. Carter b Burnup	0	c Hayward b Vine	5
E. Jones b Gill	4	c Burnup b Vine	6
J. V. Saunders b Burnup	3	not out	0
Extras (B 6, LB 2, NB 1)	9	(B 5, LB 3, NB 4)	12
	249		**248**

SOUTH OF ENGLAND

Mr C. J. Burnup c Jones b Noble	66	c Hill b Armstrong	27
R. Abel b Armstrong	55		
T. Hayward c Hill b Armstrong	106		
L. C. Braund c Hill b Noble	33	c Trumper b Trumble	13
Mr J. R. Mason c Duff b Armstrong	34	c Trumper b Armstrong	18
Mr S. H. Day st Carter b Noble	44	c Carter b Trumble	0
*Dr W. G. Grace not out	17		
Mr E. W. Dillon b Noble	8		
J. Vine not out	3	not out	0
†J. H. Board ⎫ did not bat		not out	11
G. Gill ⎭		st Carter b Trumble	14
Extras (B 26, LB 2, W 5, NB 4)	37	(B 2, LB 1, W 1)	4
(7 wkts dec.)	**403**	(5 wkts)	**87**

S. OF ENG.	O.	M.	R.	W.	O.	M.	R.	W.
Braund	26	5	88	4	21	4	78	0
Gill	24	1	98	3	21	5	59	2
Mason	8	2	27	0	6	0	31	0
Vine	2	1	5	0	21.4	7	31	7
Burnup	4.3	0	22	3				
Hayward					10	0	37	1

AUSTRALIANS	O.	M.	R.	W.	O.	M.	R.	W.
Jones	18	5	46	0				
Saunders	19	2	64	0				
Noble	32	10	89	4				
Trumble	25	6	58	0	11	1	47	3
Armstrong	34	6	90	3	11	1	36	2
Hopkins	9	2	19	0				

Umpires: G. Bean and F. Martin

to dominate the bat completely. Arnold and Tate, bowling un-changed, had the Visitors in trouble on the variable-paced pitch, to the crowd's obvious delight; only Noble, with a careful 30, and Trumble, not out for 17, were able to counter them. All out for 123, no less than eight of their wickets had fallen to Arnold.

If the Tourists were humbled by Arnold, the batsmen of the "South" were annihilated by that master of variable pace and spin, Hugh Trumble. On a pitch that suited his talents admirably, he had everyone playing and missing – even Fry! In just 16 overs and four balls he mesmerised the South completely to take 9 wickets for 39 runs, and they were all bowled or leg before. Charles Fry was top scorer with 18, before he succumbed to Saunders, out of the South's meagre 87 runs.

Going in again the Cornstalks fared little better, such was the sticky state of the pitch. Arnold and Tate were again the purveyors of ill intent, but it was Fred Tate's golden opportunity to get some of his own back for Old Trafford! Clean bowling four of his six victims, he showed how well he could operate on a wet surface. Noble again manfully played the watching and waiting game for 20 out of 91. With Ted Arnold securing the remaining four wickets, he had earned a match total of 12 for 87. This splendid bowling gave the South an outside chance with 128 to win, but, on the pitch as it still remained at lunch on Saturday, it seemed a tall order.

Apart from Hayes (11) and Fry (26), both bowled by Trumble, they never looked like getting them. With the two Victorians bowling with artful skill to the tightest of fielding, no one else reached double figures and it became a procession, the last five wickets falling for 20 runs. By half-past four the Australians had triumphed by the comparatively large margin of 61 runs. Adding another six victims to his list Trumble's remarkable analysis became 15 wickets for 68 runs, once more proving what a grand match-winner he really was and a priceless asset to his side.

The tour as originally planned would have ended at Bournemouth, but some weeks previously it was felt that something of a grand finale was called for. What better way was there than by arranging a fixture with the Players at Kennington Oval? This move was a very popular one as far as the cricketing public was concerned; they turned up in good numbers on Monday 15 September.

A strong selection represented the Players, for all its chosen members, save Vine, had represented the "Professors" in at least one of the three fixtures opposing the Gentlemen during the season; indeed, Tyldesley had been present in all of them. Abel and Hayward, of course, were appearing on their home ground. The rest of the team was Hirst, Rhodes and Haigh from the Champion County, Yorkshire; Jim Iremonger of Notts; Willie Quaife and Dick Lilley of Warwickshire; and Leonard Braund of Somerset.

AUSTRALIANS
v
SOUTH OF ENGLAND

At Bournemouth, 11, 12, 13 September.

Australians won by 61 runs.

AUSTRALIANS

V. T. Trumper c and b Arnold	10	c Woods b Tate	6
R. A. Duff lbw, b Arnold	7	b Tate	11
*J. Darling b Tate	12	c Fry b Arnold	3
M. A. Noble c Hayes b Arnold	30	lbw, b Arnold	20
S. E. Gregory lbw, b Arnold	12	b Tate	0
W. W. Armstrong c Board b Arnold	13	b Tate	14
A. J. Hopkins lbw, b Arnold	0	b Tate	0
H. Trumble not out	17	b Arnold	8
†J. J. Kelly b Arnold	6	c and b Tate	9
W. P. Howell c Woods b Arnold	2	not out	3
J. V. Saunders c Hayes b Tate	9	c Vine b Arnold	4
Extras (B 4, LB 1)	5	(B 10, LB 3)	13
	123		**91**

SOUTH OF ENGLAND

*Mr S. M. J. Woods b Trumble	6	run out	0
Mr C. B. Fry lbw, b Saunders	18	b Trumble	26
E. G. Hayes b Trumble	1	b Trumble	11
Mr E. M. Sprot lbw, b Trumble	16	c Kelly b Trumble	8
J. Vine lbw, b Trumble	5	b Trumble	0
Mr C. J. B. Wood lbw, b Trumble	17	c Noble b Saunders	1
E. Arnold b Trumble	0	st Kelly b Trumble	0
W. Brockwell b Trumble	2	st Kelly b Saunders	2
G. Gill b Trumble	14	b Saunders	7
†J. H. Board not out	2	c Armstrong b Trumble	6
F. W. Tate b Trumble	0	not out	5
Extras (B 3, LB 3)	6		
	87		**66**

S. OF ENG.	O.	M.	R.	W.	O.	M.	R.	W.
Tate	27	5	61	2	13	2	48	6
Arnold	26	7	57	8	13.2	2	30	4
AUSTRALIANS								
Trumble	16.4	3	39	9	11.3	2	29	6
Noble	12	3	28	0				
Saunders	4	0	14	1	11	1	37	3

Umpires: A. Shaw and W. Richards

On an excellent wicket for the purposes of run-getting, the Players went in and the Australian bowlers had the thankless task of trying to get them out, although as usual they were well supported by their field. Saunders and Noble were the successful bowlers, Hugh Trumble having the unusual experience, after taking 139 wickets so far on the tour in most convincing manner, of only adding one further wicket at a cost of 129 runs. All of the "Professors", excepting Vine and Haigh, made runs, Hayward (74), Tyldesley (56) and

Iremonger (66) especially so. The whole of the first day was consumed on that easy-paced pitch, and they batted on until Haigh was run out just before one o'clock on Tuesday. Feeling quite satisfied with themselves after 356 runs had been compiled, the Players were in a commanding position, but they had occupied the crease too long.

Under a darkening sky Trumper opened the Visitors' account with Syd Gregory as his partner, and they went for the runs. At 70 for one wicket – Gregory had been run out for 22 – the seemingly ever-present enemy – rain – dogged the Australians to the very last,

AUSTRALIANS *v* PLAYERS

At Kennington Oval, 15, 16, 17 September.
Match drawn.

PLAYERS OF ENGLAND

R. Abel c Hill b Noble	35	not out	32
T. Hayward st Kelly b Saunders	74	c Kelly b Hopkins	18
J. T. Tyldesley b Saunders	56	c Darling b Noble	27
W. G. Quaife c Hopkins b Trumble	31	not out	5
J. Iremonger c Hopkins b Armstrong	66		
L. C. Braund b Saunders	15		
G. H. Hirst c Duff b Noble	35	c Duff b Armstrong	23
J. Vine c Trumper b Noble	7		
*†A. A. Lilley c Darling b Saunders	16		
S. Haigh run out	0		
W. Rhodes not out	11		
Extras (B 3, LB 5, W 1, NB 1)	10	(B 7, LB 3, W 1, NB 1)	12
	356	(3 wkts)	117

AUSTRALIANS

V. T. Trumper c and b Rhodes	96	H. Trumble b Rhodes	68
S. E. Gregory run out	22	W. W. Armstrong b Vine	20
C. Hill b Haigh	81	†J. Kelly b Rhodes	0
M. A. Noble b Rhodes	4	J. V. Saunders not out	1
R. A. Duff c Hayward b Rhodes	15	Extras (B 27, W 3)	30
*J. Darling c Rhodes b Braund	28		
A. Hopkins b Vine	49		414

AUSTRALIANS	O.	M.	R.	W.	O.	M.	R.	W.
Trumble	42	10	129	1				
Saunders	26.4	11	50	4	5	1	24	0
Trumper	7	3	17	0				
Armstrong	23	3	45	1	5	0	12	1
Noble	31	8	85	3	18	7	40	1
Hopkins	5	0	20	0	6	1	22	1
Duff					2	0	7	0
PLAYERS								
Hirst	15	3	51	0				
Vine	27	8	77	2				
Haigh	26	4	64	1				
Rhodes	36.4	3	115	5				
Braund	12	1	56	1				
Hayward	3	0	21	0				

Umpires: W. A. J. West and W. Richards

robbing them of an hour and a quarter's playing time. No wonder when they returned home their fellow-countrymen joked that as long as Joe Darling and his team were about, Australia would never suffer from another drought! Once they recommenced Victor Trumper and Clem Hill delighted the "Surrey Crowd" with a fine display, punishing the bowling without mercy. Looking forward to their idol's twelfth hundred, which he seemed so well set for, they were immensely disappointed when Rhodes caught and bowled him for 96. So Victor became the Yorkshireman's 209th wicket of the season, and he was to take another four.

Not to be outdone, Hill carried on where Trumper had left off for 81, first with Duff and then with a rumbustious Darling. It was now apparent that unless more rain happened to be about overnight, this most attractive fixture would not be brought to a definite conclusion. While Hopkins sedately made 49, Trumble, as if to atone for his unsuccessful bowling, laid about himself for 68 runs – his highest score of the tour. But time was running out as, batting to the bitter end, the Cornstalks came in with 414 on the board.

There was little possibility of a result unless the Players were to collapse in remarkable fashion. Determinedly they had only to stay at the wickets and play out time; this they were able to do without much difficulty. Interest was fast waning – even Duff bowled – and a game which had commenced with the prospect of being a fascinating cricket match sadly declined to a tame draw, due to an over prepared pitch and lost playing time. A somewhat disappointing conclusion to this splendid tour of Joe Darling's Australians.

CHAPTER 16

The Tour in Retrospect

As our Australian friends departed for South Africa on their journey homeward, after nearly five months of intensive six-days-a-week cricket, they left behind them an impression of pre-eminence. When they first arrived many sporting scribes, both here and in Australia, intimated that they were, generally speaking, none too strong. Initial games did little to dispel this notion, but, as we have already noticed, the spring and early summer were abnormally cold and wet, conditions quite foreign to most of them, and their health and spirits suffered accordingly. In addition to this, injuries added to their worries, particularly that to their prime bowler, Hugh Trumble, who was kept out of the game for over five weeks. At times they were hard put to it to field a fit eleven. The remarkable thing was the resilience of these young men in being able to keep going and play, day after day, bright and zestful cricket.

After the first Test match, when they were completely demoralised for 36 runs at Edgbaston, then humiliated by Hirst and Jackson at Leeds, to the sporting press and the public they seemed a beaten side. Undoubtedly England, with her great cricket strength, would win the rubber against this eleventh Australian touring team. But the gentlemen of the press, the man who paid his sixpence, and probably most English cricketers themselves, underestimated the ability of these sun-tanned young men who never considered themselves beaten until the last ball had been bowled.

With the influenza epidemic behind them and Trumble's bowling hand healed, they began to reveal more of their true form. Playing delightfully attacking cricket they soon had quite a following with the sporting English crowds around the country. Their keenness to win, their amazingly fair and sportsmanlike approach to the game, and the genuine friendliness and unfailing good humour these young men displayed, made them extremely popular wherever they went. On first-name terms with amateur and professional alike

187

(the caste system of English cricket was quite inimical to them), they made new friendships and renewed old ones to cement the good feelings amongst all players that are so necessary for the game itself, and to promote the best of relations between the new Commonwealth and the "Mother Country".

The old "saw" – "it's bowling that wins matches" – was never more true than with the Australians, and in view of the damp pitches of 1902, Trumble and Saunders were so often the match-winners. Noble was an admirable third string, a potential wicket-taker under all conditions, and with the accurate Armstrong there were signs of coming stature. Had the season been a drier one Ernest Jones and Bill Howell would have been put to much greater use, but so often the pitches did not suit them. There were days, too, when Trumper and Hopkins had success with the ball.

Trumble's bowling record was an amazing one – 140 wickets at an average of 14.27 – and these were garnered in only twenty matches. Had he been able to perform throughout the tour, his eventual bag must have been well over 200. So often Jack Saunders operated in harness with Trumble, and his cleverness in using the damp English pitch, hitherto unknown to him, to his team's advantage made him at times more difficult to counter than his giant colleague. The results Saunders achieved of 127 wickets at 17.07 fully justified his inclusion in the touring party, but many English players thought his bowling action was, to put it mildly, suspect. However, no umpire, not even Jim Phillips, called him for throwing.

Personal misfortune, as previously related, affected Bill Howell's performance as well as the pitches, though there were times when he bowled with such determination that he carried all before him by sheer force. Considering the circumstances, his effort of 68 wickets at 17.87 was quite a fine one. It was not a very good season for fast bowlers and Ernie Jones, in common with his English brethren of extreme pace, suffered accordingly. There were one or two occasions when he bowled on a sympathetic pitch with all his old fire and sting, but he was now past his prime, had put on weight, and when his pace flagged he could be hit. Still unpassable at mid-off and a very useful tail-end hitter, he did well whenever it was possible to do so in all departments of the game.

Darling's captaincy was ever astute, always appearing to have control of the game and managing his bowling forces admirably, save for but one occasion: the last innings of the Fifth Test match when he relied too much on Saunders instead of making more use of Noble. A born leader, on and off the field, Darling, by example and a kindly firmness, encouraged his team to maintain themselves in excellent physical condition. With great powers of concentration of purpose, he kept them just as zestful in their cricket at the close of the tour as at the beginning. Ever zealous of his team's welfare, he never lost sight of the reason for which they had come: to play cricket in the best spirit of the game and, above all, to win the Test rubber. For their ultimate success, the Tourists had much to thank their outstanding captain for.

As the all-rounder of the side, Noble had to deputise for the injured Trumble at the beginning of the tour (that he did so admirably can be seen from the records), but this extra burden had its effect upon his batting. Patently quite out of form until the eve of the Third Test match, in which he did so well with bat and ball, he subsequently came good with a sprinkling of fifties, a hundred off Gloucestershire, his mammoth 284 at Sussex' expense, then a whirlwind 113 at Southampton. Hitting freely and hard whenever circumstances permitted, he ended with 1,416 runs in 48 innings. As his batting improved so his bowling seemed to leave him, but 98 wickets at 19.85 could be considered a good performance for a bowler of his type in such a watery summer.

The most remarkable feature of the 1902 cricket season was the pre-eminence of Victor Trumper over every other batsman in the game. In a very wet season, while most of them were struggling for runs, Trumper was in a class by himself, scoring 2,570 including eleven separate hundreds, the highest being only 128. That he could have scored hundreds more had he wished to do so there is little doubt, for he often gave his wicket away when he saw little purpose in keeping it up. Simply scoring runs for the sake of it never appealed to him. In matches against the counties, if circumstances warranted it with plenty of batting still to come, he would quietly give his wicket to a bowler he felt deserved encouragement, thereby allowing his team-mates to get a knock. It was the very nature of the man.

When one attempts to study his methods from the action photographs and through the eyes of those who saw him, it becomes apparent that Trumper could be compared, in the broadest terms, with Gilbert Jessop as a hitter and with Ranjitsinhji for finesse of wristy strokeplay. He combined each approach with a charming gracefulness of his own, transmuting them to a loftier plane. As A. E. Knight was to write of him: "Stylish in the highest sense, orthodox, yet breaking all canons of style, Trumper is just himself. . . . Not in his fascinating collection of strokes, nor in their frank and open execution merely lay the charm; it was a man playing away a power which was himself rather than in him."[*] Never playing himself in at the commencement of an innings (remember, "he looked upon the ball when it was red"), quite often he would hit the first ball for four runs. Always on the attack and always attempting to dictate to the bowler by going down the pitch, Trumper experimented with strokes for the sheer pleasure it gave

*A. E. Knight, *The Complete Cricketer*, Methuen, pp. 273-4.

189

him. If three identical balls were bowled to him of the same length, line and pace, they would most likely be dispatched to the boundary with a cut, a pull and a drive over the bowler's head.

Bowlers could rarely keep him quiet, indeed they had difficulty in setting a field to him, for Victor could hit almost any ball to any point of the compass round the wicket. By advancing down the pitch to fast bowlers, as well as medium or slow, he destroyed their length and would cut, hook or pull balls which were plumb on the stumps. This called for near perfection in co-ordination of eye, reflex and movement, additionally requiring nerve and a supreme confidence in one's powers. In an age of amateur batsmen who were quick scorers, even for those days, Victor Trumper was far quicker in his run-rate per ball than anybody except Jessopus. He sometimes gave chances, but with the methods he employed this was not surprising. What did surprise the onlooker who was lucky enough to see him in action in 1902, though, was thàt Trumper made the scores he did by these very methods. The utter despair of all who bowled to him, their only hope was his own charming negligence.

"So before his mighty powers fell the valiant and the brave,
And full many a reputation found a most untoimely grave,
As me Victor tramped the country, like a divastatin' wave,
Makin' 'ivry kind o' wreckage wid the bowlin'.

"He's as modest as a daisy, and as gentle as can be,
So I take me hat off to him, wid this message frank and free,
That his rivals in ould England think a match well lost to see
Victor Trumper spind an hour wid their bowlin'."*

From this lofty plane we come to the remainder of the batting, which rather fell below the known potential of the players concerned, due, no doubt, to the effect of the damp pitches and attempts to keep scoring at an energetic rate. Clem Hill was the next best bat after Trumper in both runs scored (1,614) and method, but he reached neither the heights of 1899 nor of the recently closed season at home. Still a magnificent player and difficult to dislodge when set, he seemed an easier target than previously, undergoing periods of unaccountable ill ease when the bowling troubled him. Such was the fighting spirit imbued within him, however, he seemed to be able to do something of note on the big occasion with the bat and in the long field, as at Sheffield and Old Trafford – such was his tenacity of purpose. Having four separate hundreds to his credit and many other splendid innings, it was noted how much harder he hit the ball; and there were times when Clem was unlucky enough to be dismissed by fielding as brilliant and audacious as his own.

*Guy Eden, "Victor Trumper," *Bush Ballads & Other Verses*, verses v & ix, Sisley's Ltd.

Showing great promise at all times, Reg Duff always appeared likely to make a long score and to do so, moreover, in a vigorous and buoyant fashion. That he often failed to do himself justice may have been due to his forcing style on pitches to which he was unaccustomed. An unhappy knack of getting himself out when well set was Duff's misfortune, plus the disadvantage of usually being at the wickets with Trumper. That he could still shine in his colleague's exalted company was due to his natural genius and the forcing game he played. After a healthy start with three forties, he underwent a bad patch and was temporarily dropped to number six or seven in the order, when he re-established himself in magnificent style with 182 at Bradford against "An England Eleven". Returning to number two in the next game with 98 versus Scotland, he then scored 90 off Worcester followed by 62 at Bristol and 183 – his finest innings – at Taunton. The next knocks, 57 from Surrey then 54 in the Fourth Test, were followed by another lean period; even so, he made 1,507 runs and was five times not out in fifty-eight innings.

The other two new batsmen on the tour were, strictly speaking, chosen as all-round men. Warwick Armstrong's batting was stern and capable, showing sound judgement and much patience, but there were occasions when this tall, powerfully built man would drive hard and cut with great determination. That he was very difficult to dislodge, even when beaten by the ball, is apparent from his ten not out innings, one of which was as large as 172. What surprised his opponents more than anything else was the extreme accuracy of Armstrong's leg-breaks. Even when the pitch gave little assistance, he put them down on the leg stump with such nagging persistence that he could effectively keep down the runs. The 81 wickets he claimed at 17.41 runs each is not quite the whole story, for nearly a third of the overs he sent down were maidens. A very effective performance for one who was included as just a change bowler.

An elegant and graceful bat was Hopkins, who, like Armstrong, spent much of his time in the lower batting order where there was less chance to shine. When opportunity came his way, he played some notable innings in the classic mould (particularly 80 against Notts, 105 not out versus Gloucestershire, 74 off the South of England), and there were many more in the forties, fifties and sixties from his wristy bat. Always useful as a second or third change, his medium-paced off-cutters, with considerable variety of pace, often broke up a stand. Seven wickets for 10 runs in Cambridge University's second innings and 9 for 76 at Cheltenham were his great performances, but, doubtless, that which satisfied him most were the scalps of Ranji and Fry at the opening of the abortive Lord's Test. 1,192 runs with 8 not outs and 38 wickets at 17.61 average fully justified his selection.

Joe Darling's form with the bat was not up to the standard of his previous visit in 1899, although he showed splendid touch at the commencement of the current tour with 92 and 128 from the two opening fixtures. There followed a lean period which was not overcome until mid-June, when he made 65 and 40 in consecutive innings. The respite was only temporary for again he suffered a series of low scores including two "pairs", until the two fine innings in the Old Trafford Test, his marvellous 116 in 80 minutes against Hampshire, and a spirited 67 at Harrogate. The power with which he hit was tremendous and the 1,113 runs would certainly have been increased had the season been a drier one. More than once he played a captain's innings.

The other "old hand", Syd Gregory, sadly disappointed, falling one run short of a thousand and never reaching the magical hundred. Still as immaculate as ever and always a delight to watch with his classic strokemaking, "Little Tich" suffered misfortune time and again in getting out for low scores. Even so, he performed much useful service to his side, in particular the notable 42 not out in the critical second innings against Yorkshire at Bradford, and a fortune-turning second innings of 71 at Eastbourne. But the occasion upon which he really shone was at Lord's when he made 86 off the M C C attack and looked so well set for the century he failed to achieve. As usual his fielding was superb throughout the season; for that alone he was worth his place.

Another reason why the touring side was so successful in the field lay in Jim Kelly's smart keeping throughout the season. Time and again, regardless of the state and pace of the pitch, Kelly kept to his bowlers in an ever reliable manner, never appealing unless he was certain, always neat, unobtrusive, and never showy. All the bowlers had great confidence in his powers for he so often made opportunities, such as his remarkable stumping of Braund during the critical last innings of the Old Trafford Test. He achieved the honour of being voted by *Wisden*, along with Trumper and Armstrong, one of the "Five Cricketers of the Year".

With the senior wicketkeeper maintaining such grand day-to-day form Hanson Carter's opportunities with the gloves were comparatively restricted, but he proved an able deputy, cool and reliable, neat in gathering the ball and particularly smart in taking on the leg side. It was obvious to discerning observers that here was Kelly's replacement in the Australian side, ready-made for when the older man retired.

The consistently high standard of fielding, as always with the Australians, was such a noticeable feature of the season. Whether in anticipation, ground fielding, gathering the ball, accurate throwing and catching, they as a team were in a class by themselves. Even the England side at their best, save for Jessop and Braund, could match them only at Birmingham. During the county games, except those with Yorkshire, the difference was even more marked. If individuals are to be mentioned at all, Hill, Trumper, Duff and Hopkins in the long field, Gregory at cover, Noble at point, and Jones at mid-off continually brought off daring saves and splendid catches with scarcely any fall-off in their cricket.

By winning two out of the three finished Test matches the Australians took the rubber handsomely enough, but all of the luck that was going happened to be on their side, and, considering the series as an entity, the result could so easily have gone the other way. Nonetheless, all credit is due to the Tourists for their two well-earned victories. Taking the tour as a whole, with 23 wins, 2 defeats and 14 unfinished in the 39 matches played they easily surpassed the records of all their predecessors. Of the unfinished matches, due in every case except the last to the vagaries of the weather, the Cornstalks were almost always the superior side, though they could have been beaten at Hastings by the South of England. At all times their cricket had a sparkling quality, and as entertainment value it was of the highest order. They added considerable colour and distinction to the English season and enhanced the already enormous reputation of Australian cricket.

That the eleventh touring team proved to be so outstanding is without question, but it is of absorbing interest to consider how this 1902 side of Joe Darling's compares with other great teams from the premier cricketing country. The most powerful combination of talent to visit our shores previous to the series just considered was W. L. Murdoch's, the third Australian team of 1882. It boasted five bowlers of the first rank: Spofforth, Palmer, Giffen, Boyle and Garrett; two brilliant hitters: Percy McDonnell and H. Massie; Murdoch himself and Giffen to get runs with Alec Bannerman to stonewall at one end. It was a fine fielding side, with the peerless talents of John McCarthy Blackham behind the stumps. They suffered four defeats, two of these being inflicted by the exceptional Cambridge University team of that year, but otherwise they were like lions in the land. Their crowning glory was, of course, the Oval Test match (only one was played that year) when they won a most remarkable game of low scores, coming from behind in England's last innings amid tremendous excitement to be victorious by 7 runs. This was the "match of the Ashes", the first occasion upon which an Australian eleven triumphed over the might of England on her own soil.

Warwick Armstrong's monumental team that descended upon us in 1921 must merit consideration for its record and tremendous strength. Two really fast bowlers in harness – Jack Gregory and Ted McDonald – was something new, and they were ably supported by Arthur Mailey's "bosies" and Armstrong's leg-spin. Macartney and Bardsley each scored over 2,000 runs, and were backed up by Armstrong, Ryder, Collins, Andrews and Taylor, to mention only some of the batsmen. Carter was making his last tour and Oldfield his first. The record, strikingly similar to 1902, with one game less played, was 22 won, 2 lost and 14 drawn. The opposition they encountered as they steamrollered their way around a recently war-torn England could hardly be compared to the strength that Darling's team had met nineteen years before.

And finally, of course, there is Bradman's all conquering team of 1948, the twentieth touring side: Lindwall, Miller, W. A. Johnston, I. W. Johnson, Toshack, Morris, Barnes, Bradman, Hassett, Brown, Loxton, Harvey, Ring, Saggers, McCool and Tallon. It won four of the five Test matches, all by very large margins, and was unbeaten in all its 31 first-class games. The disparity, however, between England and Australia was immense, and with the counties even more so. English cricket at that time was probably much weaker even than in 1921.

It is hardly possible to classify the respective merits of these four outstanding touring teams, each of which shattered our native game, owing to changes in the game itself, the individual players' approach to their cricket, and the fact that the circumstances and manner in which the game was played altered so profoundly between 1882, 1902, 1921 and 1948. That Bradman's and Armstrong's combinations were stronger in fast bowling cannot be denied, but in 1902 Darling's darlings had to meet a far higher standard of opposition in their daily cricket, and an England side at the very peak of its powers.

Appendix
Statistics of the Tour

Note: the matches columns indicate those games in which a player batted or bowled.

AUSTRALIAN BATTING AVERAGES–ALL MATCHES

	Matches	Innings	Runs	Most in an Innings	Times not out	Average
V. T. Trumper (NSW) .	35	53	2570	128	0	48.49
M. A. Noble (NSW) ...	34	48	1416	284	5	32.93
C. Hill (SA)	36	52	1614	136	1	31.65
R. A. Duff (NSW)	38	58	1507	183	5	28.43
W. W. Armstrong (V) ..	36	51	1087	172*	10	26.51
A. J. Hopkins (NSW) ..	37	54	1192	105*	8	25.91
J. Darling (SA)	35	51	1113	128	5	24.20
S. E. Gregory (NSW) ..	34	52	999	86	6	21.72
H. Trumble (V)	19	30	429	68	6	17.88
J. J. Kelly (NSW)	22	33	368	75	8	14.72
E. Jones (SA)	17	21	254	40	1	12.70
H. Carter (NSW)	15	20	121	31	5	8.07
W. P. Howell (NSW) ..	17	24	95	16	6	5.28
J. V. Saunders (V)	23	34	84	9*	9	3.36

In one match – against Cambridge University – the Australians were assisted by Dr Rowley J. Pope, who scored 2*.

*Signifies not out.

AUSTRALIAN BOWLING AVERAGES–ALL MATCHES

	Matches	Overs	Mdns	Runs	Wickets	Average
H. Trumble	20	948	305	1998	140	14.27
J. V. Saunders	26	749	172	2168	127	17.07
W. W. Armstrong	31	694.1	206	1410	81	17.41
A. J. Hopkins	23	242.1	67	669	38	17.61
W. P. Howell	18	497	148	1215	68	17.87
M. A. Noble	32	733	213	1945	98	19.85
E. Jones	20	548.2	145	1456	71	20.50
V. T. Trumper	14	152.3	43	415	20	20.75

R. A. Duff 20—4—48—4, bowled in five innings; C. Hill 19.5—4—59—4, in four innings; S. E. Gregory 4—0—21—0, in two innings; and J. J. Kelly 4—0—13—2, and H. Carter 1—0—7—0, each in one innings only.

AUSTRALIAN WICKETKEEPING–ALL MATCHES

J. J. Kelly .... Caught 22 and stumped 13.
H. Carter .... Caught 20 and stumped 5.
R. A. Duff .... Caught 3.

AUSTRALIAN CATCHES–ALL MATCHES

W. Armstrong 32, M. Noble 31, C. Hill 28, J. Darling 26, V. T. Trumper 24, R. Duff 23, A. Hopkins 22, S. Gregory 20, H. Trumble 19, W. Howell 15, J. Saunders 15, E. Jones 12.

AUSTRALIAN BATTING AVERAGES IN THE FIVE TEST MATCHES

	Matches	Innings	Runs	Most in an innings	Times not out	Average
C. Hill	4	8	258	119	1	36.86
V. T. Trumper	4	8	247	104	0	30.88
H. Trumble	3	6	107	64*	2	26.75
A. J. Hopkins	4	7	117	40*	1	19.50
M. A. Noble	4	7	129	52	0	18.43
R. A. Duff	4	8	129	54	0	16.13
J. Darling	4	7	109	51	0	15.57
S. E. Gregory	4	8	100	29	1	14.29
W. W. Armstrong	4	7	97	26	0	13.86
J. J. Kelly	4	7	46	39	3	11.50
J. V. Saunders	3	6	6	3	1	1.20

W. P. Howell 0, and E. Jones 0, each batted once. H. Carter, the reserve wicketkeeper, did not play in any of the Test matches.

AUSTRALIAN BOWLING AVERAGES IN THE FIVE TEST MATCHES

	Matches	Overs	Mdns	Runs	Wickets	Average
H. Trumble	3	172.4	55	371	26	14.27
M. A. Noble	5	127	41	307	14	21.93
A. J. Hopkins	3	17	5	49	2	24.50
J. V. Saunders	4	131.1	23	473	18	26.28
E. Jones	2	39	13	107	3	35.67
V. T. Trumper	4	37	11	101	2	50.50
W. W. Armstrong	5	44	10	123	2	61.50

W. P. Howell also bowled in the Birmingham match, his figures being 26—8—58—1.

AUSTRALIAN WICKETKEEPING–TEST MATCHES

J. Kelly caught 3, stumped 3.

AUSTRALIAN CATCHES–TEST MATCHES

W. Armstrong 7, C. Hill 4, H. Trumble 4, M. Noble 3, V. Trumper 2, S. Gregory 2, R. Duff 2, J. Darling 2, A. Hopkins 2, J. Saunders 1, E. Jones 1.

ENGLISH BATTING AVERAGES IN THE FIVE TEST MATCHES

	Matches	Innings	Runs	Most in an innings	Times not out	Average
W. Rhodes (Yorks.) ...	4	7	67	38*	6	67.00
Hon. F. S. Jackson (,,)	5	8	311	128	1	44.43
G. H. Hirst (Yorkshire)	3	5	157	58*	1	39.25
Mr G. L. Jessop (Glos.)	3	5	190	104	0	38.00
J. W. Tyldesley (Lancs)	4	7	245	138	0	35.00
Mr A. C. MacLaren (,,)	5	8	198	63	1	28.29
W. H. Lockwood (Surrey)	3	5	86	52*	1	21.50
R. Abel (Surrey)	2	4	73	38	0	18.25
L. C. Braund (Somerset)	4	7	115	65	0	16.43
Mr L. C. H. Palairet (,,)	2	4	49	20	0	12.25
A. A. Lilley (Warks.) ..	4	7	46	16	0	6.57
K. S. Ranjitsinhji (Sussex)	3	4	19	13	0	4.75
Mr C. B. Fry (Sussex) ..	3	4	5	4	0	1.25

The following also batted: S. F. Barnes (Lancashire), 7 and 5; F. W. Tate (Sussex), 5* and 4; and T. Hayward (Surrey), 0 and 7.

*Signifies not out.

ENGLISH BOWLING AVERAGES IN THE FIVE TEST MATCHES

	Matches	Overs	Mdns	Runs	Wickets	Average
W. H. Lockwood	2	81.1	18	206	17	12.12
S. F. Barnes	1	32	13	99	7	14.14
W. Rhodes	4	140.5	38	336	22	15.27
G. H. Hirst	3	79	18	208	9	23.11
F. W. Tate	1	16	4	51	2	25.50
L. C. Braund	4	76.5	13	210	7	30.00
Hon F. S. Jackson	4	61.1	12	209	6	34.83
Mr G. L. Jessop	2	10	2	26	0	—

ENGLISH WICKETKEEPING–TEST MATCHES

A. A. Lilley caught 11, stumped 1.

ENGLISH CATCHES–TEST MATCHES

L. C. Braund 8, A. MacLaren 5, W. Rhodes 4, F. S. Jackson 3, C. B. Fry 2, G. L. Jessop 2, J. T. Tyldesley 2, G. H. Hirst 2, L. C. H. Palairet 2, F. W. Tate 2, R. Abel 1.

THE FOLLOWING TWENTY-FOUR INNINGS OF 100 AND OVER WERE HIT FOR THE AUSTRALIANS

128   V. T. Trumper, v. Cambridge University, at Cambridge.
127   V. T. Trumper, v. Eleven Players of England, at Harrogate.
125   V. T. Trumper, v. Gloucestershire, at Cheltenham.
121   V. T. Trumper, v. Oxford University, at Oxford.
120   V. T. Trumper, v. South of England, at Hastings.
119   V. T. Trumper, v. Essex, at Leyton.
113   V. T. Trumper, v. An England Eleven, at Bradford.
109   V. T. Trumper, v. Essex, at Leyton.
105   V. T. Trumper, v. MCC and Ground, at Lord's.
104   V. T. Trumper, v. England, at Manchester (Fourth Test Match).
101   V. T. Trumper, v. Surrey, at Kennington Oval.
136   C. Hill, v. MCC and Ground, at Lord's.
125   C. Hill, v. Gloucestershire, at Bristol.
119   C. Hill, v. England, at Sheffield (Third Test Match).
104   C. Hill, v. Essex, at Leyton.
284   M. A. Noble, v. Sussex, at Brighton.
113   M. A. Noble, v. Hampshire, at Southampton.
100   M. A. Noble, v. Gloucestershire, at Bristol.
183   R. A. Duff, v. Somerset, at Taunton.
182   R. A. Duff, v. An England Eleven, at Bradford.
128   J. Darling, v. Notts, at Nottingham.
116   J. Darling, v. Hampshire, at Southampton.
172* W. W. Armstrong, v. Sussex, at Brighton.
105* A. J. Hopkins, v. Gloucestershire, at Bristol.

*Signifies not out.

THE FOLLOWING SIX INNINGS OF OVER 100 WERE HIT AGAINST THE AUSTRALIANS

138   J. T. Tyldesley, for England, at Birmingham (First Test Match).
128   Hon F. S. Jackson, for England, at Manchester (Fourth Test Match).
106   T. Hayward, for South of England, at Hastings.
104   Mr G. L. Jessop, for England, at Kennington Oval (Fifth Test Match).
104   R. Abel, for Surrey, at Kennington Oval (second match).
104   L. C. Braund, for London County, at the Crystal Palace.

Bibliography

Altham, H. S., *A History of Cricket*, Vol. I, Allen & Unwin, 1962.

Altham, H. S.; Arlott, John; Eagar, E. D. R.; Webber, Roy, *Hampshire County Cricket*, Phoenix House, 1957.

Arlott, John, *Rothmans Jubilee History of Cricket*, Arthur Barker Ltd, 1965.

Arrowsmith, R. L., *A History of County Cricket – Kent*, Arthur Barker Ltd, 1971.

Barker, Ralph, *Ten Great Bowlers*, Chatto & Windus, 1967.

Beldam, G. W. and Fry, C. B., *Great Batsmen – Their Methods at a Glance*, Macmillan, 1905.

Beldam, G. W. and Fry, C. B., *Great Bowlers & Fielders – Their Methods at a Glance*, Macmillan, 1906.

Binns, Richard, *Cricket in Firelight*, Selwyn & Blount Ltd, 1935.

Britton, C. J., *G. L. Jessop*, Cornish Brothers Ltd, 1935.

Brodribb, Gerald, *The Croucher – A Biography of Gilbert Jessop*, London Magazine Editions, 1974.

Brodribb, Gerald, *Maurice Tate*, London Magazine Editions, 1976.

Cardus, Neville, *Autobiography*, Collins, 1947.

Cardus, Neville, *The Summer Game*, Rupert Hart-Davis, 1929.

Country Vicar, A (R. L. Hodgson), *Cricket Memories*, Methuen, 1930.

Cricket: A Weekly Record of the Game – particularly the year 1902.

Darling, D. K., *Test Tussles on and off the Field*, Pub. by the Author, 1970.

Duckworth, Leslie, *S. F. Barnes – Master Bowler*, Hutchinson & Co., 1967.

Fingleton, J. H., *The Immortal Victor Trumper*, Collins, 1978.

Frindall, Bill, *The Wisden Book of Test Cricket*, MacDonald & Janes, 1979.

Frith, David, *The Fast Men*, Van Nostrand Reinhold, 1975.

Frith, David, *The Golden Age of Cricket 1890–1914*, Lutterworth Press, 1979.

Fry, C. B., *Life Worth Living*, Eyre & Spottiswoode, 1939.

Grayson, Edward, *Corinthians & Cricketers*, Naldrett Press Ltd, 1955.

Hutchinson, Horace G., Ed., *Cricket (Country Life Library of Sport)*, Country Life, 1903.

Jessop, Gilbert L., *A Cricketer's Log*, Hodder & Stoughton, 1922.

Knight, Albert E., *The Complete Cricketer*, Methuen, 1906.

Lilley, Arthur A., *Twenty-Four Years of Cricket*, Mills & Boon, 1912.

Mailey, Arthur, *10 for 66 and All That*, Phoenix Sports Books, 1958.

Marshall, John, *Old Trafford*, Pelham Books, 1971.

Morrah, Patrick, *The Golden Age of Cricket*, Eyre & Spottiswoode, 1967.

Moyes, A. G., *Australian Cricket – A History*, Angus & Robertson, 1959.

Moyes, A. G., *The Changing Face of Cricket*, Angus & Robertson, 1964.

Noble, M. A., *The Game's the Thing*, Cassell & Co., 1926.

Raiji, Vasant, Ed., *Victor Trumper*, Vivek Publications, Bombay, 1964.

Rogerson, Sidney, *Wilfred Rhodes*, Hollis & Carter, 1960.

Sewell, E. H. D., *Who's Won the Toss?*, Stanley Paul, 1943.

Standing, Percy Cross, *Cricket of Today and Yesterday*, Vols I & II, T. C. & E. C. Jack, 1902.

Standing, Percy Cross, *The Hon. F. S. Jackson*, Cassell & Co., 1906.

Thomson, A. A., *Cricketers of My Times*, Stanley Paul, 1967.

Thomson, A. A., *Hirst and Rhodes*, Epworth Press, 1959.

Trevor, Col. Philip, *Cricket & Cricketers*, Chapman & Hall, 1921.

Trevor, Major Philip, *The Problems of Cricket*, Sampson Low & Marston & Co., 1907.

Wakley, B. J., *Classic Centuries*, Nicholas Kaye Ltd, 1964.

Warner, P. F., Ed., *Cricket* (The Badminton Library), Longmans, 1920.

Warner, P. F., *Cricket Reminiscences*, Grant Richards, 1920.

Warner, P. F., *How We Recovered the Ashes*, Chapman & Hall, 1904.

Warner, P. F., *My Cricketing Life*, Hodder & Stoughton, 1921.

Webber, Roy, *Book of Cricket Records*, Phoenix, 1961.

Webber, Roy, *Test Records*, Vol. I (1877–1939), Playfair Books Ltd, 1952.

Wellings, E. M., *A History of County Cricket – Middlesex*, Arthur Barker Ltd, 1972.

Wisden Cricketers' Almanack – particularly 1903 Edition.

Woods, S. M. J., *My Reminiscences*, Chapman & Hall, 1925.

In addition, newspapers consulted for major matches: *Birmingham Post, Daily Graphic, Daily Telegraph, Evening News, Manchester Guardian* and *Yorkshire Post*.

Index

Abel, R., xii, 20, 21, 22, 53, 68, 72, 73, 74;
  (3rd Test) 84, 85, 86–87, 90, 93; 106, 112,
  114; (4th Test) 116, 117, 122, 128–129,
  132; 146, 179, 182, 183, 185; (Stats)
  197–198
Anderson, Mr J., 80, 82, 83
Andrews, T. J. E., 194
Ansell, Mr W., 95
Anthony, G., 17, 18, 19
Apted, Sam, 152
Armstrong, W. W., xi, 2, 8, 10; (v Lon. C.)
  13, 14, 15; (v Notts) 17, 18 19; (v Surrey)
  20, 21, 22; (v Essex) 23, 24, 25; (v Leics)
  29; (v Oxf.U) 29, 31; (v MCC) 35, 36;
  (1st Test) 44, 45, 48, 50; (v Yorks) 55, 57,
  59, 60; (v Lancs) 62, 63; (v Camb.U) 65;
  (2nd Test) 71; (v Eng.XI) 74; (v Derby)
  76; (v Eng.XI at Bradford) 79, 80, 81;
  (v Scot.) 82; (3rd Test) 86, 87, 89–90, 91,
  93; (v Warks) 96, 98; (v Worcs) 101, 102,
  103; (v Glos) 104, 105, 106, 107; (v Som.)
  111; (v Surrey) 113, 114; (4th Test) 122,
  123–124, 127, 128, 131, 132; (v Sussex)
  138–139, 140; (v Glam & Wilts) 139, 141;
  (v Hants) 144; (5th Test) 147–148, 149,
  151–152, 154, 156–157, 159, 161; (v MCC)
  163, 164, 165; (v Glos) 166, 167; (v Kent)
  170; (v Middx) 169, 170, 171, 172, 173;
  (v Lancs) 174, 175; (v XI Players of Eng.)
  178; (v C. I. Thornton's XI) 177, 179,
  180; (v S of Eng. at Hastings) 180, 181,
  182; (v S of Eng. at Bournemouth) 184;
  (v Players) 185; 188, 191, 192, 193–194;
  (Stats) 195–198
Arnold, E., xii, 72, 73, 74, 100, 101, 103,
  176, 177, 178, 181, 183, 184
Ashcroft, Mr E. M., xii, 75, 76
Attewell, W. (Ump.), 140

Bainbridge, Mr H. W., 39, 95, 96, 98
Bairstow, 79, 81

Baker, A., 22, 112
Bannerman, A. C., 193
Bardsley, W., 194
Barnes, S. F. xii, 61, 62, 63; (3rd Test)
  85–86, 88, 89, 93, 94; 116, 117, 118, 172;
  (Stats) 197
Barnes, S. G., 194
Barrett, Capt. E. I. M., 142
Barton, V. A., 143, 144
Bates, 39
Bean, G., 139, 140
Bean, G. (Ump.), 15, 74, 107, 111, 182
Beldam, Mr G. W., xii, 12, 13, 15, 99, 169,
  171–172, 173
Beloe, Mr H., 102
Bencraft, Dr H. W. R., 142
Bernhardt, Mme Sarah, 72
Bestwick, W., xii, 72, 73, 74, 75, 76
Binns, Richard, 56, 119
Bird, A., 100, 101, 103
Blackham, J. McC., 6, 193
Blaker, Mr R. N. R., 64, 65, 167, 170
Bland, C. H. G., 137
Blythe, C., xii, 167–168, 169, 170
Board, J. H., xii, 13, 15, 106, 107, 166, 167,
  179, 182, 184
Bodington, Mr C. H., 144
Bonham-Carter, Mr M., 31
Bosanquet, Mr B. J. T., xii, 171, 172, 173
Boucicault, Miss Nina, 72
Bowley, F. L., xii, 100, 101, 102, 103
Boyle, H. F., 6, 193
Bradford, Capt. E. R., 142
Bradley, Mr W. M., xii, 167, 168, 170
Bradman, D. G., xiii, 194
Brain, Mr J. H., 139, 141
Brain, Mr W. H., 139, 141
Braund, L. C., xii, 13, 14, 15, 32, 34, 35, 36;
  (1st Test) 39, 40, 43, 45, 47, 50; (2nd Test)
  68, 71; (3rd Test) 85, 86, 87, 89, 93; 109,
  110, 111; (4th Test) 117, 119, 123–124,

Braund, L. C., (contd)
  125, 126, 129, 132; (5th Test) 147, 148,
  149–150, 151, 153, 161; 177, 179, 181,
  182, 183, 185, 192; (Stats) 197–198
Briggs, J., 61
Brockwell, W., 20, 22, 112, 113, 114, 181,
  184
Brodribb, Gerald, 160
Brown, J. T., xii, 53, 54, 55, 58, 60, 77, 78
Brown, W. A., 194
Brown, Mr W. S. A., 105, 106, 107
Brownlee, Mr L. D., 104, 105, 106, 107, 167
Brownlee, W. Methven, 104
Buckenham, C. P., 22
Burnup, Mr C. J., xii, 68–69, 99, 166, 167,
  168, 169, 170, 179, 182
Burrows, R. D., 100–101, 103
Bush, Capt. H. S., 20, 72, 74, 106
Butt, H. R., 137, 139, 140
Buxton, 76

Campbell, Mr C. M., 80, 82
Cardus, Neville, 118, 120
Carlin, J. (Ump.), 25, 98, 173
Carpenter, H., 23, 24, 25, 163, 164, 165
Carter, H., xii, 2, 11, 13; (v Surrey) 20, 21,
  22; (v Leics) 27, 29; (v Oxf.U) 30, 31; 38;
  (v Lancs) 61, 63; (v Camb.U) 64, 65;
  (v Derby) 75, 76; (v Eng. XI at Bradford)
  79, 80, 81; (v Scot.) 82, 83; 84; (v Warks)
  95, 97, 98; (v Worcs) 103; (v Surrey) 113,
  114; 118; (v Glam & Wilts) 139, 141;
  (v Hants) 143, 144; (v Glos) 167; (v Kent)
  170; (v XI Players of Eng.) 177, 178;
  (v S of Eng. at Hastings) 182; 192, 194;
  (Stats) 195–196
Champain, Mr F. H. B., 102, 104, 165–166,
  167
Charlesworth, C., 96, 97, 98
Chatterton, W., 76
Chinnery, Mr H. B., 163, 165
Clode, H., 112, 113, 114
Coe, S., 29
Collins, Mr A., 140
Collins, H. L., 194
Coulson, H. (Ump.), 141
Cox, G., 137–138, 140
Craig, Albert, 19
Cranfield, B., xii, 32, 36, 109, 111
Crawford, Mr R. T., xii, 26, 28, 29, 78, 80,
  81
Crawford, Mr V. F. S., xii, 20, 22, 26, 72,
  73, 74, 112
Crawford, Rev. J. C., 26
Creber, H., 139, 141
Cuttell, W. R., 61, 172

Darling, J., xi 1, 2, 3; (v Lon. C.) 13, 14, 15;
  (v Notts) 17, 18, 19; (v Surrey) 19, 21, 22;
  (v Essex) 24, 25; (v Leics) 27, 28, 29;

(v Oxf.U) 30, 31; (v MCC) 34, 35, 36, 37;
  (1st Test) 38, 44, 45, 46, 47, 49, 50;
  (v Yorks) 55, 57, 59, 60; (v Lancs) 61, 62,
  63; (2nd Test) 67, 69, 70, 71; (v Eng. XI)
  72, 74; (v Derby) 75, 76; (v Yorks) 75, 76,
  78; (v Eng. XI at Bradford) 79, 80, 81;
  (v Scot.) 80, 82, 83; (3rd Test) 85, 86, 87, 88,
  89, 91, 92, 93; (v Warks) 96, 98; (v Worcs)
  102, 103; (v Glos) 104, 106, 107; (v Som.)
  109, 111; (v Surrey) 112, 113, 114; (4th
  Test) 118, 121–122, 123, 125–127, 128, 129,
  131, 132; (v Essex) 135, 137; (v Sussex) 139,
  140; (v Hants) 143–144; (5th Test) 147,
  151, 153, 156, 158, 159, 161; (v MCC) 163,
  164, 165; (v Glos) 164, 165, 167; (v Kent)
  168, 169, 170; (v Middx) 171, 173; (v Lancs)
  172, 174, 175; (v XI Players of Eng.) 177,
  178, 179; (v C. I. Thornton's XI) 180;
  (v S of Eng. at Bournemouth) 184;
  (v Players) 185, 186; 188–189, 192, 193,
  194; (Stats) 195–198
Davidson, G., 6
Day, Mr S. H., xii, 63, 99, 167, 168, 170,
  179, 182
Denton, D., xii, 53, 55, 58, 60, 68, 77, 78
Devey, J., 95–96, 97, 98, 176, 177, 178
Dillon, Mr E. W., xii, 28, 29, 31, 179,
  182
Dixon, Mr J. A., 16, 17, 19
Douglas, Mr J., xii, 169, 171, 173
Douglas, Mr R. N., xii, 170, 172, 173
Downs, Mr A., 82
Dowson, Mr E. M., xii, 20, 21, 22, 63, 64,
  65, 112, 157
Driffield, Mr L. T., 65
Duff, R. A., xi, 2, 9; (v Lon. C.) 13, 15;
  (v Notts) 17, 19; (v Surrey) 20, 22; (v Essex)
  23, 24, 25; (v Leics) 27, 28, 29; (v Oxf.U)
  30, 31; (v MCC) 34, 35, 36; (1st Test) 38,
  46, 47, 49, 50; (v Yorks) 54, 56, 59, 60;
  (v Lancs) 62, 63; (v Camb.U) 64, 65;
  (2nd Test) 71; (v Eng. XI) 73, 74; (v Derby)
  76; (v Yorks) 76–77, 78; (v Eng. XI at
  Bradford) 79–80, 81; (v Scot.) 82–83; (3rd
  Test) 85–86, 88, 93; (v Warks) 96, 98;
  (v Worcs) 101, 103; (v Glos) 105–106, 107;
  (v Som.) 109–110, 111; (v Surrey) 113, 114;
  (4th Test) 118–120, 124, 125, 128, 132, 133;
  (v Essex) 135, 137; (v Sussex) 140; (v Glam
  & Wilts) 141; (v Hants) 143, 144; (5th
  Test) 147, 150–151, 160, 161; (v MCC)
  163, 164, 165; (v Glos) 167; (v Kent) 168,
  170; (v Middx) 171, 172, 173; (v Lancs)
  173, 174; (v XI Players of Eng.) 176–177,
  178; (v C. I. Thornton's XI) 177, 180;
  (v S of Eng. at Hastings) 180, 182;
  (v S of Eng. at Bournemouth) 184;
  (v Players) 185, 186; 191, 193; (Stats)
  195–198
Duncan, Mr A. W., 82

Ebden, Mr C. H. M., 64, 65
Eccles, Mr A., 61, 63
Eden, Guy, 135
Edward VII, HM The King, 1, 12, 38, 54,
72, 75, 77, 95, 134, 145,
Evans, Mr W. H. B., 28, 30, 31, 99

Fane, Mr F. L., xiii, 22, 23, 24, 25, 134–135,
137
Ferris, Mr J. J., 6
Field, F. E., xii, 96, 98
Findlay, Mr W., 28, 30, 31, 163, 165
Fishwick, Mr T. S., 96, 97, 98
Foley, Mr P. H., 97
Forester, Mr T., 76
Foster, Rev. H., 97
Foster, Mr H. K., xii, 97–98, 101, 103, 157
Foster, Mr R. E., xii, 99, 101, 103, 177, 180
Foster, Mr W. L., 98
Fry, Mr C. B., xii, 6, 7, 9, 13, 15, 32, 34, 35,
36; (1st Test) 39, 40, 41, 42, 44, 46, 49, 50;
64; (2nd Test) 68, 69, 70, 71; (3rd Test) 84,
87, 89, 91, 92, 93, 94; 99, 106, 108, 116,
117, 126, 137, 139, 140, 157, 181, 183,
184, 191; (Stats) 197
Fry, Mr K. R. B., 64, 65

Garnett, Mr H. G., xii, 174, 175
Garrett, T. W., 6, 193
Gaukrodger, G., 100, 101, 103, 176, 178
Geeson, F., 29
Giffen, G., 6, 193
Gill, G., 108, 110, 111, 179, 182, 184
Gilman, Mr J., 64, 65
Goodacre, Mr W. B., 17, 19
Grace, Dr E. M., 102
Grace, Dr W. G., xi, 6, 12, 13, 14, 15, 32, 33,
34, 35, 36, 37, 41, 102, 104, 105, 106, 180,
181, 182
Gregory, D., 17
Gregory, J. M., 193
Gregory, S. E., xi, 2, 3, 4; (v Lon. C.) 13,
15; (v Notts) 17, 19; (v Surrey) 20, 22;
(v Essex) 23, 24, 25; (v Leics) 27, 28, 29;
(v Oxf.U) 31; (v MCC) 34, 35, 36, 37;
(1st Test) 40, 47, 50; (v Yorks) 54, 56–57,
59, 60; (v Lancs) 62, 63; (v Camb.U) 65;
(2nd Test) 71; (v Eng. XI) 73, 74; (v Derby)
76; (v Yorks) 77, 78; 79; (v Scot.) 80, 82,
83; (3rd Test) 86, 87, 89, 93; (v Warks) 96,
98; (v Worcs) 101, 102, 103; (v Glos) 107;
(v Som.) 109, 111; (v Surrey) 114; (4th Test)
121, 124, 125–126, 128, 129, 132, 133;
(v Essex) 135, 137; (v Glam & Wilts) 139,
141; (v Hants) 143, 144; (5th Test) 147,
151, 153, 161; (v MCC) 164, 165; (v Glos)
166, 167; (v Kent) 170; (v Middx) 171,
172, 173; (v Lancs) 173, 174; 176, (v C. I.
Thornton's XI) 179, 180; (v S of Eng.
at Hastings) 181, 182; (v S of Eng. at

Bournemouth) 184; (v Players) 185; 192,
193; (Stats) 195–197
Greig, Capt. J. G., 142
Gunn, G., xii, 16
Gunn, J. R., xii, 16, 17, 18, 19
Gunn, W., xii, 6, 16, 17, 18, 19, 53

Haigh, S., xii, 22, 54, 55, 56, 60, 77, 78, 85,
94, 116, 117, 118, 177, 179, 180, 183, 185
Hale, W. H., 102, 104
Hallam, A. W., xii, 17, 19
Hallows, J., xii, 61, 63, 172, 174, 175
Hammond, Mr W. R., xiii
Hardy, 111
Hargreave, S., xii, 96, 97, 98
Harper, Mr L. V., 65, 66
Hartley, Mr C. R. 61, 63
Harvey, R. N., 194
Hassett, A. L., 194
Hawke, Lord, 38, 43, 52–53, 55, 56, 58, 60,
69, 75, 84, 116–117, 118
Hawtrey, George, 72
Hayes, E. G., 20, 22, 112, 113, 114, 181,
183, 184
Hayward, T. W., xii, 20, 22, 39, 41, 42, 53,
106, 112, 113, 114, 116; (5th Test) 146,
149, 153, 161; 179, 180, 182, 183, 185;
(Stats) 197–198
Hearn, W. (Ump.), 46, 50, 114
Hearne, A., 168, 170
Hearne, J. T., 32, 33, 34, 35, 36, 37, 58, 169,
171, 173
Hesketh-Prichard, Mr H. V., 143, 144
Hill, Mr A. J. L., xii, 143, 144
Hill, C., xi, 2, 5; (v Lon. C.) 13, 15; (v Notts)
17, 19; (v Surrey) 20, 22; (v Essex) 23, 24,
25; (v Leics) 27, 29; (v Oxf.U) 30, 31;
(v MCC) 34–35, 36, 37; (1st Test) 40, 44,
47, 50; (v Yorks) 54, 55, 56–57, 59, 60;
(v Lancs) 62, 63; (v Camb.U) 65; (2nd
Test) 69, 71; (v Eng. XI) 73, 74; (v Derby)
75, 76; (v Yorks) 75, 78; (v Eng. XI at
Bradford) 79, 81; (v Scot.) 82, 83; (3rd
Test) 85, 86, 88–89, 90, 93; (v Warks) 96,
98; (v Worcs) 101–102, 103; (v Glos) 106,
107; 109; (v Surrey) 113, 114; (4th Test)
120–121, 125, 129, 130, 132, 133; (v Essex)
135, 136, 137; (v Sussex) 140; (v Glam &
Wilts) 141; (v Hants) 143, 144; (5th Test)
147, 150, 151, 160, 161; (v MCC) 164,
165; (v Glos) 165, 167; (v Kent) 168,
170; (v Middx) 171, 173; (v Lancs) 173,
174, 175; (v XI Players of Eng.) 177, 178;
(v C. I. Thornton's XI) 177, 180; (v S of
Eng. at Hastings) 182; (v Players) 185,
186; 190, 193; (Stats) 195–198
Hirst, G. H., xii; (1st Test) 39, 40, 43, 45,
47–48, 49, 50; (Yorks v Aust.) 52, 54, 55,
56–58, 59, 60; (2nd Test) 68, 70, 71; 76,
77, 78; (3rd Test) 85, 88, 89, 90, 92,

Hirst, G. H., (contd)
93; 116, 117, 118, 133; (5th Test) 146,
147–148, 150, 151, 154, 156–160, 161, 162;
177, 180, 183, 185, 187; (Stats) 197
Hole, Mr L. G. D., 82
Hollins, Mr F. H., 174, 175
Hopkins, A. J. Y., xi, 2, 8; (v Lon. C.) 15;
(v Notts) 17, 19; (v Surrey) 22; (v Essex)
23, 24, 25; (v Leics) 28, 29; (v Oxf.U) 30,
31; (v MCC) 34, 35, 36; (1st Test) 45,
48–49, 50; (v Yorks) 55, 57, 59, 60; (Lancs)
62, 63; (v Camb.U) 65–66; (2nd Test) 69,
71; (v Eng. XI) 73, 74; (v Derby) 75, 76;
(v Yorks) 75, 78; (v Eng. XI at Bradford)
79, 80, 81; (v Scot.) 80, 82, 83; (3rd Test)
86, 89, 93; (v Warks) 97, 98; (v Worcs) 101,
103; (v Glos) 106, 107; (v Som.) 109–110,
111; (v Surrey) 114; (4th Test) 121, 123,
127, 132; (v Essex) 137; (v Sussex) 140;
(v Glam & Wilts) 139, 141; (v Hants) 144;
(5th Test) 148, 151, 161; (v MCC) 165;
(v Glos) 166, 167; (v Kent) 168, 170;
(v Middx) 171, 172, 173; (v Lancs) 174;
(v XI Players of Eng.) 176, 177, 178;
(v C. I. Thornton's XI) 178, 180; (v S of
Eng. at Hastings) 179, 182; (v S of Eng. at
Bournemouth) 184; (v Players) 185, 186;
188, 191, 193; (Stats) 195–198
Howell, G. (Ump.), 82
Howell, W. P., xi, 2, 10; (v Lon. C.) 15;
(v Notts) 16, 17, 18, 19; (v Surrey) 21, 22;
(v Essex) 24, 25; 27; (v MCC) 34, 35, 36;
(1st Test) 45, 49, 50; (v Yorks) 55–56, 58,
59, 60; (v Lancs) 61, 62, 63; 67, 69;
(v Eng. XI) 72, 73, 74; (v Derby) 75, 76;
(v Yorks) 78; (v Eng. XI at Bradford) 80,
81; 84; (v Worcs) 103; (v Glos) 104, 106,
107; (v Surrey) 113, 114, 115; 118; (v MCC)
163, 165; (v Glos) 167; (v Middx) 172, 173;
(v XI Players of Eng.) 177, 178; 179;
(v S of Eng. at Bournemouth) 184; 188;
(Stats) 195–196
Huggins, J. H., 105, 107
Huish, F. H., xii, 168, 170
Hulme, J., 76
Humphries, J., 74, 76
Hunter, D., xii, 54, 56, 57, 58, 60, 77, 78,
180
Hunter, Mr W. A. N., 82

I'Anson, J., 174, 175
Iremonger, J., xii, 16, 18, 19, 183, 185

Jackson, Hon. F. S., xii, 6, 22; (1st Test) 39,
40, 42–43, 44–45, 49, 50; (Yorks v Aust.)
52, 54, 55, 56–58, 59, 60; (2nd Test) 68,
69–70, 71; 75; (3rd Test) 87, 88, 89, 92, 93;
(4th Test) 116, 117, 118, 119, 123–125,
129, 132, 133; (5th Test) 147, 148, 149–150,

153–156, 161; 177, 179, 180, 187; (Stats)
197–198
Jarvis, A. H., 6
Jephson, Mr D. L. A., 19, 20, 22, 113, 114
Jessop, Mr G. L., xii, xiii, 4, 7, 9, 13, 14, 15;
(1st Test) 39, 40, 45, 46, 47, 48, 49, 50;
(2nd Test) 67, 71; 72, 73, 74, 79; (3rd Test)
84, 86, 87, 88, 89, 90–92, 93, 94; 99, 102,
103–104, 105, 106, 107, 116, 117, 118,
119, 127; (5th Test) 146, 147, 148, 149,
150, 151, 152, 153–157, 158, 160, 161;
164, 165–166, 167, 169, 179, 189, 190,
192; (Stats) 197–198
Johnson, I. W., 194
Johnson, Mr P. R., 110, 111
Johnston, Mr A. C., 144
Johnston, Mr R. H., 82, 83
Johnston, W. A., 194
Jones, Mr A. O., xii, 16, 17, 18, 19, 177,
180
Jones, E., xi, 2, 6, 9, 13; (v Notts) 16, 18, 19;
(v Essex) 23, 24, 25; (v Leics) 27, 28, 29;
(v Oxf.U) 29, 31; (v MCC) 34, 35, 36;
(1st Test) 42, 44, 45, 49, 50; (v Yorks) 55,
58, 59, 60; (v Lancs) 63; (v Camb.U) 64,
65–66; (2nd Test) 69, 70, 71; (v Eng. XI at
Bradford) 79, 80, 81; (v Scot.) 80, 82; 84;
(v Warks) 95, 96, 97, 98; (v Worcs) 101,
102, 103; (v Glos) 104, 105, 106, 107;
(v Som.) 109, 110, 111; 112, 118; (v Essex)
135, 136, 137; (v Sussex) 139, 140; (v Glam
& Wilts) 139, 141; 166; (v Glos) 167;
(v XI Players of Eng.) 176, 177, 178;
(v S of Eng. at Hastings) 179, 182; 188,
193; (Stats) 195–197
Jupp, Mr G. W., 82

Kelly, Mr G. F. W., 28, 30, 31,
Kelly, J. J., xii, 2, 4, 6, 11; (v Lon. C.) 13,
15; (v Notts) 17, 18, 19; (v Essex) 23, 25,
27; (v MCC) 35, 36; (1st Test) 38, 44, 48,
49, 50; (v Yorks) 55, 58, 59, 60; (v Lancs)
62, 63; (v Camb.U) 65; (2nd Test) 71;
(v Eng. XI) 73, 74; 75; (v Yorks) 78; 79;
(v Scot.) 82, 83; (3rd Test) 86, 90, 91, 93;
95, 101; (v Glos) 107; (v Som.) 111; 112;
(4th Test) 118, 124, 127, 128, 129, 132;
(v Essex) 137; (v Sussex) 140; (v Glam &
Wilts) 141; (5th Test) 148, 152, 153, 154,
155, 161; (v MCC) 165; (v Middx) 171,
173; (v Lancs) 174; 176, 179; (v C. I.
Thornton's XI) 180; (v S of Eng. at
Bournemouth) 184; (v Players) 185; 192;
(Stats) 195–196
Kermode, A., 2, 61, 172, 173, 174, 175
Killick, E. H., xii, 137, 138, 139, 140, 176,
178
King, J. H., xii, 26, 27, 29, 69, 78, 80–81
Kinneir, S. P., xii, 78–79, 80, 81, 95–96, 97,
98

Knight, A. E., xii, 26, 28, 29, 41, 69, 78, 81, 189
Knutton, J., 79, 80, 81
Kortright, Mr C. J., 6, 22, 23, 25, 26, 135, 137

Lacey, Sir Francis E., 142, 163
Langdon, T., 105, 106, 107, 167
Laver, F., 2
Lawton, Mr A. E., xii, 74, 75, 76
Lees, W., 112, 113, 114,
Leveson Gower, Mr H. D. G., 20, 28, 112, 113, 114
Lewis A., 109, 111
Lilley, A. A., xii, 33; (1st Test) 39, 40, 43, 45, 46, 47, 48, 49, 50; 54; (2nd Test) 68, 71; (3rd Test) 87, 88, 89, 92, 93, 94; 95, 96, 98; (4th Test) 117, 120, 121, 124, 127, 130, 132, 133; (5th Test) 147, 148, 150, 151, 154, 157, 158–159, 161; 183, 185; (Stats) 197
Lindwall, R. R., 194
Littlewood, G., 172–173, 174, 175
Llewellyn, C. B., xii, 13, 14, 15, 32, 39, 142, 143, 144, 176, 178
Lockwood, W. H., xii, 20, 22; (1st Test) 39, 40, 41, 43, 45–46, 50; (2nd Test) 68, 71; 85, 94, 112, 113, 114; (4th Test) 116, 117, 119, 120, 121–122, 124, 125, 126, 127, 129, 132; (5th Test) 147, 150–151, 152, 154, 158, 161; (Stats) 197
Looker, Samuel J., 15–16
Lowe, Mr W. W., 99, 103
Loxton, S. J., 194
Lucas, Mr A. P., 134–135, 136, 137, 163, 165

Macartney, C. G., 193
MacGregor, Mr G., 39, 171, 172, 173
MacLaren, Mr A. C., xii, 1, 3, 5, 8, 9, 10, 11, 26, 33; (1st Test) 39, 40–41, 43, 44, 46, 49, 50; 61, 63; (2nd Test) 67, 69–70, 71; (3rd Test) 85, 86–87, 88, 89, 90, 91, 92, 93, 94; 97; (4th Test) 116, 117, 118, 119, 120, 121–122, 126, 127–128, 131, 132, 133; (5th Test) 148, 151, 152, 161; 168, 172, 173, 174, 175, 177; (Stats) 197
McAllister, P., 2
McBeth, A., 2
McCool, C. L., 194
McDonald, E. A., 193
McDonnell, P. S., 193
McGahey, Mr C., xiii, 22, 23, 24, 25, 135, 136, 137
McLeod, C. E., 2
Mailey, A. A., 193
Marchant, Mr F., 167, 170
Marsham, Mr C. H. B., 28, 29, 31, 167, 169, 170
Martin, F. (Ump.), 140, 174, 182

Martyn, Mr H., 109, 110, 111
Mason, Mr J. R., xii, 39, 116, 167, 168, 170, 179, 181, 182
Massie, H., 193
Matches, (v Lon. C.) 12–15; (v Notts) 16–19; (v Surrey) 19–22; (v Essex) 22–25; (v Leics) 26–29; (v Oxf.U) 28–31; (v MCC) 32–37; (1st Test) 38–51; (v Yorks) 52–60; (v Lancs) 61–63; (v Camb.U) 63–66; (2nd Test) 67–71; (v Eng. XI at Eastbourne) 72–74; (v Derby) 73–76; (v Yorks – 2nd Match) 75–78; (v Eng. XI at Bradford) 78–81; (v Scot.) 80–83; (3rd Test) 84–94; (v Warks) 95–98; (v Worcs) 97–102; (v Glos) 102–107; (v Som.) 108–111; (v Surrey – 2nd Match) 112–115; (4th Test) 116–133; (v Essex – 2nd Match) 134–137; (v Sussex) 136–140; (v Glam & Wilts) 139–141; (v Hants) 141–145; (5th Test) 146–162; (v MCC) 163–165; (v Glos – 2nd Match) 164–167; (v Kent) 166–170; (v Middx) 169–173; (v Lancs – 2nd Match) 172–175; (v XI Players of Eng.) 176–178; (v C. I. Thornton's XI) 177–180; (v S of Eng. at Hastings) 179–182; (v S of Eng. at Bournemouth) 181–184; (v Players) 183–186
Mead, W., xiii, 22, 23, 24, 25, 135, 137, 163, 164, 165
Medlicott, Mr W. S., 139, 141
Miller, Mr A. M., 141
Miller, K. R., 194
Milligan, Mr F. W., 54
Mitchell, Mr F., 32, 33, 34, 35, 36
Mold, A., 61
Moorhouse, 96, 98
Morcombe, Major, 62
Morgan, Mr H. E., 139, 141
Morris, A. R., 194
Moss, J. (Ump.), 60, 63, 76, 132, 165
Murdoch, Mr W. L., 13, 14, 15, 42, 193
Mycroft, T. (Ump.), 19, 60, 63, 132, 174, 178

Needham, E., 73
Newton, Mr A. E., 110, 111
Nicholls, Mr R. W., 171, 173
Noble, M. A., xi 2, 4, 8; (v Lon. C.) 13, 14, 15; (v Notts) 17, 18, 19; (v Surrey) 20, 21, 22; (v Essex) 23, 24, 25; (v Leics) 27, 28, 29; (v Oxf.U) 29, 31; (v MCC) 33, 34, 35, 36; (1st Test) 44, 45, 48, 50; (v Yorks) 55–56, 57, 58, 59, 60; 61, 62; (2nd Test) 67, 71; (v Eng. XI) 72, 74; 75; (v Yorks) 78; (v Eng. XI at Bradford) 79, 80, 81; (v Scot.) 80, 82–83; (3rd Test) 86, 87–88, 89, 90, 91, 92–93; (v Warks) 96, 97, 98; (v Worcs) 101, 103; (v Glos) 106, 107; (v Som) 109, 111; (v Surrey) 112, 114; (4th Test) 118, 121, 122, 123–124, 126, 127–128, 132; (v Essex) 136, 137; (v Sussex)

Noble, M. A., (contd)
138–139, 140; (v Glam & Wilts) 141;
(v Hants) 143–144; (5th Test) 147–148,
151, 152, 157, 158, 159–160, 161; (v MCC)
164, 165; (v Glos) 166, 167; (v Kent) 168,
170; (v Middx) 171, 172, 173; (v Lancs)
173, 174; 176; (v C. I. Thornton's XI) 177,
178, 180; (v S of Eng. at Hastings) 179,
180, 181, 182; (v S of Eng. at Bournemouth)
183, 184; (v Players) 183, 185; 188, 189,
193; (Stats) 195–198

Oates, T. W., 19
Odell, Mr W. W., 26, 27, 28, 29
Oldfield, W. A., 194
Ollivierre, Mr C. A., 74, 75, 76
Overton, W., 139, 141
Owen, Mr H. G., 22, 23, 25, 134

Paish, A., 105, 107
Palairet, Mr L. C. H., xii, 32–33, 34, 35, 36,
109, 111; (4th Test) 116, 117, 122, 126,
127–128, 132; (5th Test) 148, 152, 161;
(Stats) 197,
Palmer, G. E., 6, 193
Parnham, J., 26
Penn, Mr E. F., 65
Pepall, 82
Perrin, Mr P., xiii, 22, 23, 25, 135, 136, 137
Pike, A. (Ump.), 31, 78, 81, 180
Phillips, J. (Ump.), 20, 22, 44, 46, 50, 87,
93, 165, 188
Poidevin, L. O. S., 2, 61, 106
Poore, Major R. M., xii, 142–143, 144–145
Pope, Dr Rowley J., xii, 30, 38, 61, 63, 65,
67, 195
Porter, G. (Ump.), 15, 65, 178
Pougher, A. D., 26, 58

Quaife, W. G., xii, 78–79, 80, 81, 95, 96, 97,
98, 176, 177, 178, 183, 185
Quinton, Capt. F. W. D., 142

Radcliffe, L., 172, 174, 175
Ranjitsinhji, K. S., xii, xiii, 6, 7, 32, 33, 34,
35, 36; (1st Test) 39, 40, 41–42, 44, 49,
50; (2nd Test) 68, 69, 70, 71; 85, 106;
(4th Test) 116, 117, 122, 128–129, 132;
136, 137, 139, 140, 146, 163, 165, 189,
191; (Stats) 197
Reeves, W., 25, 135, 137
Relf, A. E., xii, 137–138, 140, 176, 177, 178
Rhodes, W., xii, 22; (1st Test) 39, 40, 43, 46,
47–48, 49, 50, 51; (Yorks V Aust.) 52, 54,
55, 56, 60; (2nd Test) 68, 70, 71; 75, 76,
77, 78; (3rd Test) 86, 88, 89–90, 93; (4th
Test) 116, 117, 118, 119, 120–122, 124,
126–127, 130–131, 132; (5th Test) 147,
150, 151, 152, 154, 159–160, 161, 162; 168,
177, 179, 180, 183, 185, 186; (Stats) 197

Rice, Mr R. W., 167
Richards, W. (Ump.), 87, 93, 103, 167, 184,
185
Richardson, C. E. (Ump.), 69, 71, 103, 161,
167
Richardson, T., xii, 6, 20, 22, 41, 113, 114
Ring, D., 194
Roberts, F. G., 105, 107
Robson, E., xii, 109, 111
Robson, Mr C., 142, 143, 144
Rodgers, R. (Ump.), 141
Russell, T. M., 23, 25, 135, 137
Russell (Glam), 141
Ryder, J., 194

Saggers, R. A., 194
Santall, S., xii, 95, 96, 97, 98
Saunders, J. V., xii, 2, 9; (v Lon. C.) 14, 15;
16; (v Surrey) 19, 21, 22; 23, 24; (v Leics)
27, 28, 29; (v Oxf.U) 30, 31; 38, 61;
(2nd Test) 67, 70, 71; (v Derby) 75, 76; (v
Yorks) 75, 77, 78; (v Eng. XI at Bradford)
81; (v Scot.) 82; (3rd Test) 84, 86, 87–88,
89, 90, 91, 92, 93; (v Warks) 96, 98;
(v Worcs) 103; 104; (v Som) 109, 111;
(v Surrey) 112, 114, 115; (4th Test) 118,
122–123, 128–131, 132; (v Essex) 134,
137; (v Sussex) 140; (v Glam & Wilts) 141;
(v Hants) 143, 144; (5th Test) 148, 149, 150,
151, 152–156, 157–158, 161; (v Kent) 168,
169, 170; (v Lancs) 174, 175; (v XI Players
of Eng.) 176, 177, 178; (v C. I. Thornton's
XI) 177, 180; (v S of Eng. at Hastings) 179,
182; (v S of Eng. at Bournemouth) 183, 184;
(v Players) 183, 185; 188; (Stats) 195–197
Schwarz, Mr R. O., 171, 173
Scott, H. J. H., 63
Sellars, T. (Ump.), 82
Sewell, Mr C. O. H., 102, 105, 106, 107,
135, 137, 166, 167
Sewell, E. H. D., 22, 23, 25, 42
Seymour, J., 79, 80, 81, 168, 170
Sharp, J., xii, 61, 62, 63, 172
Sharp, Mr W. R., 82
Shaw, A. (Ump.), 20, 22, 31, 144, 173, 184
Shaw, H. (Ump.), 170
Sheffield, Earl of, 12
Shrewsbury, A., 6, 16, 17, 18, 19, 42, 53
Silverlock, 139, 141
Simpson-Hayward, Mr G. H., 99–100, 101–
102, 103
Smith, Mr C. L. A., 138, 140
Smith, Mr E., 164, 165
Smith, W. C., 20
Smith, Mr W. (Lon. C.), 13, 14, 15, 164, 165
Smith, Mr W. (Wilts), 141
Soar, T., 143, 144
Sowden, 79, 81,
Spofforth, Mr F. R., 6, 32, 193
Spooner, Mr R. H., 61

...Mr E. M., 143, 144, 181, 184
... E., 167
...ding, Percy Cross, 34, 46, 52, 113
...ning, Mr J., 174, 175
...dman, A., 21, 22, 114
...teel, Mr A. G., 39
Steel, Mr E. E., 61, 63, 172
Stevens, Mr J. E., 141
Stevenson, Mr H. J., 82, 83, 165
Storer, W., xii, 32, 33, 35, 36, 54, 72, 73, 74, 75, 76
Stuckey, H., 2
Sugg, W., 53

Tallon, D., 194
Tate, F. W., (4th Test) 117, 118, 119, 122, 124, 126, 127, 130–131, 132, 133; 137, 138, 139, 140, 146, 176, 177, 178, 181, 183, 184; (Stats) 197
Taylor, J. M., 194
Taylor, Mr T. L., xii, 52, 53, 55, 58, 60, 68, 69, 75, 76, 77, 78, 177, 180
Terry, Miss Ellen, 72
Thomas, R., 61, 63
Thompson, G. J., 72, 73, 74, 163, 164, 165, 177, 180
Titchmarsh, V. A. (Ump.), 19, 69, 71, 107, 111
Tosetti, Mr G., 137
Townsend, Mr C. L., xii, 102, 104
Toppin, Mr C., 97
Toshack, E. R. H., 194
Trafford, Mr C. E. de, 27, 29
Tree, Herbert Beerbohm, 72
Treves, Sir Frederick, 77
Trevor, Col. Philip, 99
Trott, A. E., xii, 3, 6, 32, 33, 34, 35, 36, 169, 171, 172, 173, 176, 178
Trott, G. H. S., 6, 33
Troup, Mr W., 72, 74, 104–105, 107, 166, 167
Trumble, H., xi, 2, 3, 6, 12, 13, 19, 23, 24, 38, 61, 62; (v Camb.U) 63, 64, 65; 67, 69; (v Eng. XI) 72, 73, 74; (v Derby) 75, 76; (v Yorks) 75, 77, 78, 79, 80; (3rd Test) 84, 86, 90, 91–94; 95, 101, 104; (v Som.) 111; (4th Test) 118, 122–123, 124–125, 127–131, 132; (v Essex) 134, 136, 137; (v Sussex) 139, 140; (v Glam & Wilts) 139, 141; (v Hants) 143, 144, 145; (5th Test) 148–150, 152–160, 161; (v MCC) 165; (v Kent) 168, 169, 170; (v Middx) 169–171, 172, 173; (v Lancs) 174, 175; (v XI Players of Eng.) 177, 178; (v C. I. Thornton's XI) 177–178, 180; (v S of Eng. at Hastings) 179, 181, 182; (v S of Eng. at Bournemouth) 183, 184; (v Players) 183, 185, 186; 187, 188, 189; (Stats) 195–197
Trumper V. T., xi, xiii, 2, 5, 7–8, 9; (v Lon. C.) 13, 14, 15; (v Notts) 16, 17, 19; (v Surrey) 20, 22; (v Essex) 23, 24, 25; (v Leics) 27, 28, 29; (v Oxf.U) 30, 31; (v MCC) 34, 35, 36, 37; (1st Test) 40, 44, 45, 46, 47–48, 49, 50; (v Yorks) 54–55, 56, 59, 60; (v Lancs) 61, 62, 63; (v Camb.U) 64–65; (2nd Test) 70, 71; (v Eng. XI) 73, 74; (v Derby) 75, 76; (v Yorks) 75, 77, 78; (v Eng. XI at Bradford) 79, 80, 81; (3rd Test) 85, 86, 87, 88, 89, 92, 93; (v Warks) 96, 98; 101; (v Glos) 105–106, 107; (v Som.) 108, 109, 111; (v Surrey) 112, 113, 114; (4th Test) 118–121, 125, 132; (v Essex) 135–136, 137; (v Sussex) 138, 139, 140; (v Hants) 143, 144; (5th Test) 147, 150–151, 154, 161; (v MCC) 164, 165; (v Glos) 165–166, 167; (v Kent) 168, 170; (v Middx) 170, 171, 172, 173; (v Lancs) 173, 174, 175; (v XI Players of Eng.) 176–177, 178; (v C. I. Thornton's XI) 177–178, 179, 180; (v S of Eng. at Hastings) 180–181, 182; (v S of Eng. at Bournemouth) 184; (v Players) 185–186; 188, 189–190, 191, 192, 193; (Stats) 195–198
Tunnicliffe, J., 53, 55, 58, 60, 68, 77, 78, 177, 180
Turner, C. T. B., 6
Tyldesley, J. T., xii; (1st Test) 39, 40, 43, 44–46, 50; 53; 61, 63; (2nd Test) 68, 71; (3rd Test) 87, 90–91, 92, 93; (4th Test) 117, 119, 122–123, 132; (5th Test) 148–149, 152, 161; 172, 174, 175, 177, 179, 180, 183, 185; (Stats) 197–198

Vine, J., xii, 13, 14, 15, 137, 138, 139 140, 176, 177, 178, 181, 182, 183, 184, 185
Von Ernsthausen, Mr A. C., 28, 30, 31
Voss, Mr R. Z. H., 30, 31

Wainwright, E., 75, 78
Ward, A., 61, 63, 172, 174
Wardill, Major B. J., xii, 2, 62, 67
Warner, Mr P. F., xii, 32, 34, 35, 36, 104, 169–170, 172, 173
Warren, A. R., 73, 75
Washington, I., 54, 55, 58, 60, 77, 78, 176, 177, 178
Wass, T. G., xii, 17, 19
Webb, A. W., 143, 144
Webb, S., 61, 63, 172
Wells, Mr C. M., xii, 170, 171, 172, 173
West, J. E. (Ump.), 76, 144
West, W. A. J. (Ump.), 23, 25, 114, 137, 170, 185,
Whately, Mr E. G., 31,
Wheldon, F., 100, 101, 103
White, A. A. (Ump.), 65, 74, 137, 161
Whitehead (Ump.), 180
Whitehead, H., 26, 27, 28, 29, 78, 80, 81
Whitehead, L., 54, 75, 77, 78
Whiteside, J. P., 29

207

Williams, Mr R. A., 28, 31
Wilson, Mr E. R., 63, 64, 65
Wilson, Mr F. B., 64, 65
Wilson, G. A., 72, 73, 74, 100, 101, 103
Winter, Mr C. E., 65
Wood, Mr C. J. B., xii, 13, 15, 26, 27, 28, 29, 181, 184
Woodcock, A., 26, 27, 28, 29
Woods, Mr S. M. J., 6, 108, 109, 110, 111, 181, 184

Woof, W. A., 164, 165, 167
Wrathall, H., 72, 74, 79, 80, 81, 10̅ 106, 107, 167
Wright, Mr L. G., 74, 76
Wright, W. (Ump.), 78, 81, 98
Wyld, Mr H. J., 30, 31
Wynyard, Capt. E. G., 142

Young, H., xiii, 22, 23, 24, 25, 135, 137, 163, 164, 165